# QUIT BEGGING

*Discover the Most Profitable Busi*
*to Make Risk-Free Money with Them. Trading,*
*DropShipping, Private Label, TikTok, AirBnb, Trading,*
*YouTube and Much More*

## By

## The Golden Inner Circle

for clarifying purposes only and are the owned by the owners themselves, not affiliated with this document.

# Author: The Golden Inner Circle

**THE GOLDEN**
INNER CIRCLE

The Golden Inner Circle is an elitist group business incubator. It's a way to speed yourself up with far fewer setbacks. If you are already on track follow these enlighten entrepreneurs to take you to the next level of your potential.

Get the support you need to:

- free yourself from negative limiting beliefs

- develop a marketing strategy that works

- discover the Golden Method to improve your skills

- realize the dream of being able to work in complete autonomy

- create passive income with low-budget investments form your home.

The Golden Inner Circle is the movement that is leading hundreds of people to find a real strategy to achieve great results in the most profitable businesses such as Youtube, Instagram, Airbnb...

This series of over 20 books called "Clever Entrepreneurs in the XXI Century" is a step-by-step program that will take you from zero to the highest level of success.

The information contained within will help you to raise the dormant leader inside you, develop the King Midas' touch and to embody the NEW Golden YOU.

# Table of Contents

## Private Label Crash Course

## Youtube, Tik-Tok and Instagram Made Easy

# Short Stays Real Estate with No (or Low) Money Down

# The Golden Ratio Trading Algorithm

# The Complete Startup Crash Course

## The 9+1 Best Home-Based Business Model of 2021

# Private Label Crash Course

*Build Your First 6-Figure Business Supported by a Collection of 9+1 Profitable Strategies. Find the Best Products, Build an Enlighten Team and Start Your Personal Brand*

## By

## The Golden Inner Circle

# Table of Contents

# Introduction

A private label is where a person or corporation paying another business to make a commodity without its name, emblem, etc. The person or business then applies to the packaging their name and design. So, what sorts of items should be labeled privately? From skincare and dietary treatments and infant essentials, pet products, and kitchen utensils, pretty much all under the sun. The benefit of private labeling is that nothing innovative needs to be produced or developed by you. You can add your mark on it as long as it's not a proprietary commodity and label it yours. For the last ten years, private labels have risen by at least double the number of popular household products. In reality, there is a lot of conversation about the rise of private labels or retail brands around the world these days. Or we need to claim private brands, maybe since they are indeed labels by the end of each day. Opportunities to have ever-better-value offerings for both of us as consumers. Possibilities for everyone to push the main factors transforming the world of today and tomorrow. Yes, it's not the Private Label curse. It could well, in truth, be a present. A blessing that pushes us all to question the status quo again. A gift that pushes one to step positively with some of the main big forces that form the world of today to collaborate together more successfully and collaboratively. A blessing that is increasingly important to all of us, whether in the United Kingdom, the United States, China, or Scandinavia. If we like it or not, Private Label will soon have a single category of quick products in the country. In the last ten years, private labels have risen at least double the amount of popular consumer packaged goods brands. How did the Private Label expand at the above remarkable pace, and what lessons does it give players in the more narrowly established markets of fast-moving consumer goods? We like to think of it as a food event, but it's increasingly a complete experience of consumption. Flavors' globalization, marketers, and individuals have made Private Label a global fact. More and more, Private Label is the face of today's retailer. Comprehend it. This isn't going to go away. Act about it. Perhaps we should name them PRIVATE Companies from now on. Perhaps we might create very different tactics to survive if we began naming them brands instead of labels. Brands are concerned about combating their closest competing brand. Will they behave as though their closest advertised rival is the Private Label? Maybe they could, because maybe if they did, they might behave very differently in reality. The commodity has gone on. In turn, as Private Label has become a brand power in its own right, it has become privatized. It cannot be ignored as a single mark anymore. It's something a ton more. While taken out of context, Private Label is turning controversial for this cause, maybe more than any other, placing owners on the backhand side and retail section on the offensive. Neither group appears especially keen to publicly address it or cooperate on something outside development. Products have brought copycatting stores to court, and dealers have de-listed popular brands from their racks. There's a tiny concession space. It increasingly distorts agreed shopping habits and usage trends in order to exacerbate problems more. It is a brand that can often account for two out of three physical transactions made by your consumer. A brand that is gradually seen as an alternate product and value of parity. A company that will out-weigh and out-image any typical brand by exploiting the retailer's corporate strength and spending. A brand that can drive producers into a vicious cycle of loss in the market. A trillion-dollar market that, as you realize its sheer scale and future effects, must be the least evaluated and poorly understood industry around. An industry that in the years to come is going to get a lot larger. There would theoretically be billions of dollars of sales redirected by brand owners to this power. Are you confident your plans are ready? The remedies? But, as the solution, what do people recommend? Lower costs, increase efficiency, and be more imaginative. This is not just a remedy that you can pursue as a standard component of your business growth. It is simply not sufficient. This is an opportunity that requires the unusual and the unconventional. Or else rise to the challenge. The Private Label is a wake-up call from a brand creator. Wake up to the truth in the company. Wake up in search of a shopper. Wake up to what you might theoretically do for your company. Wake up to proactivity for real. Wake up to a chance to get the rest of the planet back into communication with your company. Private label has arisen from the conventionally held assumption that firms will benefit and conquer the competition by providing either higher value at a higher cost for their consumers (or shoppers) or fair value at a cheaper cost (retailer brands). In other terms, it's a preference between distinction (or innovation) and low cost, and it's safe to assume that only then have retailers fallen into the former to offer the latter to the shopper reliably in spades. As Coke (and Tesco) can also inform you, it pays dividends to see the brand on any street corner. However, as some of our research highlights would demonstrate, there is still a significant perception difference between Private Label and existing manufacturer labels in terms of quality/value. As long as the shopper is concerned, at least, without the other, one will not thrive, and broadly speaking, maker labels are better positioned to offer sound 'innovation' and 'value' to retailers. Just 16% of shoppers in all regions sincerely agree that a supermarket of retailer-owned goods can only be expected in the future. So, we think there is a potential for brands to constantly reinvent themselves through shopper intuition, deeper brand commitment, and creativity. The potential for retailers to continuously add value is there. The potential exists for producers to maximize their manufacturing ability and for interactions to be reinvented by agencies. But most critically, the potential is there to constantly impress and entertain the shopper, far beyond all their hopes. The other alternative frequently provided is to get yourself into making a private label. However, you may be compelled by Private Label to analyze the very simple essence of the company in which you are and to doubt whether it is strong enough to move you further. Ask for your goods. Ask how and to whom you are offering. Ask if you still are tuning into the agents of transition. Your corporate purpose issues. Ask if you have the best staff and processes to meet this crucial problem. Finally, Private Label is a concern for manufacturers alike. Knowing how to profitably manage it without undermining the very essence of the organization you are with. And the manufacturers that you work with. Yes, you may assume that you can survive without them. Yet we're advising, be very, very patient. If you want to be a genuinely successful marketing tool in terms of bringing to the shopper, you need one another. In comparison, we exist in an age in which the newspapers are building up major global supermarket chains as the latest businesses to despise. Why are you stopping this? As the messenger, you use Private Label, a messenger that not only reveals that you deliver excellent value and costs but also indicates that you think for your consumer and their long-term social needs. And you are really doing what you can to support them. Now, even more on this. The private label is, to a great degree, a hidden force. The conservative nature of the subject-matter literature tends to downplay its actual place in the world, a function far from conservative in fact, and a role in which Private Label is undeniably the single greatest influence on our businesses and goods today. Brands, engagement professionals, and scholars have consistently ignored or underestimated this. That's got to change.

# Chapter 1: Getting Started-Private Label

A private label is where a person or corporation paying another business to make a commodity without its name, emblem, etc. The person or business then applies to the packaging their name and design. So, what sorts of items should be labeled privately? From skincare and dietary treatments and infant essentials, pet products, and kitchen utensils, pretty much all under the sun. The benefit of private labeling is that nothing innovative needs to be produced or developed by you. You can add your mark on it as long as it's not a proprietary commodity and label it yours. A private label product is made and marketed under a retailer's brand name through a contract or third-party maker. You specify all about the commodity as the distributor-what goes into it, how everything is packaged, what the logo looks like-you pay to get it manufactured and shipped to your shop. This is in relation to purchasing goods with their corporate logos on them from other businesses. A successful brand identity can be the crucial base for building loyal customers, customer growth, and a competitive edge. Care of your corporate name as your company's face is how you are viewed by the audience. Without a detailed, excellently defined brand identity, the consumer might not realize who you are. In the end, you need to create a personal link. The potential exists for producers to maximize their manufacturing ability and for interactions to be reinvented by agencies. But most critically, the potential is there to constantly impress and entertain the shopper, far beyond all their hopes. The other alternative frequently provided is to get yourself into making a private label. However, you may be compelled by Private Label to analyze the very simple essence of the company in which you are and to doubt whether it is strong enough to move you further.

## 1.1 What is Private Label?

A private label product is made and marketed under a retailer's brand name through a contract or third-party maker. You specify all about the commodity as the distributor-what goes into it, how everything is packaged, what the logo looks like-you pay to get it manufactured and shipped to your shop. This is in relation to purchasing goods with their corporate logos on them from other businesses.

## 1.2 Private Label Categories

Almost every consumer product category has both branded and private label offerings, including:

- Condiments and salad dressings

- Cosmetics

- Personal care

- Frozen foods

- Dairy items

- Beverages

- Household cleaners

- Paper products

## 1.3 Different types of Private Label as profitable strategies

### Generic Private Label

Generic private-label goods are one of the conventional private label tactics used to provide the price-conscious consumer with a low-price alternative. The brand doesn't matter to these consumers. With limited advertising and no marketing, the goods are inexpensive, undifferentiated, poor inconsistency. In commoditized and low-involvement goods, these private labels are primarily present. For both discount stores in Western nations, this technique is widespread.

### Copycat Brands

In order to draw buyers, manufacturers play on the price point, retaining the packaging identical to a national brand that offers a sense of the product's similar consistency. These goods are reverse engineered, utilizing factories of identical technologies from national brand products. In wide categories that have a clear market champion, certain private labels are mostly present. In the detergent group, Massive Corporation blindly embraces the copycat brand approach. Detergents against rival products with identical packaging have been launched, albeit at a cheaper price.

### Premium store brands

Retailers now have started utilizing private labels, rather than just as a pricing strategy, as a store point of difference. Premium store brands are valued higher and are also high in performance than the national brands. Here, the customer proposal is to be the greatest brand that money will purchase. In the retailer's shop, these products get influential eye-catching locations. In the advertising, the manufacturer insists on the excellent consistency of the goods.

### Value innovators

Retailers manufacture goods that have all the value-adding characteristics and eliminate the non-value-adding characteristics in order to reduce costs, one point ahead of the copycat approach, and thus provide the customer with the best value deal. The danger of being imitated also rests in these labels. As it produces furniture under a modern market paradigm that involves self-service, assembling, and transporting yourself, Ikea is renowned for its better goods.

## 1.4 White Label vs. Private Label Dropshipping?

You can select between white label and private label dropshipping if you want to launch an online store. Both words define goods that have been branded by a reseller, but the two definitions very distinctly. Particularly to beginners, they may seem quite complicated, so let's go through each one and explain their relative benefits.

### Private Labeling

Private marking is where a company selectively makes a commodity for a store that offers it under its own name. Costco utilizes private marking, for instance, by marketing its own "Kirkland" brand that no other store can offer. As a consequence, goods with private labels are typically less pricey than national brands. Plus, they can be very lucrative if they're promoted properly. Dropshipping is a convenient method for private-label goods to be distributed. You will find a dropshipping provider if you are an online shop owner who can offer items directly to you and incorporate your branding. Dropshipping is an e-commerce market concept in which no inventory is held by the manufacturer. The retailer, instead, manages the packaging, packing, and delivery of goods to the end customer. In other terms, for dropshipping, the goods are delivered directly to consumers, and they are never used by stores.

## White Labeling

A white-label product is a manufactured product that a company makes but is rebranded by marketers to make it look as though it had been produced. Each dealer is authorized to resell the item under its own title and labeling. Unlike private labels, several retailers may market a white-label commodity. For e.g., you can have your own branding and labels on the goods that are delivered if you wish to market a product under your brand name utilizing the dropshipping business strategy. It is often safer to search at something that already has a market when it comes to items with a white mark. It's dangerous to produce goods with white marks that consumers are not comfortable with. It's safer to go for existing brands that people regularly use. As with private labels, dropshipping makes it simple to market online white-label goods. Again, the items are delivered directly from the producers to customers, and the commodities are seldom seen by dealers.

## Advantages & Disadvantages of White Labeling

You won't have to go through the complicated logistics of making a commodity in one of these two e-commerce market models. You can save a lot of time and money without significant expenditure of time and energy in product design and production. In essence, you will concentrate on selling the commodity to the target group and branding it. In order to expand your company, you won't spread yourself thin and can concentrate on other areas of expertise. So, let's go through the common advantages and disadvantages of each business model:

**Advantages of White Labeling**

There are some real benefits of the white labeling market model, including:

- **It saves time and money.**

It's just cheaper to white mark an established commodity instead of wasting resources on developing a product from scratch.

- **Gain a large profit**

In general, white label goods are exclusively marketed by suppliers and may be bought at cheap market rates.

**Disadvantages of White Labeling**

There are, on the other side, some risks of white marking, including:

- **Limited options for branding**

Because it will be the producer or retailer who makes the white label product's bottle, label, and packaging, depending on the concept, you can just decide what it will deliver for you.

- **Limited choices of products**

Just the goods that the maker produces will be preferred, and you will not be allowed to produce anything special to the market.

- **Competition is tough**

It is challenging to stand out from the other online vendors that, white-label or not, sell the same items.

## 1.5 Dropshipping Private Label

We have addressed that different dropshipping products are among the simplest methods for private or white label items to be distributed. So, let's go about how private or white label items can be dropshipped.

**Finding a supplier**

In order to achieve the sustainability of online shops, having a successful dropshipping supplier is utterly crucial. In quest of finding a directory of dropshipping vendors who sell private label facilities, you should look at business websites or just do a search on Google. Seeking a niche will allow you and your business to stand out from other retail vendors. Make sure that you conduct consumer analysis to figure out what sort of thing you would prefer to rebrand or distribute.

## Establishing the identity with the brand

A successful brand identity can be the crucial base for building loyal customers, customer growth, and a competitive edge. Care of your corporate name as your company's face is how you are viewed by the audience. Without a detailed, excellently defined brand identity, the consumer might not realize who you are. In the end, you need to create a personal link. Brand awareness must be expressed in the products, slogan, website, and packaging. It can offer a' derived from human attributes' to your brand. Brands with a very well-established personality make the brand intimately relatable, connecting consumers at a relational level and having to have the commodity in their lives. This is relevant for dropshipping products, including the private and white labels.

## Increase awareness about your label and brand

Growing your brand recognition is another important move towards building a profitable brand. If the product is fresh, then identifying your target customers and discovering ways to draw consumers to your shop is the very first thing you'll want to achieve. This is so if it's the private label dropshipping goods. Here are some forms that brand recognition can be improved without any expense:

- Build content on your website with the addition of a blog

- Developing your social network online identity

- To engage and network with more clients and get product feedback.

- To maximize your keyword scores, perform SEO.

## 1.6 Deciding What to Private Label

You might be wondering about what's a competitive commodity to private label. The secret to this phase and probably the most crucial step in beginning a private label company is researching and putting efforts into finding a good product. You ought to figure out which products/services are in the market to ensure if your product would sell. To see what people, look for on the internet and get ideas about what you can offer from there, you can use programs available online. If you intend to launch your private label company on online marketplaces, you'll want to use a testing method that actually monitors what individuals are searching for on that platform. For this, popular programs include Helium 10 and Jungle Scout. They both provide several resources to help you continue your market path with your private label.

### What Makes A Good Private Label Product?

The biggest point to hold in mind when applying for a private label for a commodity is to find one that:

**It is in strong market demand and has limited competition from sellers.**

This can help you stop being trapped with things that you will not offer.

## Has a strong margin for benefit

Taking into consideration how much the item would cost you vs. how much you will market it for. If the item is held in a warehouse, plus the expenses involved with sale online, don't neglect to take into account the delivery costs from your source to you and from you to your client, packing and storage fees.

## If you can manage the expenses

If you have a $1,000 or $10,000 startup investment budget, you need to take into consideration how many units you will need/want to buy and how much of the budget you will spend.

## How to Find Suppliers

It's time to search for a producer or trade firm that provides private label service once you have a commodity in mind that you would like to private label. You can select anywhere in the world to make your goods. And several times, the type of service/product you select would rely on where you choose to get your product made. For e.g., China might be worth considering if you are trying to sell toys or gadgets because they seem to produce a ton of these types of items at very low prices. Consider looking for Alibaba or AliExpress if you want to go on this path. Both of these platforms are bulk markets where the goods are identified by suppliers and trade houses, where you can find almost everything. Because with all our federal rules, it's a great choice to source in the U.S. whether you want to offer food, dietary foods, cosmetic goods, or something else you bring in or on your body. Check on Google for items sourced domestically. Say you're searching for vegan deodorant source, just type in Google "vegan perfume private label U.K." to get a list of companies that can use vegan deodorants for private label.

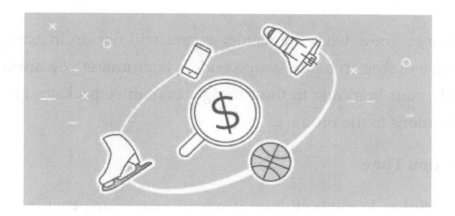

## What to Ask Private Label Suppliers

Once you've drawn up a list of possible vendors, calling each one and posing some questions is a smart idea.

## Pricing Per Unit

The price would usually already be accessible for you to see on the website for each item. However, depending on how many units you order, most manufacturers give a discount. Knowing this data would also assist you in estimating the gross margin.

## MOQ

In the private label/wholesale environment, this is a generic word used because it stands for "minimum order" or the minimum number of units you will order at a time. On their website/product listing, most vendors will mention their MOQ, although you will only have to inquire for some. The MOQ of a producer can be as few as five units, although it can be 1,000 and beyond for some. Although this may be negotiable often, asking this upfront is a smart move so that you can prepare and budget appropriately.

## Customization

It is nice to know what the factory is and will not do in advance so that you can stop trying to swap vendors later unless you are seeking to apply your branding to the package, customize packages, or make modifications to the product.

## Production Time

It is helpful to know how long it would take your provider to meet orders when your private label company continues to expand, and you continue to prepare for potential orders. Typically, the norm is around 15 days (depending on the commodity and order size), so it can go up from there.

## Response Time

Take notice of how long it takes for the supplier to get back to you, bearing in mind that you are initiating a long-term future trading partnership. You would want to make sure that your communication individual is trustworthy, prompt, and specifically addresses your questions. If your provider is based in another country, take into consideration that they are in a separate time zone and that you will not automatically obtain a reply. During their business hours, being present will allow the operation easier.

## Samples

Ask for prototypes such that the consistency and particular requirements can be measured. Many vendors can submit a sample free of charge, while others may start charging a small fee. Anyway, it's certainly not something you'd skimp on, especially if you're trying to give the highest service to your customers.

**Customizing Your Product**

In how your product can market, customizing your product will play a huge role. Question yourself, "What's going to set my version apart from the competition?" The response to this is key in having a prospective customer select your product over the product of a more known, well-reviewed business. Perhaps it's as quick as providing color combinations or getting fancy packaging, or it might be easier to enhance a function that you want more in-depth. Such customizations, such as packaging upgrades, are likely to be achieved by your supplier, and some can be accomplished through yourself or by your suppliers, such as custom marking with product specifics and a logo. Customizing the goods in any form is the main message here. Stand out by having it different (and better) than the rivals '. By basically slapping the mark on it, you don't want to sell the same exact thing as another brand.

**You are selling your Private Label product.**

You may pick anywhere to market your private-label line of items. Here's an extensive list of online sales places or suggestions on how to get into shops.

**A Personal Online Store**

Such customizations, such as packaging upgrades, are likely to be achieved by your supplier, and some can be accomplished through yourself or by your suppliers, such as custom marking with product specifics and a logo. Customizing the goods in any form is the main message here. Stand out by having it different (and better) than the rivals '. By simply yanking your tag on it, you wouldn't want to give the same product as yet another brand.

## Brick-And-Mortar

Sitting the goods on the shelf of a physical shop offers consumers the ability to see your product that they would never have dreamed of it otherwise. In other words, customers have to practically "search" for services or products they want to buy online. But if they don't think about it, they're not going to search and probably won't find it unless you pay serious bucks promoting it. If shoppers are still in a shop and happen to see it, it builds brand/product recognition at least. Fees and requirements for getting shelf-space vary by store, but it can be a decent place to start from local, family-owned stores. Read more regarding boutique collaborations or having your own storefront.

## Markets

Markers and art fairs for producers are on the increase. Consumers love to shop locally and want to help their community's artisans. They're a perfect way to get instant input from customers, too. Find out how to start trading and find craft markets at farmer's markets.

## Don't limit yourself.

Start with a variety of channels, in-person shops, and websites. You would be able to see over a span of time how many sales you create from each one, how much money each produces, etc. You should just stick doing what's profitable, then. It is certainly a road to launch your private label company, and it will be months until you can bring the goods on the market. But the trip can be well worth it if you do your product testing, pick the best source, separate the product from the market, and price it right.

# Chapter 2: Profitable Strategies in Building Six-Figure Business

For private-label products, manufacturers may raise gross margins by managing the whole supply chain from manufacture to distribution. Clothing traders have been pushing different private-label options for years. Costco has the Kirkland private-label name. Nordstrom's got Caslon. And Kohl's has Sonoma as its in-house, billion-dollar brand. Although online stores have supplied other industries with private label labels, basic products for tangible products focused on low-cost hardware and office equipment, the move to clothes implies a brazen policy expansion. Any volume seller is looking at the advantages of growing private-label brand's goods in order to drive sustainability and connect with a more aware and conscious millennial generation who are known for not being very brand loyal.

## 2.1 Private Label for Profitability

Profits are powered by private labels. A private-labeled commodity or product with parity in operation and consistency with major labels will cost manufacturers 40 to 50 percent less to develop and sell to consumers. In order to negotiate with online marketplace empires and other online suppliers who offer low-cost products without caring about reducing margins, merchants will then switch around to provide greater discounts. Online, where customers have 100 percent pricing transparency, this is especially essential. This functions on both luxury and commodity items. Building and maintaining a private label often enables manufacturers to develop exclusive goods for higher prices or to manufacture commodity products below brands at a sustainable price. To boost their inventory rotation, manufacturers are now using private-label tactics. Retail stores with services from private labels could also have more than four seasons a year. An innovative team in private label, such as the JCPenney team of 250 designers working in-house or the internal production and procurement departments of Nordstrom, will contend on an equal footing with fast-trending fashion stores like H&M.

**Factors to be Considered**

It may be dangerous to hop into this business without carefully thinking it over. Before investing and dedicating time to a privately-label approach, here are some factors to be considered:

- **Identifying low cost and high-quality manufacturer**

A colossal advantage is strong production suppliers, while poor manufacturers or suppliers are a horrific liability. Spend the effort to do it correctly. There are hundreds or thousands of suppliers capable of producing stuff that you would need. Find the producer that fits all the requirements for price and consistency; often, identifying the markets that are relevant. You may also want to learn from Portugal or Vietnam for clothing. Vietnam, South Korea, and China have manufacturing expertise in electronics. Take note that costs for suppliers differ greatly depending on the order's size.

- **Strengthen the Skills in Design and Procurement**

The private label includes relationships with producers of agricultural and consumer goods, component retailers, multinational warehouses, and distribution suppliers. Will you broaden the current partnerships between suppliers? If not, determine whether to consult the staff or purchase the expertise that will render the retail company a key competency of the strategy regarding the private label. Consider a completely dedicated bet on vertical trading, too.

- **Using brand pricing and external signs as guiding principles for pricing policy**

Research your rival brands closely while designing your own products under the banner of a private label. Retailers ought to make up their mind whether to generate the product as a luxury product and expend marketing expenses or to position it as an alternate brand by selling below national labels. If product attributes can be readily contrasted and placed as a substitute brand, it is important to consider the price point of comparable goods to position them correctly against competitors' national brand/products label brands. In other situations, were comparing features is not something very straightforward. Retailers can use a number of internal market pointers for pricing, such as site traffic, ratings, consumer feedback, and retailers can recognize the popularity of the product. Today, if a commodity is popular/interest-generating, but the converging performance is low, this can cause a price reduction/promotion intervention.

- **Acknowledge the differences in categories and manage them smartly**

Consumers can browse for functionality within a particular perceived cost sub-set for white and hard goods. Buyers searching for features are opting for a dryer or washing machine. Potential customers are looking for other qualities, such as cloth, shape, trendiness, for soft items like clothing. Those features deter similarities.

- **Decide Efficient Customized Label Blend**

The best combination of private label and branded items has to be determined by retailers. Are buyers looking for a feature in a certain product category or range on the website? Collecting web search data can help marketers make a choice. They have to remember the client base as well. If the consumer pool is predominantly 28- to 51-year-old buyers, private label goods can be more value aware and prefer small-scale proliferation.

- **Implement Algorithmic, Data-Driving Pricing Methods**

With constantly evolving customer preferences, at every given level in time, you should be able to recognize demand levels and continually seek the optimum price value. Factor in leveraging algorithms based on technology systems to easily evaluate price levels and strategies; when priced carefully with supporting data, private-label brands also deliver unexpected revenues. For e.g., the commodity was priced well below the national brand by a generic manufacturer of merchandise with a very well private label refrigerator brand, just to experience a drop in revenue. The store began checking multiple price ranges, steadily pushing up the segment. Sales started to fall with the first $200 onwards. And, magically, revenue and traffic boomed until the price reached a hidden barrier. This sounds counterintuitive, but the private-label company has already been put in a competitive area with national labels in the view of the consumer. Instead of seeing it as a lower quality commodity, clients began to see it as domestic brands. They were prepared to move since the price levels were always cheaper than domestic brands. In a considerably more profitable buyer zone, it was repositioned by moving the idea up the continuum. If consumers interpret things the same way with analytic pricing, the same SKU will gain double the profits. These are some of the most important elements in successfully initiating your private label initiative at any major retailer. Going over these basics will strip the efforts of the bulk of danger.

## 2.2 9+1 Pricing Strategies

**Want to maximize profit on your product sales?**

Aside from other publicity and business tactics, a strong pricing policy is indeed something you need to concentrate on. When setting the price for your goods or services, what considerations do you consider? When determining the prices for your goods or services, there are a number of considerations, including:

- Production cost

- positioning strategies

- competitor's products

- Distribution cost

- Target consumer base

When buying a commodity, price is a very important consideration for a buyer. A productive pricing system can also have a profound influence on the company's performance. And often, it decides whether or not the organization can succeed. So, what are those tactics you should suggest in order to improve the revenue and be more profitable?

## Premium Pricing

Marketers put rates higher than their competitors or rivals for this promotional policy. However, it is used where there is a major competitive edge, and a relatively cheaper price is safe for the marketer or the organization to charge. For small businesses that offer exclusive services or products, high pricing is perfect. A corporation, however, can check that the packaging of the goods, its promotional campaigns, and the décor or luxury facilities of the store all fit to maintain the fixed price.

- **Example of Premium Pricing**

Let's take the example of luxury specialty retail stores that charge you a little extra but sell you exclusive styles and tailored clothing.

## Penetration Pricing

To try to draw buyers? Ok, this technique is going to help you with the purpose. Lower rates are given on utilities or goods under this strategy. Although this technique is used by many emerging firms, it does appear to lead to an initial reduction of profits for the business. Over time, though, the growth of product or service recognition will drive revenues and allow small businesses to stand out. In the long run, as a business succeeds in entering the sector, its costs always end up growing to represent the condition of its role in the sector.

## Economy Pricing

The advertisement expense of a service or commodity is held at a low in this strategy. The technique is used during a certain period where the organization does not invest much in promoting the service or product.

## Example of Economy Pricing

The first few budget airlines, for instance, are offered at low rates in discount airlines to fill in the jet. A broad variety of businesses, from discount stores and generic grocery manufacturers, use Economy Pricing. The technique, though, maybe dangerous for small firms when they lack the market scale of larger corporations. Small companies can fail to make a sufficient profit with low rates, but strategically tailoring price-cuts to your most loyal customers or consumers may be a successful way to guarantee their loyalty for years to come.

## Price Skimming

This technique is meant to assist enterprises in focusing on the sale of innovative services or goods. During the preliminary process, this strategy means setting high prices. The rates are then reduced steadily when the competitor's goods or services arrive on the market. When the product is first released in the marketplace, this price approach produces an image of exclusivity and good quality.

## Psychology Pricing

This method of pricing deals with a client's psychology. For e.g., setting the price of a ring at $99 is likely to draw more clients than setting prices at $100. But the concern is, in terms of a very limited gap, why are consumers more drawn to a product's former price? Psychology suggests that on a price tag, customers prefer to give greater attention to the first digits. When stores apply $0.99 on product tags of $1.99 or $2.99, you can find identical promotional strategies. The purpose of this approach, therefore, is to build an image of greater value for the consumer.

## Bundle Pricing

How often have you been persuaded to purchase a multipack of 6 packets for $2.99 instead of purchasing one packet for $0.65? Or an SMS kit instead of texting on the individual rates? Without sacrificing efficiency, we all enjoy commodities that cost us less. This is why package selling is a success for both the vendor and the consumer and is profitable. The vendor gets to sell more of their inventory, and for less cost, the consumer gets to purchase the product in bulk. For instance, if bundle package of chips is for $1.30 and 3 multipacks for2.50$. The probability of purchasing three packs is more than purchasing only one. Bundle pricing enhances the worth sense when you are actually offering your consumers anything for free.

## Value Pricing

This technique is used when external forces such as increased rivalry or unemployment cause corporations to offer valuable promotional offerings or goods, e.g., combo offers or value meals at KFC and other restaurants, to sustain sales. Quality pricing lets a buyer know like for the same price, they are receiving a ton of product. In several respects, profit pricing is analogous to economic pricing. So, let's make this very clear that there is added benefit with regard to service or product in value pricing. Generally speaking, price cuts should not rise in value.

## Promotional Pricing

Promotional pricing is a really common method for sales and can be used in different department stores and restaurants, etc. Part of this promotional policy are methods such as money off coupons, Buy One Get One Free, and promotions.

## Cost-based Pricing

This method entails determining cost-based rates for the commodity to be made, shipped, and sold. In addition, a fair rate of profit is usually added by the corporation or sector to compensate for the risks as well as initiatives. Businesses such as Walmart and Ryanair are seeking to become low-cost suppliers. These businesses may set lower rates by constantly lowering costs whenever feasible. This undoubtedly contributes to lower profits but better profits and revenues. Companies with higher costs can, therefore, often rely on this approach to pricing. Yet, in general, in order to demand greater profits and rates, these businesses purposely generate higher costs. The aforementioned techniques are the most widely adopted strategies used by corporations to increase profit from sales of their product or service. In its own unique way, any pricing strategy is effective. Therefore, consider your marketplace and other conditions before selecting a pricing plan for your good or service to bring the most out of the strategy used. Therefore, becoming mindful of the competitive place when setting a price is important. What the clients or buyers anticipate in terms of the price should be considered in the marketing mix.

## 2.3 Best Practices in Private Label Branding

Can you recall when generic or non-national branded items with large black lettering and bad product consistency indicated simple white or yellow packing materials? After the unmemorable early days of supermarket labels, stores have clearly come a long way. In fact, many private label labels today are practically indistinguishable from their producer-branded equivalents on the shelves.

### Align with and support the master (retail) brand

It is certainly no accident that some of the best private label company portfolios are those that tend to be in tune with the supermarket master brand's positioning and strategic purpose. Preferably, their positioning is strongly complementary to the supermarket master brand, enhancing the latter's equity and beneficial relationships.

**Bring differentiation to the category; fulfill unmet customer needs.**

When their products are additive to the supermarket, or better still, the overall competition, private label labels are maybe at their strongest. One way to achieve this is to bring the category to something completely differentiated. Another similar approach is to resolve consumer expectations that are not fulfilled by the big national labels. Importantly, this difference can be more than just a cheaper price than the brands of the manufacturer. In the good or service offering itself, private label labels can often be exclusive. Safeway is a perfect illustration of introducing distinction to the market and thereby addressing an increasingly unmet desire of the customer. Finally, creativity is another form in which private label labels may offer category and consumer distinction.

**Establish clear boundaries for private label brands**

There is also a temptation to expand it everywhere and anywhere in the shop once retailers effectively establish a good private label brand. This extends horizontally across types of goods and vertically across ranges of price/value. However, the tendency to over-extend or dilute the private label brand properties is resisted by better practice retailers.

## Define brands based on emotional attributes

Since they feel an intrinsic bond to them, customers prefer to gravitate towards (and stay faithful to) products. There is no more for products with private labels than for brands with national suppliers. For private label labels, it is important that they stand for something more than just price/value and much more than a commodity attribute. They need to have an emotional advantage to which customers may connect. This essential nuance is understood by marketers that have become popular with exclusive labels and find ways to distill emotional equity through their private label brands.

## Distinguish brands with a distinct identity and appropriate brand linkages

Finally, a distinctive and highly identifiable visual identity is established by leading label labels and embraces a clear messaging approach. They still maintain clear rules specifying the degree to which the private label mark may and should be identifiably affiliated with the supermarket master brand. An attractive visual presence and strategically advantageous brand design are undeniably part of what makes private label companies popular or leads to their downfall if overlooked.

## 2.4 Positives and Negatives of Private Label

### Advantages

There is a legitimate explanation for retailers that are involved in flooding their stores with items with their brand name. Many of the main benefits of goods with private labeling include:

- **Handling Production**

Third-party suppliers operate at the behest of the supplier, providing full influence over the ingredients and consistency of the goods.

- **Control overpricing**

Retailers may also assess sales cost and efficient selling due to leverage over the product.

- **Adaptability**

In reaction to growing consumer demand for a new feature, smaller stores have the opportunity to move rapidly to bring a private label product into development, whereas larger firms might not be involved in a product or niche category.

- **Managing branding Decisions**

The company name and package concept produced by the manufacturer carry private label items.

- **Managing profitability**

Retailers monitor the amount of profitability their goods offer due to control over manufacturing expenses and pricing.

- **Increased margins**

Private labels enable manufacturers to sell and raise the profit margin more competitively on their goods. Compared to producing brands, several manufacturers gain 25-30 percent higher profit profits on private labels.

- **Customer loyalty**

Nowadays, consumers want goods manufactured locally, and they would like more if they enjoy the private label products. You would be the only outlet who would be willing to supply them with such goods. It is challenging to win the trust of individuals in the retail sector.

## Disadvantages

As much as you have the financial capital to spend in creating such a commodity, the risks of introducing a private label brand are few. Primary drawbacks include:

- **Manufacturer dependency**

Since the manufacturing of your product range is in possession of a third-party vendor, working with accomplished businesses is critical. Otherwise, if the manufacturer gets into challenges, you might lose out on opportunities.

- **Difficulty building loyalty**

In a number of retail stores, existing household brands have the upper hand and can always be found. Only in your shops can your goods be sold, restricting consumer access to it. Restricted supply, of note, may also be an asset, providing clients an incentive to come back and purchase from you. Although private label goods are usually offered at a lower price point than their brothers of the corporate name, certain private label brands are also branded as luxury products, with a higher price tag to show it.

## 2.5 Keys to Private Label Greatness

As of late, we are doing a lot of innovative work in the Private Label sector, and here is a good refresher of The Core Values that we believe in for developing our own labels that are strategically convincing. We also see that there are particular fundamental stories in their creation throughout all great store brand cases, but there are seven values that they must abide by to be genuinely strategically convincing.

### Principles of Equity and Environment

From a branding and design point of view, there has never been more interest in the grocery store and how we connect, affect purchasing decisions, and even construct theatre inside it. This is real in every part of the world. Of course, there is a reverence we all have to have for the cultural uniqueness of the grocery store, from country to country, since some customers are in the store just once a week, to other food and market experience where customers connect every day. Even with these diverse regional variations in frequency, familiarity, and satisfaction inside the retail shop, there is a common emphasis on making the store brand function more credibly and more convincingly with consumers in general.

## The equity connection

Immersing oneself in the retailer's overarching goal, its perception and equity distinction as it is now, and what is achievable in the future is important. To achieve this, the right branding collaborators coordinate with the senior brass of the distributors with which they operate, as well as the organization's top merchants and store name specialists. They take into account all the main targets for which a merchant is fishing and then see how to enhance store brands as being one of the key tools to accomplish their task. Store products strengthen the retailer's total equity and vice-versa, and they struggle because they do not.

## Environmental support

A kit can only do too many. Your store brand will get overloaded if it does not have the off-shelf environmental help in the vast stream of 40,000+ items that many of the largest supermarkets carry today. Beyond the box, give it existence and speech. To help your brand, use the theatre in the shop.

## Be preferential

For supermarket brands, own products, exclusive brands, and the like, there are loads of common nomenclatures. "But whatever the language, don't treat your store brands to the larger national brands as weaker "stepchildren. Don't be afraid to handle your supermarket labels preferentially in the store, beyond the incisive box template for your company. In their importance, in their distribution of space, in their positioning of shelves, and in their show and cross-merchandising all throughout the shop. No need to apologize to the CPGs or succumb to the study of planograms.

## Don't blindly follow.

For years, there has been a "follow the herd" attitude of store labels, and today it still persists. Because of what Walmart has achieved with Such Prices, many retailers we talk to now are terrified of "white" packaging. So often, individuals are hyper-attentive to the competition and norms and what's going around the market of store labels. The bottom line is that you can build your own vision in a very creative and special way. Do not blindly obey the naming conventions, color conventions, or typically mundane price-centered store brands set by broad categories and how they have traditionally behaved in order to reconsider anything intelligently.

## Three layers have to work together.

Make sure you are not concerned with visual language alone with the positioning of the store labels and how they are to be fully distinguished for the future. This is the responsibility of a number of production agencies, who feel they are only employed to rewrite the store brand's aesthetic vocabulary. If we want to encourage these products to be produced differently, we need to understand how the graphic language is created, indeed, but also how it is structurally packaged and the language we use to orally convey the item. Graphic, systemic, and verbal languages all cohesively operate together.

**Steve Jobs never asked the consumer.**

Apple is one of the world's most creative and well-thought-out, profitable enterprises. When questioned what Steve Jobs felt about research in a New York Times report and how Apple uses it to direct new product creation, he replied, "None... it's not the job of consumers to know what they want." There are so many retailers that use research to store products in their innovative development phase, and this is a mistake. Customers will still turn to the protection and what is comfortable with them, but if they are the only sounding board, you will not have the most creative performance.

**On the brand's positioning**

In using the name of the shop on the individual store brand packaging, there are no universal guidelines, just as there are no generalizations to create about how large the store brand should stretch. Both of these brands had a very definitive strategic positioning when producing Greenway, Hartford Reserve, and Via Roma for A&P, and this relationship that established the role of the company was a very significant part of the process. Clearly describe it, know that you want to distinguish the brand rather than sheer costs, own it thoroughly in the consumer's head, and correctly reiterate it. In the development of an ambitious store brand platform, these ideals would suit you well because they are standards that the best supermarket brands live by with true conviction. The name brand industry continues to be guided by continuing innovative creativity, a true steel hand in spreading out from the single "price" veil, and to be persuasive in their own right. And store brands need to be promoted with vigor, motivation, and media support.

# Chapter 3: Finding the Products & Starting Your Personal Brand

You should concentrate on creating a reputation before you start your company, one that is recognizable and valued, and a private label benefits both you and the retailer or supplier you select. The first move with your organization is importing the goods you choose to market, products that do not crack easily, which have satisfaction for the customer. The second and most significant move is to make your brand known to current and future clients. The more customers remember your brand, the higher it is possible that your revenue rate will be. Through selecting producers or suppliers who will submit your goods via Private Label, you will help this along. This operates by encouraging the consumer to position their orders with you, then deliver them to the retailer and directly dispatching the product. The return home address would be that of the company in most situations, but for Private Label, this will be yours. This ensures that whether they have any concerns or queries, the consumer would assume that the service/product has come from you, and they will only contact you. This helps you build up a brand reputation, but using trustworthy vendors, depends on you, and you deliver top-quality customer support. In general, manufacturers are willing to use private labels since it suggests that they do not have to be interested in any consumer problems. To sum up, while you are looking to get your brand out and develop a company without leeching on mainstream online market place/websites' popularity, a private label makes perfect sense. It will require a bit extra time to select a supplier since you must do the job yourself and guarantee that you work for the right supplier. Still, you will also gain a better profit when you take responsibility for the client support and are willing to negotiate the supplier's rates. A private label is where a person or corporation paying another business to make a commodity without its name, emblem, etc. The person or business then applies to the packaging their name and design. So, what sorts of items should be labeled privately? From skincare and dietary treatments and infant essentials, pet products, and kitchen utensils, pretty much all under the sun. The benefit of private labeling is that nothing innovative needs to be produced or developed by you. You can add your mark on it as long as it's not a proprietary commodity and label it yours.

## 3.1 How to Start Your Private Label Brand from Scratch?

Because of its profitability and consumer benefits, private labeling has boomed in prominence in recent years. To distinguish between larger vendors, more and more sellers create their products on and off e-commerce marketplaces. With 50 percent of one of the online markets, private labeling vendors, the rivalry is fierce. You need to realize what you're doing if you want to excel. To start a strong private label, you need the know-how, expertise, and money. When you place your logo and name on a standardized commodity, private labeling is. This separates the brand from related rivals and retailers. You have full power over your brand, with a private label. You establish a distinctive identity that is essential for successful promotion and the acquisition of consumers. Customers, not goods, are faithful to labels. Customer satisfaction and repeat business may be created through the private label. In the market, you still have the power of your price and place. A private label on the online marketplace enables you to build a different collection of items only for your product. This gives real estate devoted to your brand and assures that you are not vying against other retailers for the Buy Box. Since they get higher value, clients love private labels. Private-label goods are usually cheaper, but major stores' efficiency is the same, if not higher. In reality, at least one form of private label product is purchased by approximately 98 percent of customers. Depending on their lifestyle, customers may even buy goods. One study showed that clients prefer private labels for the price and choose them based on expertise. They buy from private labels that they most associate with. Ultimately, in a sea of rivals, a private label separates the name, allows you greater leverage over your revenues, and appeals to a niche client target. So, you have agreed to launch a private label of your own. The measures to take to help you start a profitable private label from design to launch are below.

## 3.2 Understand the costs of private labeling

Before digging deeper into a private label, it's important to consider the initial start-up costs. In comparison to reselling, private tagging is more costly. However, this capital input usually results in a better return on your expenditure in the long term.

### Manufacturing

Typical development expenses, such as supplies, processing, manpower, and transportation, would have to be accounted for. You may need to consider the customization charge, too. For customizing a product with your mark, packaging, or specs, most manufacturers will charge a fee.

### Brand

Even to design the brand itself, you would require money. To create the logo and package template, you'll definitely want to employ a graphic artist. To stress the voice of your company, you will also want to develop a content strategy.

### Marketing

Marketing is a significant part of private labeling. Customers don't know about your company, so to become more noticeable, you need to spread knowledge. A large cost may be generated through ads such as promoted and boosted blogs. A website creator and domain name would presumably both need to be charged for. For any other unforeseen fees or modifications that pop about at the beginning of the start of a new company, you can also add a sizable buffer.

- **Choose the products you want to sell**

The majority of corporations and labels start with a commodity. The brand is how you create your cash and profits. The item is the guiding force of your business. Starting a commodity with your name helps determine your margins, demand, and availability. The brand is the consumer service, but you will need to offer your consumers a valuable product in the end. You would typically choose a branded commodity that you place your own logo on while you market a private label. This suggests that a single generic product begins with your "brand." How do you further build and broaden your branding using that product? You want high-rank and high-margin units when buying a commodity. To lower warehousing and shipping costs, you will want thin, lightweight goods. If the first product you offer doesn't work out or you choose to shift paths, you can still move goods. The aim is to stick less to one commodity than to use product testing as a prism in your overall business and niche instead. You should also accept complimentary commodities with this in mind. If you market key items, you want to think of a range of similar goods that would still blend with your brand when choosing key products. For starters, you can grow inside the travel domain or beverage industry if you sell travel mugs. You will market some eco-friendly home products as well if you sell environmentally efficient cleaning products.

- **Define your target market**

Who is the perfect consumer for you? Who would be more willing to buy your unique product? This can assist you in deciding the sorts of goods you are trying to produce and how you are going to promote such products. The consumer is your market and your brand's secret. Getting a well-defined target demographic is more relevant than ever, considering the current condition of the economy. No one is willing to afford to target everyone. By approaching a niche segment, small enterprises may successfully compete with big firms. Many firms say they are targeting "anyone interested in my services." Others say they are targeting buyers, renters, or stay-at-home moms in small businesses. These priorities are all too common. Targeting a certain market does not mean that you exclude entities that may not follow the standards. Instead, focus marketing helps you to concentrate your advertising money and brand message on a single demographic that is more inclined than other markets to purchase from you. This is a means of meeting prospective consumers and creating a business that is far more accessible, accessible, and effective. For instance, an interior design business might opt to sell to households between the ages of 34 and 63 with incomes of $160,000-plus. The business could opt to approach only those involved in kitchen design remodeling and conventional designs in order to define the segment any better. This business may be broken into two niche markets: parents on the move and baby boomers leaving. It is much simpler to decide where and how to advertise your brand with a well-specified target audience. To help you identify your target market, here are some ideas.

**Look at your current customer base.**

Who are your new clients, and why are they buying from you? Look for features and desires that are popular. What ones do other businesses carry in? It is also possible that your product/service will also help other individuals like them.

## Check out your competition.

What are your adversaries targeting? Who are the clients at present? Don't try the same business. You might discover a niche market they are missing.

## Analyze your product/service

Write up a description of each of the product or service specifications. List the advantages it offers next to each function. A graphic artist, for instance, provides high-quality design services. The advantage is the picture of a professional organization. More clients would be drawn to a professional image when they perceive the business as professional and trustworthy. So, basically, attracting more clients and earning more profits is the advantage of high-quality design. When you have your advantages identified, make a list of persons that have a need that suits your benefit. A graphic designer may, for instance, opt to approach organizations involved in increasing their consumer base. Although this is already too common, you now have a foundation on which to proceed.

## Choose specific demographics to target.

Find out not only who wants the products or service and also who is most willing to order it. Consider the reasons that follow:

- Location

- Education level

- Occupation

- Gender

- Ethnic background

- Marital or family status

- Age

- Income level

- Ethnic background

**Consider the psychographics of your target.**

Psychographics is a person's more intimate traits, including:

- Personality

- Values

- Interests/hobbies

- Attitudes

- Lifestyles

- Behavior

Assess how your service or product would blend with the lifestyle of your destination. How and where is the item going to be used by your goal? What characteristics are most enticing to your goal? What media for details does your goal switch to? Can the newspaper read the destination, check online, or attend unique events?

**Evaluate your decision**

Make sure to consider these issues after you have settled on a target market:

- Are there enough individuals that meet my criteria?

- Is my goal actually going to benefit from my product/service?

- Are they going to have the use for it?

- Do I know what guides my aim to make choices?

- Can they afford my service/product?

- With my post, may I meet them? Are they readily accessible?

Don't smash the goal so far down there. Know, there is more than one niche opportunity you may have. Consider how, for each niche, the marketing message can be different. If you can successfully hit all niches with the same post, then maybe you have broken down the market so much. Also, if you notice that there are only 50 individuals that match all of your requirements, you may need to reevaluate your objective. Finding the right combination is the trick. You might be wondering, "How do I gather all this data?" Attempt to look online for analysis that others have done on your aim. Look for posts and blogs in publications that speak to or around the target group. Check for blogs and sites where thoughts are shared by people in the target market. Check for sample findings, or try doing your own survey. Ask for input from the new clients. The hard part is identifying your target demographic. It is much simpler to find out which platforms you should use to attract them, and what advertisement campaigns can connect with them if you know who you are approaching. You should give it only to people that suit your requirements instead of delivering direct mail to anyone in your ZIP code. In identifying the target demographic, save money and have a greater return on investment.

- **Consider your differentiating factor.**

You've settled on demand and a commodity. Now, what is going to make you distinctive in your business from your competitors? Look at the rivalry. What is their emphasis? And where are they missing? A perfect spot for you to put the brand is the field that they struggle the most. You could find, for example, that all of your rivals have a formal language; with your brand, you might take a goofy and enjoyable tone. In order for it to become a good differentiator, it doesn't have to be a big improvement. The core of your identity becomes your differentiator. Keep in mind that price may also be a defining factor. You would get a different demographic and competition than a cheap or discounted commodity, whether you are quality or luxury product.

- **Create your brand look**

Your "brand" consists of the goods, the demand, and the distinguishers. Yet, it is your material and aesthetic as well. You need a clear emblem that represents the name while private labeling is used. How you are and where the stuff comes from, the logo tells. This emblem can be included in all communications, packaging, and marking. Be sure it's accessible as a corporation and website prior to picking the brand name. This would mean that you do not infringe on any patents or fight with companies with identical names. To build the logo and package template, you'll definitely want to employ a graphic artist. This is the perfect approach to make things look respectable and trustworthy to the private label.

- **Create an experience**

A brand is, ultimately, more than a slogan, though. Your "brand" is how your business is experienced by the client. It's a consistent way for your audience to communicate. You need to work out how consumers can uniquely perceive your brand based on brand differentiation. What is your content going to look like? What could you provide that is unique to the experience of your brand? You may produce visually enticing social media photographs, for instance, that contribute to the lifestyle around your dog collars. Or you should make sure that you react to and respond to any social network statement or post. To keep your label on the edge, you can use special and exclusive packaging. Build an atmosphere, and you can turn your one-time consumers into long-term customers.

- **Find a supplier**

Acting with a good provider is an important aspect of private marking. The manufacturer must have private labeling expertise so they can help you make a return from your products. For a variety of consumers, several overseas factories will produce a standardized commodity and modify such items with private packaging for marking. You collaborate with a retailer, for instance, that produces bottles of water and T-shirts. They have ten buyers, each with their own special emblem written on the bottles, that offer water bottles. A customization and packing fee will normally be paid by the factory.

- **Build the brand**

You have put yourself in a role, built a differentiator, and found a supplier. It's time to start developing your organization now. You have to:

- Name and image copyright.

- Website configuration

- Creating a voice on social media

- Shape an LLC

Just like you would like any other legal corporation, recognize your e-commerce firm. You need yourself, your goods, and your income to be covered. You would also like to start naming the lists with online items. A private label means you don't have to fight for a Buy Package. "With a different page for your branded goods, you hold your own "real estate." In line with the brand background, this is a good chance to customize the listing.

## 3.3 Choosing the Right Products

Choosing the best market and the right goods to spend your efforts on is the greatest challenge you would have to conquer. This decision is vital to the success or failure of your company. The only biggest mistake you're going to make is selecting a product based on your own interests or personal preferences, particularly if you want to create a genuinely profitable company. You have to provide what other customers want, not what you want. Especially if you are not the type of individual to embrace patterns or the type of individual that is always perceived to be "outside of the box." We can't tell you what products to offer, but we can definitely give you some ideas about how to pick the right ones.

### How to choose the right product

Your organization would have an uphill struggle to become profitable without a strong product portfolio. It may seem impossible to try to find out what you are trying to market, with potentially millions of items out there. The item you chose will also pose other concerns that you may need to work on. For starters, shipping may become an issue if you are planning to sell freezers. Depending on where the clients work, whether you are selling alcohol, there could be regulatory limits. Market analysis can sound daunting, but knowing the product can cater to the people you are going to attract through your site is important. You should monitor the industry dynamics if you already have an understanding of what you intend to do to see how the commodity is actually performing on the market. If you are really not sure what you'd like to offer, trends can still be helpful to you. Business dynamics will offer you an indication about what items consumers are purchasing or are interested in buying at the moment. Look for items that address a dilemma the target group is experiencing. If your consumer is fed up with the current product range, open a unique and better product to deliver them. Choosing a commodity that is not reasonably available nearby or a national brand that is coveted by a region outside of where it is actually accessible may also be a brilliant choice. Another recommendation is to find a service/ product based on your target audience's interests. This may be in the shape of a new TV show that is beginning or a fashion trend. It often applies to aiming for a difference in chances. If you choose a product that many different competitors are already selling, find something that you can do differently or better than everybody else. This can be an enhanced product characteristic, a market that your competitors totally miss, and maybe something in your marketing plan. If you are trying to market a commodity-based on something that is trending at the moment, ensure that you capitalize early on the pattern. There tend to be more individuals who buy the product at the beginning of a trend. Everybody else is now also moving along to the next thing if you get on the hype train at the end of the trend. Do not wait too long to profit on a trend in the market unless you think that you're going to revive a dead trend. When you make your choices, it is important to take into account product turnover. It would take a lot of time and resources on a product range that varies year after year to guarantee that the product selection is held up-to-date and does not include last year's choices, which could no longer be eligible. A reduced churn product would enable you to engage in a more informative website that will be applicable for a longer time span. Don't be frightened of looking at smaller segments and niches of products. Although there may be fewer prospective customers, there will also be less competition, making it easier to get it to the top of the search engines and much more cost-effective in terms of marketing. The right product is an essential part of your success. Take your time and also don't rush into the first good-looking product.

**Looking for Product Ideas**

There is no need to start a shop without a commodity to sell. Begin with something you already have, or how you can fix your own issues or the challenges of people you meet before you start looking for fresh ideas on what you can sell. There are some ways to consider:

- Which items or niches are you involved in?

- What items are your mates excited about?

- Which challenges do you have with your own life?

- Whose goods can address this?

- What kind of firms are based in your community?

- Can they be translated into a definition online?

- What will organizations in your culture cater to individuals outside of your community?

- In other areas of the planet, what items are trending?

- Is there a need inside your society for them?

- Will you build in your society a market for them?

- Is there a certain sector you like to be interested in if you are confused regarding products? In that industry, what products are popular?

- What items can you find useful from that industry?

- In other online retailers, what items are popular?

- Will this commodity have a niche that you should specialize in in sales?

- What's the social curation website trend?

- Is there an undiscovered thing out there that individuals would want to see open to them?

## 3.4 Building a Team and Starting your Personal Brand

### Choosing the Right Supplier

It can be tricky to pick a supplier for your private label company, but it can help you to realize that there are a variety of suppliers who have been doing this for several years. Some lead the industry in broad industries, and this may be the perfect place to get started in your new company since the goods you offer are already established and have gained appreciation from the market. You can have to trade-off or work in restricted strategies with your profitability, and you need to be careful in reviewing the terms and conditions of each corporation, but each of these can create a backdoor into which you can start a profitable long-term business. Not all private labels are made equally, and to guarantee that your organization is effective, you want to make sure you chose the best provider. There are certain items that your provider wants to provide and some things that are less essential but can have greater convenience. Any of the items you'll be searching for in a provider include:

- Will the retailer have members who are knowledgeable?

- Will the supplier devote them to a particular entity committed to your account?

- Are they invested in being advanced technologically?

- How can you send orders?

- Where are they situated?

- Are they a coordinated business?

- How fast are their orders shipped?

- How are they keeping you throughout the loop on product returns and items out of stock?

- How fast can they send you the tracking details and purchase order?

- What payment types do they approve?

- What kind of fees are they charging?

It may seem impossible to locate the legal firms and distinguish them from the fraudulent as you are searching for a provider. There are some tricks to choosing a decent provider for private labels. One crucial point to bear in mind when you start approaching suppliers is that they could very well be the secret to selecting the best supplier, even though they are not the right match for you. Make sure you always ask every supplier you meet if they can guide you in the appropriate path to reach a supplier that suits your company. As they're in the business, they are sure to have connections that will help you and are typically prepared to share the details. Looking at social media is another way one can improve the chances of having a reliable supplier to deal with. Often, through a family member, neighbor, or acquaintance who might be in the industry or meet someone in the industry, you may find a lead. Any lead is a successful lead, even though it leads to a dead end. In order to strengthen the partnership, you have with your supplier, there are a few items you should do:

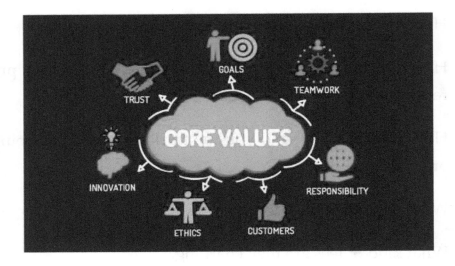

- Pay on time to develop trust and then become a reliable client.

- Set simple and realistic targets if an estimation of the goods you plan to sell in a specified period is requested

- Remember that they have other clients and do not belong to you alone.

- Learn what you need when you put orders to speed up the operation.

- If there is a malfunction, do not accuse the representative, but collaborate with them to find a remedy.

- Knowing somebody on a personal level seems to make them more likely to help you out. Build relationships with your delegate

- Train them to identify what you need, such as fresh product photos and product update updates, items out of stock, and products were withdrawn.

## Finding the Right Suppliers and Working with Them

The one crucial part you have to do before you continue the quest for the right suppliers is learned how to say the difference between a true wholesale supplier and a department store that works like one. The manufacturer orders their stock from a genuine wholesaler and delivers far higher deals than a supermarket would. To create a good organization, you need to be able to do all of the following:

### Have Access to Exclusive Distribution or Pricing

Being able to negotiate unique product agreements or exclusive prices would offer you the advantage without the need to import or produce your own product to sell online. These are not quick items to arrange, and you can notice that you are still out-priced, and at wholesale rates, some private label brands would still offer the same or equivalent. You need to find a way to persuade the buyers that the commodity you sell is of greater quality than the competitor, whether you can have exclusive distribution, particularly if the competition sells a knock-off product at a cheaper price. This is where the website's "about us" page becomes much more useful as it is a good way to share the fact that you are unique to the product.

### Sell at the Lowest Possible Price

You will rob clients from such a chunk of your niche market if you are willing to sell your goods at the lowest costs. The main thing is that since you actually won't be able to appreciate the gain, you are destined to struggle. The low price is not often the primary motivating factor behind the choice of a consumer to shop. Customers seem to choose to invest their cash on the best benefit and lowest cost of a commodity. This suggests that you ought to persuade them that the best decision is to invest a little extra cash in your goods, so there is less downside and more appeal to them.

## Add Your Value Outside of the Price

Think in terms of having data that complement the items selected. A real capitalist can fix challenges, and at the same time offering goods at high rates. In your unique niche, make sure you give suggestions and insightful recommendations. Your customer support is one extremely efficient way to bring value to the goods outside of the costs. If you are willing to address all the queries of your consumer without needing to call you and are willing to respond to any emails easily, your store website will stick out from the rest.

# Conclusion

A private label is where a person or corporation paying another business to make a commodity without its name, emblem, etc. The person or business then applies to the packaging their name and design. So, what sorts of items should be labeled privately? From skincare and dietary treatments and infant essentials, pet products, and kitchen utensils, pretty much all under the sun. The benefit of private labeling is that nothing innovative needs to be produced or developed by you. You can add your mark on it as long as it's not a proprietary commodity and label it yours. Dropshipping is a convenient method for private-label goods to be distributed. You will find a dropshipping provider if you are an online shop owner who can offer items directly to you and incorporate your branding. Dropshipping is an e-commerce market concept in which no inventory is held by the manufacturer. The retailer, instead, manages the packaging, packing, and delivery of goods to the end customer. In other terms, for dropshipping, the goods are delivered directly to consumers, and they are never used by stores. There is a legitimate explanation for retailers that are involved in flooding their stores with items with their brand name. Third-party suppliers operate at the behest of the supplier, providing full influence over the ingredients and consistency of the goods. In reaction to growing consumer demand for a new feature, smaller stores have the opportunity to move rapidly to bring a private label product into development, whereas larger firms might not be involved in a product or niche category. You should concentrate on creating a reputation before you start your company, one that is recognizable and valued, and a private label benefits both you and the retailer or supplier you select.

The first move with your organization is importing the goods you choose to market, products that do not crack easily, which have satisfaction for the customer. The second and most significant move is to make your brand known to current and future clients. The more customers remember your brand, the higher it is possible that your revenue rate will be. Through selecting producers or suppliers who will submit your goods via Private Label, you will help this along. This operates by encouraging the consumer to position their orders with you, then deliver them to the retailer and directly dispatching the product. To sum up, while you are looking to get your brand out and develop a company without leeching on mainstream online marketplace/websites' popularity, a private label makes perfect sense. It will require a bit extra time to select a supplier since you must do the job yourself and guarantee that you work for the right supplier. Still, you will also gain a better profit when you take responsibility for the customer support and are willing to negotiate.

# Dropshipping Business Model on a Budget

*The Risk-Low E-Com Guide to Create Your Online Store and Generate Profits with less than 47$*

*By*

**The Golden Inner Circle**

# Table of contents

# Introduction

With very little startup expenses, dropshipping is an innovative business model.

A dropshipping business is where an owner finds a collection of distributors to deliver and offer goods for their website. However, as in an e-commerce business, instead of owning the merchandise, a third party does much of the distribution and logistics for them. That third party is usually a wholesaler, who on behalf of the business "dropships" the consumer's goods.

When you start a retail shop, there are several factors to consider, but among the most significant aspects, you have to decide whether you'd like to store inventory or have a wholesale distributor. You must purchase goods in bulk, stock, unpack and send them to customers of your products if you want to store inventory. You may, therefore, contract the phase of storing, packaging and exporting to a drop-ship supplier by picking a wholesale distributor. As direct fulfillment, a drop-ship supplier is often described, but both definitions may be used to define the same service.

The wholesaler, who usually manufactures the product, delivers the product at the most basic, any time anyone buys a product, and you get a part of the sale for the product marketing.

Unless the client puts an order for it, you don't pay for the thing.

Dropshipping is an internet-based business model that draws novices and experts alike to choose a niche, create a brand, market and earn money, with probably the minimum entry barriers.

# Chapter 1. What is Dropshipping?

Dropshipping is a retail model of e-commerce that enables retailers to offer goods without maintaining any physical inventory. The company sells the product to the buyer through dropshipping and sends the purchase order to a third-party seller, who then delivers the order directly on behalf of the retailer to the customer. Dropshipping sellers may not need to spend in any commodity stock, inventory or storage room and do not manage the phase of fulfillment.

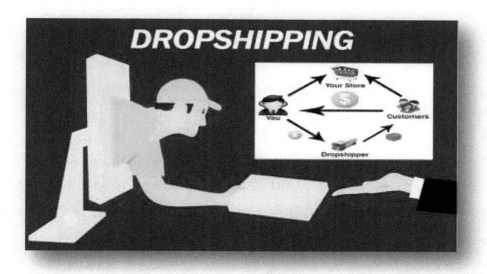

Dropshipping is a form of retail fulfillment, where the goods are ordered from a third-party retailer instead of a store stocks products. The goods are then delivered directly to the customer. This way, the vendor doesn't have to personally manage the product. A familiar sound? Maybe not, but dropshipping is a fulfillment model utilized by 35 percent of online stores.

This is mostly a hands-off process for the store. The retailer doesn't have to buy stock or, in any manner, meet the orders. The third-party retailer, instead, takes control of the product itself.

For startups, dropshipping is great since it does not take as much as the conventional sales model. You don't have to prepare, pay overhead, & stock merchandise in a brick-and-mortar store. Instead, you start an online shop to purchase bulk goods and warehouse space from vendors that already have products.

In dropshipping, the merchant is solely responsible for attracting clients and handling orders, ensuring you'll be a middleman effectively. Despite this, through pricing up the goods you offer, you can gain the lion's share of the profits. It's an easy model of business, so one that can be really successful.

Millions of entrepreneurs switch to dropshipping to get started because it takes less hassle and capital. That's why you're probably interested. And the best of all news? Through dropshipping, you can create a company right from your laptop that is profitable in the long term.

There are several pitfalls and benefits, of course, and it is essential that we check at them before you launch your own e-commerce dropshipping firm. However, once you realize the positives and negatives of dropshipping, it'll be a breeze to learn how to do so effectively.

## 1.1 Benefits of dropshipping

For aspiring entrepreneurs, dropshipping is a smart business move to start with, which is accessible. You can easily evaluate multiple business concepts with a small downside with dropshipping, which helps you to think a lot about how to pick and sell in-demand goods. Here are a couple more explanations why dropshipping is a popular business.

## 1. Little capital is required

Perhaps the greatest benefit to dropshipping is that an e-commerce website can be opened without needing to spend thousands of dollars in stock upfront. Typically, retailers have had to bundle up large quantities of inventory with capital investments.

For the dropshipping model, unless you have already made the transaction and have been charged by the consumer, you may not have to buy a product. It is possible to start sourcing goods without substantial up-front inventory investments and launch a profitable dropshipping company with very little capital. And since you are not committed to sales, as in a typical retail sector, there is less chance of launching a dropshipping shop through any inventory bought up front.

## 2. Easy to get started

It's also simpler to operate an e-commerce company because you don't have to interact with physical products. You don't have to take stress with dropshipping about:

- Paying for a warehouse or managing it
- Tracking inventory for any accounting reasons
- Packing & shipping your orders
- Continually ordering products & managing stock level
- Inbound shipments and handling returns

## 3. Low overhead

Your overhead expenses are very minimal, and you don't have to deal with buying inventory or maintaining a warehouse. In reality, several popular dropshipping stores are managed as home-based enterprises, needing nothing more to run than a laptop & a few operational expenses. These costs are likely to rise as you expand but are still low relative to standard brick-and-mortar stores.

## 4. Flexible location

From almost anywhere via an internet connection, a dropshipping company can be managed. You can operate and manage the business as long as you can effectively connect with vendors and consumers.

## 5. Wide selection of goods to sell

Because you don't really have to pre-purchase any items you market, you can offer your potential clients a variety of trending products. If an item is stored by vendors, you will mark it for sale at no added cost at your online store.

## 6. Easier for testing

Dropshipping is a valuable form of fulfillment for both the opening of a new store and also for company owners seeking to measure consumers' demand for additional types of items, such as shoes or whole new product ranges. Again, the primary advantage of dropshipping is the opportunity to list and likely sell goods before committing to purchasing a significant quantity of stock.

## 7. Easier to scale

For a traditional retail firm, you would typically need to perform three times as much work if you get three times the amount of orders.

By using dropshipping vendors, suppliers would be liable for more of the work to handle extra orders, helping you to improve with fewer growth pains & little incremental work.

Sales growth can often bring extra work, especially customer service, however companies which use dropshipping scale especially well comparison to standard e-commerce businesses.

## 8. Dropshipping starts easily.

 In order to get started, you need not be a business guru. You don't really require some past company knowledge, honestly. You will get started easily and learn the rest while you move along if you spend some time to learn its basics.

It is too easy to drop shipping, and it takes so little from you. To help you out, you don't need a warehouse to store goods or a staff. You don't need to think about packaging or storage either. You do not even have to devote a certain period of time in your shop every day. Surprisingly, it's hands-off, especially once you get underway.

All of this means that today you can begin your company. Within a matter of hours, you will begin getting it up and running.

You're going to need some practical skills and the right equipment and tools. You will be equipped with the skills you have to jumpstart your own dropshipping company by the time you've done it.

## 9. Dropshipping grow easily.

Your business model doesn't even have to alter that much at all when you scale up. As you expand, you'll have to bring more effort into sales and marketing, but your daily life will remain almost the same.

One of the advantages of dropshipping is that when you scale, the costs do not spike. It's convenient to keep rising at a fairly high pace because of this. If you choose to build a little team at any stage, you can manage about anything by yourself, too.

## 10. Dropshipping doesn't need a big capital.

Since you need very little to start a dropshipping business, you can get underway with minimal funds. Right from your desktop, you can create a whole corporation, and you do not need to make any heavy investment. Your costs would be reasonably low even as your company grows, particularly compared to normal business expenses.

## 11. Dropshipping is flexible.

This is one of the greatest advantages. You get to be a boss of your own and set your own regulations. It's one of the most versatile occupations anyone can try.

With just a laptop, you can operate from anywhere, and you can operate at the hours that are most comfortable for you. For founders that want a company that fits for them, this is perfect. To get stuff done, you won't have to lean over backward. You choose your own pace instead.

Dropshipping is indeed flexible in that it allows you plenty of space to create choices that fit for you. Whenever you choose, you can quickly list new items, and you can change your plans on the move. You should automate it to work when you're gone, whether you're going on holiday. You get the concept prospects are limitless.

## 12. Dropshipping manages easily.

Because it doesn't need you to make several commitments, with no hassle, you can manage everything. When you have found and set up suppliers, you are often exclusively liable for your e-commerce store.

# Chapter 2. How Dropshipping Works

Dropshipping functions by third-party suppliers, which deliver goods for each order on a just-in-time basis. When a sales order is received by the retailer, they transfer the requirements to the supplier—who manufactures the product.

While dropshipping is used by many e-commerce retailers as the base of their business processes, dropshipping can be used successfully to complement traditional retail inventory-stocking models. Because dropshipping does not create any unused surplus inventory, it may be used for analysis purposes before committing to sale on a marketplace, such as testing the waters.

Dropshipping works because, with the aid of a third party such as a wholesaler or an e-commerce shop, a dropshipper fulfills orders to deliver the goods for an even cheaper price. The majority of dropshippers offer goods directly from Chinese suppliers because the prices of most products in China are very poor. If the wholesaler's price is 5 dollars for a product. A dropshipper sells it for $8 and retains $3 for himself. The bulk of dropshippers target nations with higher purchasing power.

## 2.1 Awareness about the Supply Chain

You'll see the word "supply chain" a lot in here. It seems like a fancy lingo for the business, but it actually applies to how a product transfers from seller to consumer. We'll use this to explain the method of dropshipping.

## 2.2 The Supply Chain Process

You, the merchant, are only one puzzle piece. An effective dropshipping mechanism depends on several parties all acting in sync together. The supply chain is just that: producer, supplier, and retailer coordination.

You should split down the supply chain into three simple steps:

- The producer manufactures the goods and supplies them to wholesalers & retailers.

Let's say maker A is manufacturing bottles of water. They are marketed in bulk to manufacturers and wholesalers after the bottles come off the assembly line, who switch around & resell the bottles to dealers.

- Suppliers and wholesalers market the products to dealers.

For a particular type of product, a retailer like yourself is searching for a supplier. An arrangement to operate together is then reached between the retailer and the supplier.

A little point here: Although you may order directly from product producers, purchasing from retailers is always much cheaper instead. There are minimum purchasing criteria for most suppliers that can be very high, and you will still have to purchase stock & ship the goods.

So, purchasing directly from the producer might seem quicker, but you would profit more from buying from distributors (dealing with the little profit).

Suppliers are often convenient since all of them are skilled in a specific niche, so the type of items you need can be quickly identified. This also implies that you'll get started to sell super quick.

- Retailers sell goods to buyers.

Suppliers & wholesalers should not market to the public directly; that's the task of the retailer. The last move between the product & the consumer is the supplier.

Online stores from which customers buy goods are provided by retailers. The merchant marks it up again to reach at the final price after the wholesaler rates up the items. By "markup," we apply to fixing a premium that covers the product's cost price and gives you a benefit.

It's that! From start to end, it is the whole supply chain. In business, it's a simple but crucial concept.

You may have noted that no other group has been alluded to as a dropshipper. That is because there is no particular function for "dropshipper." Dropshipping is actually the activity of somebody else delivering goods. Technically, producers, retailers, and merchants will all be dropshippers.

Later on, we'll discuss how to start a retail dropshipping company in this guide. In other terms, you can learn how to become a trader who buys commodities from wholesalers to market to the public. This may indicate that through an online storefront, you sell through eBay or even your own website.

Remember what it's like for the consumer now that you realize what the supply chain is like.

## 2.3 What is Fulfillment?

Order fulfillment that's all the steps a corporation requires in having a fresh order and bringing the order into the hands of the customer. The procedure includes storing, picking & packaging the products, distributing them and sending the consumer an automatic email to let them know that the product is in transit.

## 2.4 The Steps to make Order Fulfillment

There are some steps involved in order fulfillment, which are as under:-

## 1. Receiving inventory.

Essentially, there are two approaches for an eCommerce company to manage inventory. It can decide to receive & stock the in-house inventory, or it can employ an outsourcer for eCommerce order fulfillment to take control of the inventory and other associated activities. The organization would be liable for taking stock, inspecting the product, marking, and maintaining the inventory method if it opts for the first alternative. If the business wishes to outsource or dropships, the order fulfillment agent or supplier can perform certain duties.

## 2. Storing inventory.

If you plan to stock the inventory yourself, after the receiving portion is finished, there'll be another list of assignments waiting for you. Shelving the inventory and holding a careful watch on what goods come in and what goods are going out would be the key activities on the list so that you can deliver the orders without any complications.

## 3. Processing the order.

Businesses who outsource order fulfillment do not have to get through the nitty-gritty of order delivery since they actually move on to their partner's order request and let them manage the rest. This is the phase where the order is taken off the shelves, shipped to a packaging station, examined for any damage, packed and transferred to the shipping station for businesses who handle their own product.

## 4. Shipping the order.

The best delivery strategy is calculated based on the scale, weight and precise specifications of the order. A third-party contractor is typically contracted to complete this phase.

Returns Handling. For online shoppers, the opportunity to refund unwanted goods quickly is a big factor in the purchase phase. You ought to design a crystal straightforward return policy that is readily available to all the customers and workers to ensure the receipt, repair and redemption of the returned goods are as successful as practicable. It will help you prevent needless confusion and errors by making this step automated.

# Chapter 3. Why dropshipping is one of the best way to make money in 2021.

According to Forrester (analyst) Reports, the magnitude of online retail revenues would be $370 billion by the end of 2017. In comparison, 23 percent, which amounts to $85.1 billion, would come from dropshipping firms. To many businesses, like startups, this sheer scale alone is attractive.

An online retailer following this concept appears similar to its traditional e-commerce competitors by appearance. Dropshipping may be a well-kept mystery in the e-commerce world as consumers just think about the goods, price and credibility of the shop rather than how the goods are sourced and who delivers the shipments.

In summary,' dropshipping' is a business strategy in which the supplier does not directly hold the inventory or process the orders in his or her control. Both orders are delivered directly from a wholesaler and delivered. This encourages the supplier to concentrate on the business's selling aspect.

Many major e-commerce names, such as Zappos, began with dropshipping. For those that seek motivation, billion-dollar dropshipping internet store Wayfair or the milliondollarBlinds.com are top examples today.

Five explanations of how the dropshipping business strategy appeals to both startups and experienced entrepreneurs are offered below. These issues in traditional e-commerce have been nagging challenges, which can be addressed with the dropshipping model immediately.

## 3.1 Dropshipping Is The E-Commerce Future

It seem that dropshipping will be the future of e-commerce. Here are some main reasons which explain this concept.

Sourcing of Product:

Conventional e-commerce stores must directly import supplies from wholesalers, frequently based in various countries. They often need goods to be bought in bulk and are then shipped prior to being promoted and distributed to the local warehouse. A lot of time, money & resources are required for the whole phase. The presence of expensive intermediaries, such as banks, freight shipments and export-import brokers, also involves it.

The dropshipping model, however, enables manufacturers to market goods for large quantities of each product without needing to think about sourcing. The entire method is substantially simplified with just a turn-key e-commerce storefront such as Shopify and a dropshipping software like Oberlo. The retailer may choose to notify the distributors via e-mail to tell them that their supplies are now being shipped to the store. The most of the procedure can be quickly handled from the dashboard, such as uploading product images, updating pricing and order monitoring.

## Storage

A traditional e-commerce store, particularly as it carries multiple or large products, requires large storage spaces. It might be imaginable to store ten to 100 items, but storing 1,000 or 1,000,000 items will cost a real fortune that is not within the reach of a start-up. This high warehouse rent issue is addressed by the dropshipping model since the goods remain with the distributor or wholesale retailer until they are bought.

## Order fulfillment

Many pioneers of e-commerce do not foresee investing most of their time picking, packaging and delivering orders. They should, of course, outsource the order fulfillment for ease to a boutique e-commerce fulfillment, such as ShipMonk. The dropshipping model, however, facilitates hands-free shipment, since the whole packaging and shipping process is in the possession of the wholesaler or distributor.

## Cataloging & photography

A conventional e-commerce shop owner has to take professional-quality images of items that may be very pricey, like a decent digital camera, a light panel, lighting and some more. For a dropshipping control software, this issue is fixed, as the "product importing" function allows for instant picture import.

## Scalability

Wayfair.com is a major online dropshipping store that holds 10,000 vendors of more than eight million items. Yes, $8 million. By this business model, such huge scalability is made possible.

Because the retailer just has to work on the publicity and customer care aspect, they don't have to think about the warehouse's rent and other operating expenses skyrocketing.

In conclusion, the dropshipping paradigm offers the ability for tiny startups with minimal capital to contend with large and medium online stores comfortably, rendering the field of e-commerce an equal environment for everyone. That being said, plan in the future to see more e-commerce shops adopting this model.

# Chapter 4. Niche And Product Selection

You want a business to start, but the thing that holds you down is the market niche that you feel you need to pick. And, honestly, it can be tricky: you might mention all your interests & passions and yet feel like you haven't hit the singular thing that you were expected to do.

Yet, it can trigger paralysis to place some sort of burden on yourself to choose the very right niche.

Certainly, in choosing a suitable niche business, you like to do your careful research, but it's easier to get up and run than to wait around. You will try ideas that way, enter the market earlier, and benefit from the victories and losses. That way, too, you can still take what you have gained from previous attempts, so step on with fresh concepts if the first company does not take off.

## 4.1 Steps how to search your right niche

Using the following five methods to find your niche, whether you're unable to determine or you need more information to work with.

### 1. Identify your interests & passions.

This could be something that you have achieved before. But, if you haven't, quickly make a compilation of 10 topical passions and areas of passion.

Business isn't easy, and it can challenge you at any stage. If you work in an area you don't care for, the likelihood of leaving will increase significantly — especially like a first sole proprietor.

This doesn't mean that a better match has to be found. You can stay with it if you are excited about any part of running the business. If you don't care about the issue, you might not be able to easily find the drive to persevere within.

### 2. Identify problems that you can solve.

You're able to get to narrow down your choices with your list of ten topics in hand. You first need to identify challenges that your target clients are facing to build a viable enterprise, then decide if you can potentially fix them. Here are a few items you should do to find issues in different niches.

### 3. Research your competition.

There is not always a bad thing in the presence of competition. It can actually show you that you've discovered a market that's lucrative. Although you do have to do an in-depth analysis of competing pages.

Build a fresh spreadsheet and start tracking all the competing websites that you can find.

And find out whether there's already an opening in the crowd to stick out. Are you still willing to rate the keywords? Is there really a way to distinguish and build a unique offer for yourself? Here are some indications that you will enter a niche and flourish, even though it is already covered by other sites:

- Content of poor quality. In a niche where several company owners are not delivering high-quality, informative content that suits the viewer, it's easy to outrank the competitors.
- Lack of transparency. By establishing an authentic and accessible identity in a niche where most platforms are faceless and unnecessarily corporate, many internet marketers have disrupted whole industries.
- The lack of paid competitiveness. If you have noticed a keyword with a relatively high search rate but little competition with paying ads, there is undoubtedly a potential for you to upset the business.

**4. Determine the profitability of the niche.**

You need to have a fairly decent understanding now about what niche you're about to get into. You might not have limited your selection down to a particular region of the topic, but you've certainly noticed a few suggestions that you feel pretty good about. It's important to have an idea at this stage about how much money you have the opportunity to make in your niche. A fine way to go to continue your search is ClickBank.

So, browse the category's best brands. That is not a positive indication if you can't locate any offers. It could mean that the niche could not be monetized by someone.

You're in luck if the quest throws up a good amount of products — just not an excessive amount of products. Take notice of pricing points such that your own goods can be marketed in a fair way.

Bear in mind, though, that you may not have to launch your organization with your own product offering. You should collaborate in your niche with product makers, marketers and site owners to start earning commissions when working on your innovative solution.

## 5. Test your idea.

You are now prepared with all the knowledge you need to pick a niche, and checking your proposal is the only thing needed to do. Setting up a landing page for pre-sales of a product you're producing is one easy way to do this. Through paying ads, you will then push traffic to this page.

That doesn't actually mean that you are not in a viable niche, even though you don't get pre-sales. Your message may not be quite correct, or you haven't found the right deal yet. You will maximize conversions by using A/B split testing to figure out whether there is something preventing the target group from taking action or not.

You will sell to two fundamental markets: customer and corporation. Such divisions are reasonably clear. "For example, if you sell women's clothes from a department shop, shoppers are your target market; if you sell office supplies, companies are your target market (this is referred to as "B2B" sales). In certain instances, for example, you could be selling to both corporations and people if you operate a printing company.

No company, especially a small one, can be everything to all individuals. The more you can describe your target group broadly, the stronger. For even the larger corporations, this method is recognized as building a market and is crucial to growth. Walmart and Tiffany are also stores, but they have somewhat different niches: Walmart caters to bargain-minded customers, while Tiffany tends to luxury jewelry buyers.

"Some entrepreneurs make the error of slipping into the "all over the map" pit instead of building a niche, believing they can do many things and be successful at all of them. Falkenstein warns that these individuals soon learn a difficult lesson: "Smaller is larger in market, and smaller is not across the map; it is extremely focused."

## 4.2 Creating a good niche

Keep in mind these important to create a good niche:

## 1.  Make a wish list.

Who do you like to do business with? Be as descriptive as you are capable of. Identify the regional spectrum and the kinds of firms or clients that you want your organization to target. You can't make contact if you do not really know whom you are going to do business with. Falkenstein cautions, "You must recognize that you can't do business with everyone." Otherwise, you risk leaving yourself exhausted and confusing your buyers.

The trend is toward small niches these days. It's not precise enough to target teens; targeting adult, African American teenagers with the family incomes of $40,000 or more is. It is too large to target corporations that market apps; it is a better aim to target Northern California-based firms that offer internet software distribution and training that have sales of $15 million or more.

## 2. Focus.

Clarify what you intend to sell, knowing that a) to all customers, you can't be all items and b) smaller is better. Your specialty isn't the same as that of sector you are employed in. A retail apparel corporation, for example, is not a niche but a sector. Maternity clothes for corporate mothers" may be a more specific niche."

Using these strategies to assist you in starting this focus process:

- Create a compilation of the greatest activities you do and the talents that are inherent in many of them.
- List your accomplishments.
- Identify the important things of life that you've experienced.
- Look for trends that reflect your personality or approach to addressing issues.

Your niche should emerge from your desires and expertise in a normal way. For instance, if you spent 10 years of working in such a consulting firm and also ten years working for such a small, family-owned company, you may actually have to start a consulting company that specializes in limited, family-owned businesses.

## 3. Describe the customer's worldview.

A good corporation utilizes what Falkenstein called the Platinum Rule: "Do to the others as they're doing to themselves." You will define their desires or desires as you look at the situation from the viewpoint of your prospective clients. Talking to new clients and recognizing their biggest issues is the perfect approach to achieve this.

## 4. Synthesize.

Your niche can begin to take shape at this point when the opinions and the desires of the consumer and desire to coalesce to create something different. There are five attributes of a Strong Niche:

- In other terms, it relates to your long-term view and carries you where you like to go.
- Somebody else needs it, consumers in particular.
- It is closely arranged.
- It's one-of-a-kind, "the only city game."
- It evolves, enabling you to build multiple profit centers and yet maintain the core market, thus guaranteeing long-term success.

## 5. Evaluate.

It is now time to test the product or service proposed against the five requirements in Phase 4. Perhaps you'll notice that more business travel than that you're ready for is needed for niche you had in mind. That indicates that one of the above conditions is not met-it will not carry you where you like to go. Scrap it, and pass on to the next proposal.

## 6. Test.

Test-market it until you have a balance between the niche and the product. "Give individuals an opportunity to purchase your product or service, not just theoretically, but actually put it out there." By giving samples, such as a complimentary mini-seminar or a preview copy of the newsletter, this can be accomplished. "If you spend enormous sums of cash on the initial trial run, you're possibly doing it wrong," she says. The research shouldn't cost you a bunch of money:

## 7. Go for it!

It is time for your idea to be implemented. This is the most challenging step for many entrepreneurs. But worry not: if you have done your research, it would be a measured risk to reach the business, not simply a chance.

# Chapter 5. How to start dropshipping business in 2021

It's not easy to learn the way to start a dropshipping company, as with any type of business. Nevertheless, it's a perfect first move in the world of business. Without keeping any inventory, you may sell to customers. You do not have to pay upfront for goods. And if you are passionate about your new venture, in the long term, you will create a sustainable source of revenue.

In this complete dropshipping guide, suggest taking the following market and financial moves if you are considering dropshipping.

Others are mandatory from the start, and others are only a smart idea, so it will save you time and stress down the line by coping with them up front.

Dropshipping is a method of order fulfillment that helps shop owners to deliver without stocking any stock directly to buyers. If a consumer orders a commodity from a dropshipping shop, it is delivered directly to them by a third-party retailer. The client pays the selling price that you set, you pay the market price of the vendors, and the rest is benefit. You never need to maintain goods or spend in inventory.

You are responsible for designing a website and your own label, as well as selecting and promoting the items you choose to offer in the dropshipping business strategy. Your corporation is therefore liable for the expense of shipping and for setting rates that result in a reasonable profit margin.

**Steps For Starting A Dropshipping Profitable Business**

Learn to find high-margin products, introduce them to your business, and easily begin selling them.

## 1. Commit yourself for starting a dropshipping business

Dropshipping, as in any other business, needs considerable effort and a long-term focus. You're going to be deeply surprised if you're looking for a six-figure benefit from 6 weeks of part-time employment. You would be far less likely to get frustrated and leave by entering the organization with reasonable assumptions regarding the commitment needed and the prospects for benefit.

You'll need to spend heavily when beginning a dropshipping venture, utilizing one of the two following currencies: time or funds.

**Investing time in dropshipping business**

Our recommended strategy, particularly for the first dropshipping developers, is bootstrapping & investing sweat equity to develop your company. For various factors, we prefer this method over spending a huge amount of money:

- You will understand how the organization works inside out, which, as the enterprise expands and scales, will be crucial for handling others.
- You would know your clients and business personally, helping you to make smarter choices.
- You would be less inclined to waste huge amounts on vanity ventures that are not vital to success.
- You will build some new talents that will enable you a stronger entrepreneur.

Realistically, most persons are not ready to leave their work in order to ramp up their own online shop for six months. It might be a little more complicated, but even though you're already doing a 9-to-5 job, it's surely feasible to get underway with dropshipping, assuming you set reasonable standards for your customers about customer support and delivery times. When you continue to expand, as much as working capital and profitability allow, you will move into working long hours on your company.

Both companies and entrepreneurs are specific, but it is feasible to produce a monthly income stream of $1,000-$2,000 within 12 months of working around 10 to 15 hours per week to develop the firm.

Excited regarding starting a new business but not knowing where to begin? This informative guide will show you how to identify great products with strong sales potential that are newly trendy.

If you have the choice of working long hours on your company, that's the best option to increase your profit prospects and the possibility of good dropshipping. It is particularly beneficial in the early days to concentrate all the energies on publicity when creating traction is essential. It would normally take approximately 12 months of full-time jobs based on our knowledge, with a heavy focus on publicity for a dropshipping firm to replace an annual full-time salary of $50,000.

For a very small payout, it might sound like a lot of work, but bear these two points in mind:

When the dropshipping company is up and going, it would actually require considerably less time than from a 40-hour-per-week work to maintain it. In terms of the reliability and scalability that the dropshipping paradigm offers, much of your expenditure pays off.

You establish more than just a revenue stream when you develop a company. You also build an asset that you will market in the future. Be sure that when looking at the true return, you remember the equity valuation you are accruing, and also the cash flow produced.

## Investing money in dropshipping business

By spending a lot of capital, it is feasible to develop and grow a dropshipping company, but we suggest against it. We attempted all methods to growing an enterprise (bootstrapping it ourselves vs. outsourcing the procedure), and while we were in the trenches doing much of the work, we had the most progress.

In the early stages, it is vital to have someone who is profoundly involved in the company's future to construct it from the ground up. You would be at the hands of pricey engineers, developers, and advertisers who will easily eat away whatever money you produce without knowing how your organization operates at any stage. You don't have to do everything it yourself, but at the start of your company, we highly advocate becoming the primary motivating power.

To have your company started and operating, you would, though, require a modest cash reserve in the $1,000 range. For limited administrative costs (like web hosting and dropshipping providers), you may need this and to pay some incorporation fees, which we will cover below.

## 2. Dropshipping business idea to chose

The second phase in studying how to launch a dropshipping company is to do the market research required. You want to find a niche you are interested in and make choices based on how effective it can be, almost like though you were starting a grocery shop and checking at the numerous sites, rivals, and developments. But the fact is, it's tricky to come up with product concepts to offer.

Niche goods also have a more passionate client base, which, through increasing awareness about the items, will make marketing to unique audiences simpler. A good entry point to begin dropshipping without cash could be health, clothes, makeup goods, appliances, phone accessories, or yoga-related pieces.

Any instances of dropshipping stores in a niche may be:

- Dog bow and ties for dog lovers
- Exercise equipment for fitness
- iPhone cases and cables for iPhone owners
- Camping gear for campers

To try the dropshipping business ideas, you may also use the appropriate techniques:

Google Trends could really help you identify whether, as well as the seasons in which they tend to trend, a product is trending up or down. Notice the search volume is not indicated by Google Patterns. But if you're using it, be sure to use a keyword tool such as Keywords Everywhere to cross-check your data to determine the popularity of the product in search.

### 3. Do competitor research

You want to check about your competitors so that you know what you're trying to sell in your shop and appreciate the way they operate. Your competitors may have great success hints which can help you develop a better marketing strategy for your dropshipping firm.

Limit your study to only five other dropshipping firms, like one or two major players such as Walmart or Ebay, if your business has a number of competitors (that is a positive thing in dropshipping). It will help you remain centered and prepare your next phase.

### 4. Choose a dropshipping supplier

Choosing a supplier for dropshipping is a crucial move towards creating a profitable dropshipping business. A dropshipping company does not have any goods to ship to consumers without vendors and would thus cease to operate.

At this stage, you analyzed what goods you want to offer and realize that they can be profitable, and you want to know where to find a provider of dropshipping that provides you with the high-quality service that you need to grow. By linking Oberlo to the online store, eCommerce platforms such as Shopify provide a plug-and-play style alternative to find possible suppliers.

## 5. Build your ecommerce store

An eCommerce platform such as Shopify is the next what you need to launch a dropshipping business. This is the home where you deliver traffic, offer goods, and payments are processed.

These type of platforms makes the e-commerce website simple to create and launch. It is a complete commerce service that connects you to sell and receive payments in several ways, like online, sell in different currencies, and conveniently manage products.

To use e-commerce websites, you don't need to become a programmer or developer either. They have resources to assist with anything from domain name ideas to logo design, and with the store creator and Payment processing themes, you are quickly able to modify the feel and look of your store.

## 6. Market your dropshipping store

It's time to talk about promoting your new shop, now that you know to start a dropshipping firm. You may want to bring more work into your marketing and promotional activities while developing the dropshipping business strategy to stick out in your market.

You will invest time working on selling and supporting the company in the following ways, with too many stuff about dropshipping being processed:

- Paid ads (Facebook & Google).

For a Facebook ad, the average cost is about 0.97 cents per click, that's not too bad if you're new to social media advertising. Facebook ads are extensible, goods can perform ok on them, and they click into the desire of people to purchase momentum. You can run Google Shopping Ads and target lengthy keywords that are more likely to be purchased by shoppers. Typically, with Google ads, there is more price competition, but it might be worthy of your time to check it out.

- Influencer marketing.

You may have a low funds for marketing your business as a new dropshipper. Influencer marketing is also an affordable way to target audience because individuals are more likely than traditional advertising to trust influencers. When you go this route, start negotiating an affiliate fee versus a flat rate with the influencer. It's a win-win situation, as every sale they're going to make money off, and the cost is going to be less for you.

- Mobile marketing.

Smartphone marketing is a broad term referring to a company that connects with clients on their mobile phones. You can start with a VIP text club, for example, and encourage website users to sign up for the exclusive promotions & deals. Or provide client support through Messenger in a live chat session with shoppers. You can create automated qualified leads, customer loyalty, and cart abandonment campaigns with a mobile marketing tool such as ManyChat to drive sales and profits for your dropshipping business.

Stay updated on what channels are operating and which are not, as with any profitable online business, especially if you invest money in them like paid ads. You can always adjust your marketing plan to lower costs as well as maximize revenue as you keep growing and improve your business.

## 7. Analyze your offering

You should start looking at the consequences of your diligent work after you've been promoting and operating your dropshipping company for some time. Any analytics will help you address some critical online shop queries, like:

- Sales

What are my channels with the highest performance? Where am I expected to put more ad dollars? What else are my favorite items for sale? What are my greatest clients?

- Behavior of shoppers

Do citizens buy more on their laptops or cell phones? For each unit, what's the conversion rate?

- Margins of profit

Why are the most profitable pieces and variant SKUs? What do my month-over-month revenue and gross income look like?

To track web traffic over time and optimize your search engine optimization activities, you can even use resources like Google Analytics & Search Console. Plus, you review the results monthly to guarantee that your overall plan succeeds with your business, whether you are utilizing third-party software for your social network or messenger marketing.

You want to build a data-informed analytics framework while building a dropshipping e-commerce store. Remain compatible with what you evaluate over time and calculate the consistency of your store against simple KPIs. This will encourage you to make better choices for your store, so move your small business over time to the next level.

# Chapter 6. How To identify Best Suppliers For Your New Dropshipping Business

Dropshipping is a model for eCommerce that is increasingly attractive. That is because launching a dropshipping company is simpler (not to say less expensive) than managing inventory for a traditional digital storefront.

The whole model of drop shipment is focused on the retailer doing its job well and delivering orders timely and effectively. It goes without saying, therefore, that identifying the appropriate supplier is one, if not the most important, and a step towards creating a successful brand. If an order is messed up by your supplier/seller, you and your organization are liable, so the trick is to find someone who adheres to the schedule and is open to discuss any problems

The advantages and disadvantages of dropshipping are well known, but it has become far less obvious that the most significant part of beginning a dropshipping business is choosing the right vendors for your WooCommerce shop. Until now.

## 6.1 The Importance of Selecting The Right Suppliers

A special model for eCommerce is Dropshipping. To retain their own inventories, conventional online retailers compensate. Those expenses are all but offset by dropshipping, so dropshipping would not need substantial start-up investment.

In the other side, dropshipping suggests that you place the destiny of your eCommerce store in the possession of others.

With the dropshipping system, retailers focus on wholesalers, manufacturers, and dealers who meet the orders of the retailers.

The dropshipping puzzle has several parts, and for the greater image, each component is critical. Among those pieces, one of the most significant is dropshipping suppliers. In reality, the finest dropshippers know that a dropshipping eCommerce store can make or break the efficiency and overall reliability of dropshipping suppliers.

## 6.2 Finding Your Dropshipping Suppliers

It needs you to partner with manufacturers, wholesalers, & distributors to start a dropshipping business. You want to identify vendors who improve the dropshipping business rather than compromise it.

**Research Your Products**

You have to figure out what types of things you can sell before you can start finding and working with vendors.

You want to address queries in specific, such as:

- Where does the item come from?
- How long would manufacturing take?
- How is it done?

Are there factors of height or weight which might make fulfillment more complicated or more costly?

The purpose is not expertise; however, you want to get to know the goods so that you can help determine which ones are suitable for dropshipping.

**Understand the supply chain and recognize the considerations**

You need to get familiar with dropship supply chain after nailing down your goods. In other terms, you should to know how it works for dropshipping.

For dropshipping, the items never really go into the hands of the dealer. Instead, an order is issued by the retailer, and a supplier who manages packing and delivery initiates fulfillment. In this way, the dealer is like the director of a dropshipping company.

You can't sell goods if you don't have reputable vendors, which suggests that you don't have a dropshipping business.

You need to get familiar with dropship supply chain since nailing down your products. In other terms, you need to understand how it functions for dropshipping.

For dropshipping, the items never really go into the hands of the dealer. Instead, an order is issued by the retailer and a supplier who manages packing and delivery initiates fulfilment. In this manner, the retailer is just like the director of a dropshipping company.

You can't sell goods if you don't have reputable suppliers, which suggests that you don't have a dropshipping business.

**Search for Dropshipping Wholesalers on Google**

You will identify the major vendors for your preferred commodities or product types with a Google search.

When you build a preliminary list, by studying the next few queries, take notice of the various characteristics of dropshipping suppliers.

- What is supplier location?
- Will the retailer link with your WooCommerce shop so that fresh orders are immediately submitted for fulfillment?
- What (if any) is the sum of minimum order (MOQ)?
- What support (e.g., mobile, email, chat, etc.) does the provider offer?
- What kind of range of items does the retailer offer?

**Subscribe to Dropshipping Suppliers Directories**

And if lots of choices pop up in the Google searches, directories will bring even more options. For a broad selection of items, these repositories comprise of web lists of dropshipping vendors and wholesalers.

You should recognize that some of the finest are premium directories, such as Salehoo and Worldwide Labels, implying they need paying subscriptions. There are a lot of free directories accessible that you can access at no fee, like Wholesale Central. Free directories, though, are occasionally obsolete. Newer vendors do not exist, and suppliers are also listed who are no longer in operation.

Usually, premium directories vary in cost from $20 a month for lifetime access to a few hundred bucks. You can find the expense of a premium directory to be beneficial, with free directories often hit-or-miss. There are also premium directories, like Doba, explicitly customized for dropshipping.

**Figure Out Your Competitor's Suppliers**

It follows that you must see what your competitors do if you want to be successful in the dropshipping field. Do any acknowledgment, in fact, to see which manufacturers are meeting their requirements.

There are a lot of methods to do this, but testing the markets that the competitors sell is the best.

If the supplier is not listed on the page, by making your own order, you will always show the supplier. Since the retailer is pleased, an invoice or packaging slip from them would possibly be included with the shipment. To ask about a partnership with your own dropshipping company, you can then contact the supplier directly.

**Attend Trade Seminars**

Trade shows have been considered to be an efficient place for manufacturers to set up and grow their companies. So, if you haven't been to a trade seminar  yet, add it to the end of the list of to-do events.

You network with other participants within dropship supply chain, like distributors and dropshipping wholesalers, at trade shows. You get an insider's view on current and future products that you should introduce to your online store. For dropshipping businesses, you even get to "talk shop" face-to-face, which is also the most successful way to do business.

## Join Industry Groups and Networks

Trade shows facilitate with locating vendors for dropshipping firms, yet another effective resource is business networks and groups.

The majority of retailers, like the identities of their dropshipping vendors, are not willing to share the secrets of their performance. The individuals who enter business groups, however, want to share, learn, & develop. Through being part of the dropshipping network, you will get valuable insight from industry professionals. Your colleagues, for instance, might recommend better suppliers or alert you about suppliers in order to avoid.

## Connect with the Manufacturers

Not all manufacturers supply to consumers directly, although there are those who do. Until picking vendors for your eCommerce dropshipping shop, suggest reaching out to the producers of the goods that you will market.

You have far higher margins when a producer chooses to be the distributor than with a traditional retailer or wholesaler. Manufacturers, on the other hand, frequently impose minimum order amounts that could need bigger orders. You might find yourself with considerable inventory to deal in this situation, which is intended to circumvent dropshipping.

Ask the vendor to recommend vendors for you if a manufacturer won't work with you. A recommendation, after all, indicates that the agreements and commitments between a manufacturer and a supplier is successful. For that cause, it is definitely worth putting suggested vendors on your list of possibilities.

**Order Samples**

There's no substitution for firsthand knowledge, no matter how many feedback or testimonials you find. This is why ordering samples is the next phase in finding the correct dropshipping suppliers for the business.

Ordering samples teaches you a few key things about a supplier. First one is that you get to know the product's consistency yourself.

The second is that you will see how delivery is done by the retailer, and what shipment packaging seems to if a different vendor is involved, and how long it takes to ship and distribute. Suppliers will execute the requests, so buying samples provides you with an idea of what your clients will feel.

**Confirm Contract Terms & Fees**

You compiled several options, removed any but the most suitable possibilities, ordered tests to assess certain vendors, and decided on your dropshipping company with the right supplier (or suppliers). Negotiating deal conditions and payments is the last option left to do.

New businesses with unproven consumer bases have fewer bargaining leverage relative to mature companies with established customer bases. When it comes to communicating the margins, this is especially true.

Since dropshipping means that you don't have to hold your inventory, there would be low margins. The bulk of inventory costs and expenditures involved with meeting your orders is borne by your supplier(s). With dropshipping, because prices are smaller, gross margins are often lower than if you stored and delivered orders personally.

With margins generally poor, the fees concerned may be the biggest distinction between vendors. Such suppliers, for instance, charge flat per-order rates that are applied to the overall cost of the goods. Per-order payments typically vary from $2 and $5 to cover delivery and shipping costs (although big or unwieldy goods can require higher fees).

In the end, you want to select the supplier(s) that satisfies your specifications and give contracts of appropriate terms.

# Chapter 7. Setting Up Your Dropshipping business On A Budget

The establishment of a dropshipping company as an eCommerce business is a perfect way to earn money. Managing a business without the hassle of product and shipping logistics is the most convincing aspect of a dropshipping store

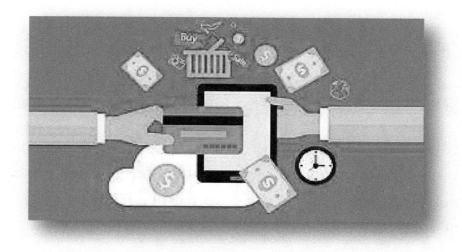

You have already heard stories from businessmen about how costly it is to start a business. This involve accounts of hopelessly pursuing buyers or firms failing because of bleak financials to remain afloat. Do not let this scare you from launching a dropshipping store, as this model enables you to offer low-risk products.

What you need to do is get the orders and call the supplier-the rest is up to them.

There are very few financial barriers associated with the establishment of a dropshipping store when it comes to financing the company. In fact, with around zero initial investment, you can get underway with an online store.

Here's a 7-step feasible plan for launching a dropshipping shop on a budget shoestring.

## 1. Research Your Options

You'll need to do some research before beginning some form of business.

It requires getting online and finding out the competitors that offer related goods. To see just what each has to suggest, you'll also want to spend a little time investigating the future vendors and distributors.

Each shipping group will have a specific way of doing stuff and pricing models, therefore pay careful attention to those specifics so that you can ensure that you team up with your dropshipping store with the right party.

## 2. Create a Plan to Stick

You'll need to get a solid plan in progress before you can launch your business activities. A budget is used with this. It's important to decide what your budget is, whether you have $100 or $500 to get underway and ensure that you adhere to it. The easiest way to achieve so is to maintain good track of all your spending to guarantee that as you start up your store, you do not go over the budget.

## 3. Find Your Niche

In reality, many believe that it is an impossible task. It may be really challenging to appeal to all. Instead, rather than attempting to market could product under the sun, choose the goods focused on a particular niche.

Select a particular area of the business, such as organic pet food or dog clothes, if you decide that you want to market animal-related items.

When you can refine your attention down, you can have a much higher sales rate, and you are more likely to be noticed when customers are looking for a particular form of a product. Your small shop can get lost in the noise of competitors if your focus is too big.

## 4. Set Up Your eCommerce website

This is the phase through which you finally launch and set up your site with a dropshipping store.

Three of the most successful eCommerce sites accessible to sellers today are Shopify and Wix. It's quick to get started, as well as its user-friendly interface, also for sellers who are not especially tech-savvy, makes configuration and maintenance easy.

With monthly prices of less than $40, Shopify and Wix are both inexpensive alternatives, making it a perfect way to get off on a budget in the digital marketplace. You may also open a Modalyst store to boost the delivery and streamline the distribution process.

You're able to move on to the next stage after you have set up a simple online storefront that has your products selected.

## 5. Make Meetings With Your Suppliers

When it comes to choosing which provider to use it for your dropshipping shop, there are lots of decisions out there. Because you've done your homework in phase one already, now is the moment where your decision is formalized. Through entering into a contract with the commodity distributor(s) of your choosing, you will do so. Any of the most successful shipping partners makes it simple to get started, and in no time, unlike having to pay such upfront costs, you will be on your way.

The most relevant issues you are asking your prospective suppliers are:

- Do you keep all products in stock?
- How do you care the returns?
- What is your normal or average processing time?
- In which areas do you ship to? Do international shipping available?
- What kind of support did you offer?
- Is there any limit for orders?

You would have a solid understanding about how your suppliers conduct their company until you meet a supplier who addresses certain questions to your satisfaction. In addition, as a seller dealing for them, you'll realize what you need to do. You're on the path to a successful working partnership at this point.

## 6. Start Selling

Oh, congratulations. In launching your online store, this is one of most exciting steps. It's time to add your product details to your website and start selling until you have all your arrangements and agreements in order.

If customers are not aware of the products, you will not have enough sales, to begin with. You'll want to waste more time and money on ads if this is the case. By beginning with low-cost advertisements on Instagram and Facebook, or advertising on blogs as well as other websites which have a common audience, you will keep advertising costs reasonably small.

## 7. Optimize Your Site

You should take some time to customize the website until you have some revenue and knowledge under your belt. You can do all this earlier in the process, but waiting to see what is really working before you start to make changes is often a good idea.

There are a broad variety of customization choices for sites such as Shopify and Modalyst, including templates that change the way your website looks and plugins to can customize how your website works. The primary aim here is to tweak the site in ways that make it smoother for your clients and more organized.

As you've seen, all it takes to set up an online store is a few steps, and most of them don't need any money. You're not lonely if you're excited about being an owner of an eCommerce company just don't have a ton of money to launch with. This is why so many platforms are accessible that make it easier to get started without investing a million in the process.

Making sure that it works and prepare a strategy that you will use to guide you when keeping under your budget by setting up your dropshipping business, no matter how small it might be.

# Chapter 8. Mistakes To Avoid When Developing Your Dropshipping Business

In an environment that jumps at the chance to make a business deal quick and convenient, Dropshipping tends to have a no for retailers. It might seem like, now, acquiring the goods and marketing with a bit of savvy are your only worries. Yet, if you wish to hold the company afloat, you should not forget about the client's perspective. True, the boring duties of inventory, order filling, and then ensuring shipping can be passed on.

The dropshipping company, however, does not waste any time thinking about the feelings of your client. How do you assume if your client is going to be satisfied? The buyers are the ones who put the money back. Anything falls out the window if they're not satisfied. You would need to consider the duties and what failures typically trigger it all to backfire in order to completely enjoy the advantages of utilizing dropshipping.

Here are a common mistake that leads to the failure end of your dropshipping business, so you should hold these mistakes in mind all the time.

# 1. Worrying About Shipping Costs.

While shipping costs might be a doozy, it's never productive to stress. In this area, you will need to decide under which your priorities lie. Shipping prices can vary all over the board, depending on where orders come from. This stress can be relieved by setting a flat rate and generally evens out with time. Not only does this make things easier for you, but it's also simple and easy for customers.

# 2. Relying Much on Vendors.

By putting much trust in such a vendor, a good number of crises can arise. For example, they may go out of business or increase their rates on you if you only use one vendor. They might run out of the items that you expect them to supply. Where would you be then? This is why there should always be a backup for you. It is smart to write up the contract with your vendors for your own insurance to remain aware of your requirements. This will ensure that everyone involved has agreed to uphold what you demand.

# 3. Expecting Easy Money.

Dropshipping, as we've already established, offers a degree of ease that can seem to make your work easier. Yet, you can't ignore how critical your product is in marketing and all the competition you're going to face. This involves analysis and the creation of a unique approach that will allow the product more attractive than that of anyone else.

## 4. Making Order Difficult to Access.

When you assure your consumers a simple and quick procedure, they'll want to see the proofs. Set approximate location-based ship dates and require suppliers to keep you posted on the status of the order so that you can keep the consumer aware. This way, you can track shipments whenever you anticipate them to come longer than expected and easily fix issues.

## 5. Not Enough Brand Display.

Through dropshipping, it may be hard to guarantee the brand remains to be seen in the customer's overall experience. You may not want people to forget regarding you, so it's important to insert as many locations as possible into your brand. You should have customized packing slips, stickers and custom exterior packaging to hold the name included after delivery. Sending a follow-up thank you message or a survey to remind about of you and prove them you think for their feedback at the same time is also not a bad idea.

## 6. Return Complications.

If you do not have a system for returns set up, things can get messy very quickly. You and your vendor will have to establish a refund policy to avoid this. Customers are going to wait for their refund expectantly, and being disorganized on that front and will not make them feel good. They may also need guidelines explaining how or where to return the product. Organizing a structure for this will save a good amount of confusion and irritation for both you and the client.

## 7. Selling Trademarked Products

When most people learn about dropshipping and realize that it is not that complicated to do the process, they picture all the things they might sell and make a quick buck.

Many of these goods are items which have been trademarked by a manufacturer. Selling these goods without the manufacturer's specific consent to be a retail agent will lead you to legal issues. This can not only lead to the end of your online shop, but you can also be held personally responsible.

You should, consequently, look at generic items which you can add to your variety of products for sale. Best still, you should swap in goods with white marks. They are plain goods that are available to those who rebrand them through the manufacturer. You will order and get these items customized to suit the brand and display them.

## 8. Picking the Wrong Field

Once you have abandoned thoughts of selling any product you come across, by concentrating on one field, you can develop your dropshipping business.

You might, however, select the wrong niche in which to operate. Maybe you should pick a niche that isn't lucrative. This may be that it's out of vogue or it's simply not meant for shopping online.

Therefore, to see what will earn you money, you have to do proper market analysis. "Market research" might sound like a complex process in which only major brands participate.

Simple Google searches will, therefore, show you what individuals are interested in and where they purchase them.

## 9. Poor Relationship With Suppliers

Your vendors are part of your business; they promise that you have the best goods and that they supply your consumers with them. You can be inclined, though, to consider them as workers and handle them as though they are in the hierarchy on a lower rung.

They're not. They are your friends, without whom it would be effectively dead for your dropshipping business. Therefore, you can establish a better relationship with them.

This will have its benefits. When negotiating costs for commodity stock, a strong partnership will work in your favor.

## 10. Lowering Price To Extreme Levels

Reducing your prices to knock out your competition is also one of the dropshipping failures to avoid.

This is a logical way for you to rise your dropshipping business, you might think. You could have been no farther from the facts. Very low prices indicate to potential customers that your product may be of poor quality.

## 11. Poor Website Structure

The progress of your dropshipping company depends on the shopping experience your clients have when they browse your online store.

Thus, you have to make sure everything is convenient for them. However, you could rush through the process of establishing your website due to low barrier for entrance into dropshipping. Many beginners do not have the coding skills required to construct an online store.

In conclusion, the primary interest is the customer's experience. Although inventory management and shipping are not your responsibility, you can also ensure that all is well handled. All of these dropshipping failures can be prevented with adequate preparation and careful management, and the business can better manage.

# Chapter 9. Smooth Running tips for Your Dropshipping Business

Well, you've done your research, decided to agree on the right dropship goods and roped in the right possible supplier. All of you are planned to begin dropshipping goods and make the mullah! Setting up the company, though, is typically one thing, but a totally different ball game is to manage it on a day-to-day basis. Even if it's a dropshipping company, there are various facets of running a business that you have to remember as a retailer: marketing, refunds, refunds, repairs, inventory, distribution, customer service, and far more. So dive into all these different aspects of managing a dropshipping business.

So far, when covered a lot of details, it involves everything from the fundamentals of dropshipping to the nuances of finding a niche and managing the business. You should have much of a base by now to begin investigating and establishing your own dropshipping company comfortably.

It's possible to get confused and lose track about what's really necessary, with too much to consider. That's why we've built this list of key elements for success. This are the main "must-do" acts that can make the new company or ruin it. If you can perform these effectively, you would be able to get a bunch of other stuff wrong and yet have a decent probability of success.

## 1. Add Value

The most important performance element is making a good roadmap on how you will bring value to your clients. In the field of dropshipping, where you can contend with legions of other "me too" stores carrying related items, this is critical for both corporations, but even more so.

With dropshipping, it's reasonable to think you're marketing a product to consumers. Yet good small merchants realize that they are offering insights, ideas and solutions, not just the commodity they deliver. You assume you're an e-commerce seller, but you're in the information industry as well.

If you can't create value by quality data and advice, price is the only thing you're left to contend on. While this has been an effective technique for Walmart, it will not help you grow a successful company for dropshipping.

## 2. Focus on SEO and marketing

The opportunity to push traffic to the new platform is a near second to providing value as a main key factor. A shortage of traffic to their sites is the #1 concern and annoyance faced by modern e-commerce retailers. So many retailers have been slaving away on the ideal platform for months just to unleash it into a community that has no clue it exists.

For the success of your company, advertising and driving traffic is completely necessary and challenging to outsource well, particularly if you have a limited budget and bootstrap your business. In order to build your own SEO, publicity, outreach and guest posting abilities, you have to consider taking the personal initiative.

Within the first 6 - 12 months, where no one know who you are, this is particularly crucial. You need to devote at least 75 percent of your time on publicity, SEO and traffic development for at least 4 to 6 months after your website launch, which is right, 4 to 6 months. You can start reducing and coast a little on the job you put in until you've built a strong marketing base. But it's difficult, early on, to bring so much emphasis on advertising.

## 3. Marketing Your Dropshipping Business

Marketing is indeed a subjective field, and that there are a billion strategies which can be used to position your brand successfully whilst driving awareness and sales of your brand. It will even help you root out the remainder of the market if the approach is well planned.

## 4. Social Media Source

Social networking is one of the most efficient ways to promote, advertise, attract clients and share content, so when social networks are now used for digital marketing, it comes as no surprise. For example, Facebook has more than 1.7 billion active members from diverse walks of life, and it is this diversity that makes it so appealing to online marketers.

One thing to note is that it's important to content. No matter how perfect a platform is or how good the product you are offering is, without high quality content backing it up, it means nothing.

## 5. Customer Ratings & Reviews

A few bad customer ratings will actually ruin a business in dropshipping business model. Think about it: As you order online from websites like ebay and aliexpress, the quality ranking and what other consumers had to tell about it will be one of the determining purchase variables, too, with decrease delivery. A few positive feedback will also give you an advantage over the competition because that is what will help you convert traffic to your website successfully.

## 6. Email Marketing

In a digital marketer's pack, this one of the most neglected tools. To keep your clients in the loop for any major changes within company, email marketing may be used: Price increases, promotions, coupons, content related to the commodity, and content unique to the industry are only some of the forms email marketing may be utilized.

## 7. Growth Hacking

Growth hacking is a cheap but highly productive way to get online creative marketing campaigns. A few definitions of growth hacking involve retargeting old campaigns and featuring in your own niche as a guest writer for a popular website. Any of this commonly involves content marketing.

# Chapter 10. How To Maximize Your Chances Of Success?

There are only a couple more tips you should adopt to maximize the chances of long-term growth if you are willing to take the plunge and attempt dropshipping. Second, that doesn't mean you can approach a dropshipping business because it's risk-free simply because there are no setup costs involved with purchasing and managing goods. You're also spending a lot of time choosing the right dropshippers while designing your website, so consider it as an investment and do careful preliminary research.

## 1. Things To Remember

What do you want to sell? How profitable is the surroundings? How can you gain clients and distinguish yourself? Inside the same room, is there a smaller niche that is less competitive? When they find a particular market and curate their goods like a pro, most individuals who operate a purely dropshipping model have seen the most growth, ensuring that any last item they offer is a successful match for their niche audience with their brand.

After you develop your list of possible dropshippers, carry out test orders and then watch for the items to arrive, thinking like a consumer. How long can any order take? What is the feeling of unboxing like? What is the commodity standard itself? This will help you distinguish between possible dropshippers or confirm that positive consumer service is offered by the one you want.

Note that the goods themselves may not be the differentiator for your business.

After you have chosen your dropshippers and products, note that the products themselves may not be the differentiator for your business. So ask what else you should count on to make the deal. This is another explanation why test orders are a wonderful idea since they encourage you to obtain the item and explain its functionality and advantages as a client might. In a way which really shows it off, you can even take high-quality, professional pictures of the product. Armed with exclusive explanations of the goods and images that are separate from all the other product photos, you would be able to start standing out.

Your bread and butter is definitely going to be a well-executed campaign strategy, so devote time and money on each section of it, from finding your potential audience to interacting with influencers on social media in your niche. Targeted commercials can be a perfect way to kick start your site to bring your name on the mind of your client base.

When it relates to your return policies, delivery contact and customer support, ensure your ducks are in a line. You'll need to do what you could to serve as the buffer between a dropshipper and your client if something goes wrong somewhere in the process. Understand the typical cost of return for each item so that you will notice whether it is large enough to denote a quality issue. If you suspect a consistency problem, talk to your dropshipper or try a different supplier to your issues.

Eventually, note that dropshipping is not a model of "all or nothing." Many of the more profitable corporations follow a hybrid model, making or shipping in-house some goods and employing dropshippers to fill the gaps. The dropshippers are not the key profit-drivers for these firms but are instead a simple, inexpensive way to provide clients with the "extras" they can enjoy. Before you put it in-house, you can even use dropshipped products for upsells, impulse sales, or to try a new model.

As long as you consider the above tips to ensuring that the one you chose is suitable for your business needs, there is definitely a lot to learn from the streamlining and flexibility of using a dropshipper. You will make your dropshipping store run for you in no time with a little of research, negotiation, and setup!

# Conclusion

So that concludes our definitive dropshipping guide. You now learn how to set up to kick start your new dropshipping business if you've made it here. Starting up your own business often involves a certain degree of dedication, effort, and ambition to make things work, much as in every other undertaking in life. It's not only about building the business but also about pushing through and knowing how to manage it on a daily basis.

The greatest feature of dropshipping is that you will practice in real-time by checking your goods and concepts, and all you have to do is drop it from your shop if anything doesn't work. This business concept is indeed a perfect opportunity for conventional business models to try out product concepts. Dropshipping creates a secure place to innovate to see what happens without incurring any substantial damages that will surely give business owners the courage to state that they have a working idea of how the market works. The dropshipping business model is an interesting business model to move into with little initial expense and relatively little risk.

A perfect choice to drop shipping if you are only starting to sell online and would like to test the waters first. It's a great way to start your business, even if the margins are low.

As dropshipping can still get started with little investment, before they build their market image, businessmen can start with that too. Ecommerce sites such as Ebay, Shopify, Alibaba and social networking, such as Instagram, Twitter, Reddit, provide vast expertise in user base and content marketing. It also helps newbies to know about establishing an online store, optimizing conversions, generating traffic and other basics of e-commerce.

That's what you need to learn about beginning a dropshipping. Just note, it's not the hard part to launch your dropshipping store, the real challenge is when you get trapped, and your stuff is not being sold. Do not panic, and keep checking as it happens. You're going to get a product soon that sells well.

# Youtube, Tik-Tok and Instagram Made Easy

*A Collection of Filters, Entertaining Topics and Viral Trends to Gain 10k Followers and Generate Passive Income*

**By**

**The Golden Inner Circle**

# Table of contents

# Introduction

Don't think you can compete against millions of creators and influencers? Well, let's set one thing straight, not only can you do it but also how you can do it. Working smarter, not necessarily harder, makes all the difference.

This book is for those who wish to make a name of themselves by leaving behind a reputation, legacy on social media platforms. Or maybe, all you want is to be able to do what you love for a living and offer that to the world. Either way, you're in the right place.

If you haven't been able to make much of a passive income from these social platforms for a while now, you should know it's probably not you; it's the platform. This book aims to provide an insight into these social platforms by teaching you how to increase your audience by changing some basic habits and teach you a few new tips, tricks, and tactics you can use by first understanding their working. 10,000 is perhaps the right number of followers to be considered literally as an influencer/brand, get paying offers, and raise your account's value.

It may be sluggish as you try to win the starting few followers, but it does get a little easier after that. Understanding the algorithm plays a crucial role in enlarging your audience. YouTube, Tik Tok, and Instagram use algorithms to recommend various creators. Once you understand how their algorithms work, you can easily reach a larger variety of users. By gaining an active audience of about 10K, YouTube, Tik Tok, and Instagram may consider paying attention to your content, and you could even gain more than 10,000 depending on your consistency.

Now, you are probably thinking "easier said than done", right? Well, don't worry, this book is solely there to make these things easier. To provide a how-to gain 10K followers quickly, An easy-to-use reference to aid your growth on social media platforms (i.e., YouTube, Tik Tok, and Instagram.)

Try not to read this book as a novel; rather, truly study it and apply it in your daily practices to notice change and improvement in your channel/account/profile growth.

First, this book will teach you why earning a passive income through YouTube, Tik Tok, and Instagram is the way to go, especially in this day and age, next, how each platform has its own way of working and different method to win over the platform to your side. And then, if you're having a tough time generating content for these platforms, the last part will teach you how you can remove your creativity block and let your muse come to you. Last but not least, Afterthoughts will give you that push you need to get cracking, radiating motivation and energy to really get you started.

# CHAPTER I: Why it's One of the Best Ways to Earn

In current times, the Internet is available in almost every part of the world. People interact, learn, and enjoy through platforms. More specifically, YouTube, Tik Tok, and Instagram. Since 2020, most people have spent their time at home, and so usage of these social media platforms has grown excessively. People discovered hidden talents, curiosity, and inspiration so much more than before.

Even if people hadn't spent half their time on their phones or other electronic devices, there are so many advantages of working on YouTube, Tik Tok, and Instagram for a passive income.

## 1.1: Freedom of Speech

YouTube, Tik Tok, and Instagram are the kind of social media platforms that allow an individual to really do anything and everything they want, needless to say, as long as they follow community guidelines.

"I do not agree with what you have to say, but I'll defend to the death your right to say it." ~ Voltaire

From a thriller, a short film to kids toy reviews, from gameplays to reactions, whatever. These are platforms where even the smallest of people have a voice, and they can make it known. Your creativity can literally pay the bills and put food on the table. And there can always be an endless supply of creativity, that is if you know where to look.

What could you possibly want more than being able to do what you love for a living? It's the ideal dream. And there are so many advantages of being able to do what you enjoy for a living.

## High Efficiency

You become more useful and productive with your work as you can be excited for the next day. Your work won't even feel like a job, and so you would find yourself more relaxed as it wouldn't feel like a burden, finding other things to do in your spare time would be exciting too.

## Inspiration

When you're having a tough time, doing what you love can spark inspiration and motivation in you. Once you feel inspired, your ideas run like a high-quality car engine, and it can sometimes even get difficult to do all these amazing things you have in mind.

## New Perspectives

When you are following a boring schedule every single day and spend most of your time thinking about what you would do once the weekends here, you should realize you're doing it wrong. When working on a social media platform, you don't have a boss; in fact, you are your own boss, much like running a business. You set timings that are best suited for your work, and as being a public figure is constantly exciting, you won't find yourself in the same routine each day. Sure, you would probably have some ups and downs, but at the end of the day, you work for your own satisfaction and so view life from a different point of view than those who work solely because they feel they have no choice.

## Better Wellbeing

Working on your chosen niche on these social platforms sounds fun and enjoyable, and it is. What you probably didn't know that being happy is great for your health. In fact, it's a lot cheaper than being miserable and stressed for every day of your life. It even relieves all that stress, mental and physical tension.

## 1.2: Fame

### An Audience

Working on being a public figure or influencer gives you an audience that cares for you; they show an interest in your content. It could make you a role model for them, or they see your content to put a smile on their faces, it could help them in some basic struggles they didn't know they had until they saw your work.

Your followers/subscribers may value your opinions on certain topics and appreciates you and your content in the respective niche. And being validated for your effort would make anyone happy.

They even help you grow by giving honest feedback and so you can easily tell what it is they like about your content.

### Opportunities

Fame grants you several chances to work with well-known brands or companies. Whether that be in sponsored advertisements or partnerships for products (i.e., perfume, apparel, electronic gadgets, games, etc.)

For example, maybe you're a sports-focused content creator, you could get offers from sportswear companies to model with their products!

Not only brands but also popular public figures would notice you, and you'd be given numerous opportunities to work with them, especially if you're in the same niche as them. When an already successful creator acknowledges and validates your content, they bring in their fans to your work, ultimately broadening your audience.

For instance, YouTuber Lilly Singh, also known as superwoman, grew so big on YouTube that she now hosts a late-night show called "A Little Late with Lilly Singh" on NBC. She not only released a film that entailed her world tour but also a book named "How to Be a Bawse: A Guide to Conquering Life," which made it to New York Times best-seller list. She also won a substantial number of rewards on multiple award shows over the years and made her own music videos, and so much more. Her Niche? Entertainment. And it's an understatement to say she entertained.

@lilly with @malala Via Instagram

Of course, it didn't come easy to her, but with time, her channel grew and not only on YouTube but also across other platforms like Instagram.

Like her, once you obtain that loyal audience, you could try new things whenever you want, but not too much, or you may drive your audience away. You'd be able to work on creative projects. (i.e., Liza Koshy acted in a tv show and other showbiz related content, PewDiePe who made not one but two games with another company as well as a YouTube original show called "Scare PewDiePie", Joey Graceffa who made his own YouTube original show called "Escape the Night".)

## 1.3: Money

The obvious reason for earning through YouTube, Tik Tok, and Instagram? The Money. Succeeding on any social platform often promises good fortune. Influencers often buy new cars, houses, editors to help them with their work, maybe even a new oven!

You'd finally be able to finish that bucket list. Get something for the people you care about! And most importantly, once you get that money you've been waiting for, be grateful and don't take it for granted.

YouTubers like Lilly Singh made use of their money by making her profile a little more professional by hiring a team and basically becoming a CEO of her team. A lot of influencers do live charity streams, raise money, or donate for the poor and needy in several ways as well. Well, that's not all she did with her money she spent it for fun too as I'm sure you can as well do whatever you want with it.

### Merchandising

You would be able to sell your own products, which would be your signature merch (people would recognize it as yours). Often influencers get sweatshirts, T-shirts, caps, posters, phone covers, etc. This increases your profits as well as advertising yourself. You get something to represent yourself with and receive more recognition.

# CHAPTER II: YouTube

## 2.1: How it Works

To know how to easily get 10,000 subscribers on YouTube, you first need to be able to understand the YouTube software's working and how you can use it to your advantage.

### Video

YouTube is a free space where creators can store videos, pictures, and posts. But their main focus is the videos that various people of all types upload. Google owns it, and its search engine is the second largest around the globe. YouTube videos can be embedded into other websites as well.

Moreover, YouTube recommends videos that are viewed by a similar audience to the one a user is currently watching.

Being successful through YouTube won't happen in a week. You have to be prepared to go through the rough patches as well as the smooth ones.

### Analytics

There is a reporting, and self-service analytics tool on YouTube which provides intel regarding every video you upload so YouTube can help you easily keep track of how many views each video receives, what type of people are watching your content (age group, where they are from, and such).

It can provide data about:

1. The age groups and genders it is commonly seen by.

2. The statistics: comments, ratings, and views.

3. The countries your content is mostly seen in.

4. The first time your video was recommended to a user, either when they are watching something similar or when your video was recommended when they search a keyword.

5. In the first instance, your video was embedded in a website by a third party.

## Advertising

YouTube embeds features that allow various businesses to promote their content to users who may have an interest in it, aiming at clients by subject and demographics.

The advertisers pay you each time someone in your audience views their Ad. They can decide the areas in which the Ad will show, the amount of payment, and the format.

## Channels

Create your own niche, don't constantly jump from one genre to another, or your audience will never remain consistent.

## 2.2: The Content

## Watch Time

Videos that consist of a higher watch time get recommended frequently on the main YouTube homepage. So how do you increase it? Pattern Interrupts.

These result in making your videos more vibrant, which prolongs the viewers' attention span.

A pattern interrupt can be jump cuts, graphics, different camera angles, and cheesy humor. It can put a smile on the watcher's face or catch them off guard, which keeps them watching.

**Trends**

Keeping up with the current times is vital for small channels to grow. Trends are one of the catalysts of increasing your audience.

PewDiePie Via YouTube

As of February 2021, most YouTubers stream live, do how-to tutorials, DIY's, etc.

Things like the chubby bunny challenge, Reddit reactions (cross-platform), spicy foods challenge, etc., gives more room for the creator and audience to get to know one another. The goal is to make them feel like your friend, so they feel comfortable enough to come back.

**Create longer videos.**

Making long videos (10+ minutes) actually gives your video a higher rank in YouTube's search results in most cases. Of course, if you make the video longer with not much to add, then it will still be lowly ranked as users will prefer not to waste their time.

And definitely avoid making videos longer than an hour because it's likely the viewers' attention gets diverted.

## Like, Share, and Subscribe

At any point of the video, remind your viewers to subscribe, but make sure you don't keep mentioning that along with 'Like, Share, and hit the notification bell' as this tends to irritate the viewers due to the fact that they just want to watch the video. Keep the message short and maybe even humorous to attract the viewers.

## Link more videos at the end.

If the users watch more of *your* content, they will probably subscribe. So, promoting your videos will definitely increase the chances of them watching it as it would be convenient for them to just click on that instead of going to your channel and surfing through there.

## Quality over Quantity

Viewers can never be fooled by the number of videos you upload every week, they value the effort and time put into each piece of content, and they are well aware that you are as human as they are.

Do try maintaining a schedule just to let your viewers know when they can expect a video, but don't force it, or it will not be valued.

## Thumbnail and Video Title

Your thumbnails should be eye-catching and interesting, as it is the first thing they see when they are introduced to your channel. It's your first impression. Make sure it's a high-quality image.

If it's a professional website, a simple and sleek thumbnail will do. If it's a vlog or an entertainment purpose video, an exciting title with an image of the most important part of the video in place of the thumbnail would fit nicely.

For example, if you want to give your review on a certain product, give a strong statement as a title that would be intriguing for people to watch (i.e., 'Why I think the new Tesla cars are amazing', 'Why Harry Potter actually makes no sense', 'Public Speaker Reacts to PewDiePie')

## More Content

At the end of your videos, hint at what you'll be doing next so your viewers can come back for more.

Keep track of your subscriber magnet. In analytics, creators can see what type of videos made by you have the most views. So, start by focusing on those. Obviously, don't make a hundred parts on the same topic, but keeping track of your subscriber magnet can help a lot.

## 2.3: Channel Profile

Keep an attractive and creative Channel with intriguing art styles, so it shows the work put in your banner. It welcomes the viewers. Here are some examples:

Jaclyn Lovey Via YouTube: here, Jaclyn made a minimalistic banner with her video update schedule and her genre of videos mentioned, so newcomers do not have to search for it; convenience.

jacksepticeye Via YouTube: Jack, a successful YouTuber with over 20 Million views, categorized all his videos in playlists so users can access any genre of his videos anytime. Also, notice a signature logo, and he mentioned all his handles, brand links too.

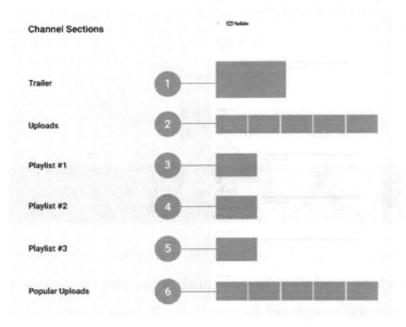

Make an exciting and persuading channel trailer. Preferably short and catchy, show the best you can here because these viewers came specifically to your channel, and you want to keep them there.

Organize the Channel page in a way that's convenient to the viewers.

Check out this basic layout:

Mention other platforms you use so they keep up with you if they don't rely on YouTube.

In 'About', make sure you provide at least 300 words about yourself, what kind of content you put out into the world, and why you think they'd be interested. If you have an upload schedule (please do), then mention                    that                    as                    well. Persuade the viewers to subscribe by the end of it. Keeping a polite tone in your descriptions, whether it be a channel description or video description, gives the viewer a positive and kind tone. They wouldn't particularly enjoy watching someone who talks in a manner of giving orders rather than guiding or entertaining (depending on your content subject).

Make sure you use well-known keywords that describe your content. (i.e., Crash courses, funny, motivational, etc.) so the YouTube algorithm          can          detect          these          things. Here's an easy comparison:

A:

Via YouTube

B:  Via YouTube

Which is a better Description of the YouTuber? I hope you say B, because it is, in fact, B.

Categorize your videos into playlists. For example, if you are running a gaming channel, make sure long gameplays are divided into separate videos but put together in one playlist after you upload them. Not many people watch 4-hour gameplays all at once, especially when you are starting as a small channel. But suppose you divide your gameplays into videos and edit them to cut out the boring bits. In that case, they may enjoy watching multiple short videos, which would be around 15-20 minutes each- depending on your preferences.

## 2.4: Interactivity

Replying to comments is the best and simplest way to gain more subscribers. The more you interact with your viewers and give importance to their feedback, the longer they stay.

"When creators take the time to interact with their local community, it can encourage audience participation and ultimately result in a larger fanbase." ~ YouTube.

Creator Hearts- you can heart your favorite comments to recognize comments from your public. By doing this, the viewer gets a notification, and this keeps interactivity high by leading them back to your channel. These notifications receive 300% additional clicks than normal.

Once you get a handful of people that are consistent in watching your content, you can even ask for their opinion on anything related to the video or even an idea for the next video. To engage your community is perhaps the most important thing, especially when you are a growing channel. Doing Q&A videos every once in a while acknowledges the audience and engages them more.

Recently, YouTube updated, and now Creators can interact with their audience with polls and posts as well as comments. Using these frequently to keep your audience there is vital.

### Shine Theory

Needless to say, they'd be more excited by a famous YouTuber replying to their comments, but you could be famous soon enough too! So, building a community that promotes each other does help. This concept comes from the Shine Theory.

Shine Theory is a long-term investment, where two individuals, creators, or consumers, help each other by means of advertising or engagement depending on the platform it is being used.

# CHAPTER III: Tik Tok

## 3.1: Down the Rabbit Hole

Over 2 billion people have downloaded Tik Tok all around the globe. Especially during the global pandemic, literally, everyone seems to have this app on their phone- and even if they don't have the app, it is taking over the apps they *do* have.

Tik Tok is super addicting, and the main reason for this is that each video is no longer than one minute, which gives viewers quick entertainment / tips / motivation.

Tik Tok famous is a word the vast majority seems to be throwing around as if it is a solid career, but the problem is, they all act as though it's a comfortable ride without even putting their back into it! Though it's a little more complicated than that, and you'd know that. But don't worry, here's a step-by-step guide to how you can be Tik Tok famous in no time.

This is the kind of platform that anyone can get into, from a 7-year-old to a 70-year-old *anyone*. Most people follow overnight after one of your Tik Tok's go mega-viral. Without further ado, let's start with all the things you need to remember to get 10 000 followers on Tik Tok.

## 3.2: The Algorithm

The Tik Tok algorithm was updated recently at the start of 2021, due to which a number of views on Tik Toks have started to go down. They did this because Tik Tok realized Tik Toks could go viral for almost anyone and a lot of creators' content was against community guidelines, so the early adopter advantage is lost. A way to tackle this is- keep pumping out more content. These algorithms will keep updating throughout the years, but the best you can do is give the viewers a reason to watch.

## 3.3: Your Profile

### Username

Choose a simple yet unique username. One that is familiar to your niche would be most preferred as it would make users find you conveniently. (i.e., if your Tik Toks are travel-focused, you can call yourself JourneysInLife)

### Bio

Think of an intriguing Profile Bio. Something
welcoming, relatable, original, fun, and interesting your followers would enjoy. And definitely mention your niche to clarify your target audience. Often really good bios consist of a call to action (i.e., follow for a cookie).

Upload a Photo (high-quality image not to look cheap). Link your other social media handles like Instagram, YouTube, etc.

## 3.4: The Content

### Target Audience

Before blindly making videos, you need to consider what kind of audience you're aiming for. Firstly, they use Tik Tok. If you think editing videos the same way you'd edit a YouTube or IGTV video will work, you're wrong. Every platform is unique in its own significant way, so you need to pay attention to how Tik Tok is entertaining and focuses on that.

Is it family-friendly content for youngsters? Short tutorials for artists? Perhaps it's professional cooking for beginners. You need to think about your audience's geolocation, age group, gender, so on and so forth.

This is an approximate age breakdown:

- Age 55+: 5%

- Age 44-53: 2%

- Age 34-43: 7%

- Age 24-33: 15%

- Age 17-23: 41%

- Age 13-16: 26%

## What's your Niche?

Delivering high-quality videos (in both quality of the video and content) is the most basic important thing. Don't steal content from other underrated creators, or it will have dire consequences like getting banned.

Make it unique, edit your videos with your ability if you can because people get tired of seeing the same editing design used by the Tik Tok app. There are various editing apps
like ViaMaker, Zoomerang, Quik, InShot, Funimate, etc.

## Quality

You need a really powerful hook in the first 3 seconds the keep the viewers wanting to watch more. Your job is to do everything and anything to keep the viewers from clicking away then make them interested enough to follow!

To do this, you need a significant number of pattern interrupts-graphics, different camera angles, etc. It could be as easy as starting with a greeting or as concrete as taking the time to explore or finishing your wish list. A trend disrupts you to exciting new locations, both visually and psychologically. It jolts you away from your comfortable perceptions and rituals and then into broad freedom of possibilities.

Better quality videos are pleasing to the eye, and they will likely continue watching until it ends. Sometimes Tik Tok degrades your videos' quality, and the reason this happens is that the data saved on your app has been turned on often than naught. This feature is on means the Tik Tok application downloads your mobile data while you watch videos. This decreases the resolution of your clips too. So, to tackle this, you can turn off the data saver feature.

## Collabs

Collaborating with some people you have good chemistry with really improves shares as it would be increasing both your and the other Tik Tokers views/follows another branch of Shine Theory.

Not just that, but Tik Tok allows you to reply to other influencers Tik Tok with your own, right? Use that! Make your reply unique and interesting to get them and other viewers to notice.

When it comes to collaborations with companies, sponsorships sound nice but try not to overdo it. While looking for new celebrities to partner with, be sure to review how many supported videos are posted. When a majority of their latest material is paying for updates, their commitment rate will not last. Alternatively, search for influencers with a decent amount of organic, non-sponsored material. As they probably have fans interested and involved.

**Going Viral**

When you post a video on Tik Tok, your creativity has the potential to ignite a chain reaction.

To get a decent amount of exposure, engage in trends, challenges, and duets. Put your own twists on patterns that captivate individuals. Paying attention to and bookmarking popular clips can prove useful to use it for inspiration. In Tik Tok, there are so many viral challenges. Engaging in various challenges will increase your visibility to the network and encourage you to get far more follows.

On the majority of your Tik Toks, for now, at least, use recommended and trending songs. Positive content almost always has more views, something quirky and enjoyable with a warm tone. Using a trending song is the next move (except when your music is original or a video idea in particular to a kind of sound.)

This is the reason why using trending songs is clever: basically, Tik Tok is a little wired in regard to trending songs to promote videos. It wasn't a random occurrence that Tik Tok also works with record companies; they work together to promote the artist's music in the app to improve the sales of the album and raise the likelihood that the song can hit the top rankings. Tik Tok practically dominates the music world. A mere peek at the week's Top 100 tunes. Most of those best hits on Tik Tok are those that are mega-famous. How do you know what tunes everyone's listening to? Simply choose one of the suggested tracks the platform recommends when you make your film.

Get on top of all those trends, except with a surprise. Do the idea of popular dances or rising clips, but add a twist on it and make it something of your own. You need to balance trending videos with fresh material when you're a small producer. A Tik Tok clip received millions of views, and that account got about 10,000 Tik Tok followers; it just happened overnight.

However, once you receive those views, you shouldn't anticipate the next day to be filled with that much fame, because you will probably be disappointed. Once you get over a million views, then you need to keep up the work or probably work even harder than before to keep everyone there.

Make sure you don't take part in really cringe trends, though!

**Using Hashtags**

Utilize hashtags as much as you can, especially hashtags that are trending. This actually matters because the Tik Tok algorithm detects these hashtags and recommends your content accordingly.

The cleverer and simpler your hashtags are, the higher your videos get ranked on Tik Tok, which in result increases your views and likes. Along with being in contact with record labels, Tik Tok often works with companies/brands, and their drives are almost always attached with a hashtag. This encourages your videos on people's For You Page during the duration of the campaigns.

1-2 hashtags are preferred. Go to the Discover tab and take 1-2 trending and 1-2 broad hashtags or tags related to your related to you exclusively and trendy.

Most Popular: #tiktokers #lfl #bhfyp #follow #explorepage #followforfollowback #explore #meme #tiktokdance #viral #memes #tiktokindia #photography #tiktokindonesia #k #cute #art #youtube #instagood #fashion #likes #bhfyp #likeforlikes #trending #music #funny #tiktok #instagram #love #like
**Timing Matters!**

What time you decide to post your content actually matters. When most people are online is when you'd want to put out videos and this depends on your geolocation heavily. If you're careful, you can get twice the followers you'd normally get.

Posting late at night (not too late), afternoon, and early morning tend to be the best times as most people would be looking through their phones then.

But that's just an average. To be more specific, go into your account analytics and content section, look at the past 7 days and what times your content was viewed most often, then make your posting times according to when your most interactive followers were active to make it as convenient for them as possible. Also, take into consideration the timings more well-known Tik Tokers in your niche are posting.

## Repost and Share.

Sometimes, your video doesn't do as well the first time but reposting it several times a day and week can drastically change that because sometimes your followers just miss it. Saying things like 'Posting again till it goes viral' or 'Reposting since it didn't do too well last time' can really make a difference.

Sharing your videos on every other social media platform (i.e., Instagram, Twitter, Facebook, etc.)

## Engagement

You need to turn your viewers, commenters, and likers into followers, especially at such an early stage. Basically, your early squad needs the spa treatment. To do this, perhaps the most important thing is engaging with your community. Interacting with them as much and as often as you can is vital to Tik Tok's growth.

Reply to each and every comment. People love viewing comments seeing their opinion was acknowledged would be a satisfying feeling for everyone. Credits: wired

Follow everyone, and I mean everyone that has interacted with your account in any way.

Go Live every single day, and it really boosts your page. Even if you're super busy, go live and work!

If you receive hate comments, reply back with a bit of humor! However, if it's constructive criticism, show interest, and try actually considering their opinion, this can really help your account develop.

Ask questions in your videos, so they feel the need to reply in the comments. This is a little trick most creators use.

**Staying Consistent**

Posting regularly is important. Post multiple times a day (considering the timings) and try avoiding uploading content right after each other, or it will not be pushed to the For You page.

Stockpile videos: If you have a day off, film as much content as you can so you can still upload videos if you're too busy another day. Posting 3-6 times a day is an ideal amount.

**Duration**

The duration of each video is preferred to be 11-17 sec long. The ideal time for something to be pushed out into the algorithm. And you'd get a good amount of watch time. Keep it shorter than you think it needs to be.

Tik Tok revolves around fun and concise videos, so if yours is too long than they would like, Tik Tok may decrease your rank on the For You page.

**Ask them to follow, like, and comment.**

The easiest method to improve the number of followers you have is by asking the viewers to 'double tap!' or 'let me know what you think in the comment section'; these things remind viewers to give you some sort of feedback on the content you create.

Asking for engagement in every video for a *very* brief period of time in the video and saying it in the description is important. Make sure it isn't mentioned for longer than 2-3 seconds, or the viewer will get bored and click away.

**Keep all your content accessible.**

Never delete any of your Tik Tok videos because it's likely your posts won't do well right away; you need to give it time. Your previous posts can go viral any time, so never keep them private or delete them.

There have been many times a Tik Toker posts a video, and it gets hardly 500 views in the first night, but about a few weeks later, it starts to become trending again, and you get a thousand more views.

**Judge Yourself**

Not to the point, you put yourself down, of course, but realistically judging yourself to keep track of your work is important.

How will this video contribute to your growth?

Is it interesting for people in my own niche?

Why would it be interesting?

What themes can I use to make this better?

If the most popular Tik Toker in my niche saw this, would they be impressed?

Take these things into consideration when you're done with certain Tik Toks.

## Follow Guidelines

Especially with the recent 2021 update, you don't want to get on Tik Tok's bad side. Make sure you aren't copying someone else's work on your own profile, as that would really degrade your account.

Funded partnerships may not be as clear to Tik Tok as they are to other social networking sites, but that wouldn't imply that the very same FTC laws do not apply. Tik Tok celebrities are expected to report advertising with a transparent and obvious message that the material is funded or promoted.

Do not, under any circumstance, attempt to get free followers. This will never help you really grow. And it can have really adverse consequences later on if you are serious about Tik Tok as this is seen as a way to steal from Tik Tok. Trying to buy free followers will never get you the triumph you thrive for.

## Stitch- The Tik Tok Feature

This adds yet another way for the user to interact with material that is created and posted every day by the creative Tik Tok users. Stitch is a feature the company called which enables a user to put in snippets of another Tik Tok video in yours.

How can you use it?

1. Search for the video you want to stitch and then click on 'Send to'.

2. Click on 'Stitch'

3. You can pull only 5 seconds out of the video, so choose wisely.

4. Make the rest of the video you want to put in with the stitched snippet.

5. Stitch them all together!

In the settings menu, you may select if you want to allow others to stitch your material. This is accessible on the Security and Confidentiality tab underneath "Settings and Privacy." You could allow or remove Stitch for any of your clips. Conversely, this feature can be customized for every clip you post.

**Stay Stress-free**

Don't try to push out more content forcefully, if your audience sees that you are, they would easily be able to get that your content came from a negative mindset. Keep it fun, enjoy making the clips, actually show your positivity.

Having a healthy mindset further nurtures your creativity and gets your ideas flowing, and you need as much of that as possible. Being authentic with your followers is key.

A few different tactics that have proved effective, such as constructive self-discuss and positive envisioning, can achieve encouraging thought.

Here are a few tactics that would prove beneficial for you to prepare your brain in thinking positively to get you started with generating content.

Concentrate on the good stuff. A part of our life is inconvenient situations and obstacles. Look at the constructive stuff once you're faced with one, regardless of how minor or relatively meaningless they are. You may still discover the ultimate positive aspect of any inconvenience if you search for it, even if it's not readily apparent.

Train with appreciation. Studying kindness has been shown to alleviate depression, boost self-esteem and promote endurance in some very trying situations. Image friends, experiences, or stuff that give you any type of warmth or delight, and struggle to convey your thanks at least once every day. This could be a thank you to a co-worker for assisting with a job, to a significant one for cleaning dishes, or to your cat for the affection they have provided.

Keep a diary of thanks. Research studies have reported that putting down stuff you're thankful for will boost your motivation and your state of wellness. You could do that by writing in a thankful diary daily or by setting down a range of items that you're happy for the days when you're going through a rough time. Using this to generate ideas even if it's really far-fetched should prove useful.

Find your motivation, whether that be intrinsic or extrinsic. You get to create the kind of content you like on Tik Tok, any kind! Use that as your passion and drive to work harder and do better.

**Let's take a look at a few Tik Tokers**

Daniel here has already made 10 parts of the same category and he still has millions of views. Why? Because he doesn't do the *same thing each* time of course, he changes it up, builds better for the next parts. His idea is original, unique, and entertaining!


But be careful not to overdo it, you can't go making 50 parts of the same theme as that would really just stretch it out too much and no one enjoys a guest who overstays their welcome.

**daniel.labelle** ✔ Daniel LaBelle

If people lagged. Part 10

♫ original sound - Daniel LaBelle

2.9M

16.3K

50.8K

daniel.labelle Via TikTok

Zach shows a clip of the most absurd idea there is: fishing in your house, using these surprises and then a pattern interrupt which involves him falling into the water really is an odd sight to see though very entertaining and unique.

Because of this, a large number of people shared his video and commented in it to share their thoughts.

zachking Via TikTok

# CHAPTER IV: Instagram

## 4.1: About You

Instagram is used by everyone in almost every part of the world. It's so popular because Instagram uses imagery rather than text, and people are extra quick to respond to that. It's easier to understand and process visual data rather than heaps of words. And so, visual marketing is blowing up.

The main focus on Instagram is are images. Captions are put out of the way and under the image for that exact reason.

Portrait photography is perhaps the most popular amongst the flock of imageries on Instagram. And most of these images are almost always edited by third-party applications (i.e., Snapseed, VSCO, Adobe Photoshop Express, Polarr).

Not just images, but also Boomerangs, IGTV videos, filters (of which most are created by users), stories, etc. These things push engagement to the front lines.

Naturally, every time Instagram's algorithm changes, it impacts every person who accesses it. You need to make sure you aren't going against the current of those waves. Because the fact is that their algorithm is constantly judging posts all over the globe and deciding which users can see each moment they open the app.

Instagram's algorithm works on machine learning, which makes the way your posts are ranked constantly changing. This book has the most recent details about how to deal with the algorithm to push you further in the marketing campaign and to keep developing engagement with your followers.

Ever since Instagram halted the inverted response in 2016, each specific feed on the site has been arranged as per the algorithm's guidelines.

As per the official @creators handle of Instagram, this concluded in a pleasant result for everybody. Basically, saying they won't be changing it back.

## 4.2: Ranking Factors

### Genre/Niche

Design your account, configure it in a way people can know precisely what they can expect from you. After which, you post intriguing content that your audience will enjoy instantly. If people have liked those kinds of posts before, the system is much more likely to display them.

For example, Let's say Steven came in contact with a verified account. He will probably see more posts from that account, especially if he saw more content from there.

Simply put, users who communicate with content similar to yours are probably going to come across your account as well.

### Timing

Recent posts are always going to be recommended more than others. So, just like Tik Tok, posting in timing when your followers are normally active is vital.

People who spend over an hour scrolling on Instagram are obviously going to see numerous kinds of posts from top to bottom compared to someone who spends hardly a few minutes will only see only the top-ranked ones.

Instagram portrays the best at the top of users' feed every time the user activates the application. So, someone who follows hundreds of thousands of accounts will most likely miss a fair number of posts from people they are even really close to.

**Engaging Your Audience**

Just like every other social media platform, Instagram wishes for users to stay on the app as much and as long as possible as long as they are interested. As an end result, the software cranks up profiles in which the followers are already conversing. This guarantees that the stress on community participation is essential for advertisers and developers.

Credits: mavsocial.com

Sliding in DMs, tagging one another in blogs, and consistently posting comments all are acts that imply a strong bond among users as well as likes, shares, and views.

## 4.3: What You Need to Do

### Pay Attention.

Seeing your Instagram stats is, perhaps shockingly, a few of the easiest ways to get insight into not only how your viewers think but also how the application looks at you.

Could you send everyone much of the same, or twists on the subject? Will they want better photos or videos? Just how many views come from hashtags? What kind of content is going to wow the audience?

Insights tell you did well, so it's up to you to work out where to run from that performance.

### Keep It Coming

Some type of involvement, and figuring out where the intended crowd is. To have a grip on the Instagram algorithm, you have to create bonds with your followers first. And because the volume is simple to compute and accomplish than performance, the first item on the agenda is to create a social media posting schedule to stay on track.

What is consistency? Mean for Instagram? This is exclusive to your niche. As you just started, start with the way you want to progress. Think about what's affordable for the team to create.

If you draw viewers with a spark, three stories, two posts, and one IGTV video per day produced a certain amount of perception. Volume and layout selections would depend on the resources you currently have. And what's most critical, however, is to concentrate on publishing posts that you feel proud of regularly.

**Reposting is Key.**

Even after you have a nice schedule, you're following and knowing what your followers expect, pushing content out into the world isn't simple like butter on jam. Recycle, change-up your best work. Now, not only do you know Instagram wants it, but it also saves a lot of time.

You could transform the videos to gifs, similar pictures to a slideshow, and use pictures used in another photo shoot for multiple reasons, throwbacks, and repost on stories.

Just use the same thing but be extra creative with it.

**Collaborating with Other Influencers & Brands**

Keep an eye on what other public figures in your niche are up to, and if possible, try to do a collab with them.

Perhaps the easiest way to naturally broaden your scope to fresh eyes is to seek a suitable friend with a complimentary following while still attracting the viewers' interest with appropriate different perspectives. The outcome may very well provide an added strength from Instagram if the partnership is as enjoyable for your community as it would be for you.

Though you need to make sure that the person you choose to partner with is suitable and legitimate, as other influencers will judge you based on who you collab with, it is probably best if you do a detailed background check before setting a collab date with them.

As that influencer will be bringing in their audience, you need to see what kind of followers they have and their analytics. Making sure you don't bring in the wrong crowd who would go away as soon as they came. You could check this by looking at their engagement on posts. If the person you are intending to collab with is genuine and interactive with his/her audience, you should probably go for it.

As searching through every single person, you could collab with would take a significant amount of time, you could use means like Ninjaoutreach, Meltwater, GroupHigh, Newswire, Cision Communications Cloud, etc. This software allows you to make your listing in its database, making things a lot more convenient for you as time is, in fact, of the essence.

The kinds of sponsorships you could get fall into three basic categories: large accounts (120K followers) get at least $400 per sponsored post, middle-class (3K-100K followers) get at least $150, and small accounts (less than 3K) get around $100 or less.

After making a list of the sponsorships you'd like to go for, you need to send each one your pitch. But not in the first text, of course, that would be not polite. Tell them why you're interested in the subject they put out and communicate with them. Once you know what they want exactly, you could develop an amazing pitch.

Next, you need to plan your influencer publicizing campaign. Make sure you keep interacting with the influencers so you can get an insight into what they think. Consider other people's opinions to make a master plan using the influencers and your creativity.

As soon as you have initiated your campaign, please keep track of how it's doing and keep adjusting it accordingly.

An example:

@omayazein partnered up with a brand called Modanisa and gave her audience a discount code, which in turn gets a lot of shares, and she has about 1 Million followers!

@omayazein Via Instagram

**Reward Them**

As discussed before, Instagram values engagement A LOT, so give your audience what they want! When your audience shares your posts on story or DM, comments and likes push your posts to the top instantly.

The goal should be to create a kind of commitment and passion that motivates individuals to advocate and empower themselves. The service could do the job for you if you already have an outstanding Business-to-consumer service. Anything other than that, you would need to find means of subtly encouraging individuals.

Please stop posting everything sent to you from your community. Compile the latest and integrate material into the digital plan of your content whenever appropriate. And bear in mind that merely reposting the stories of other users has also been specifically noted as something that would not include your stories on the Explore List, so make sure you remain imaginative and on topic.

Like your followers' and viewers' comments, reply to each one, even the haters. Try getting into a conversation with them. Interact with them through stories, polls, use trending filters.

Ask questions on your stories and share them, be humorous, genuine, everything and anything interesting. It could be 'what's your opinion on….' Or 'what's your most embarrassing story!', etc.

If they reply to your stories, make sure you reply!! And not after days at a time, but as soon as you can. Enjoy your time with them. Really try and understand what they wish to see from you. Unless they're just there to hate on you, then you should probably ignore it or if you could do something creative with it (while following community guidelines), go for it.

Follow influencers that are familiar with your niche. This can link other people that are interested in your type of content to you. Not just follow, but also like and comment on their posts, share it!

(Another way of utilizing the Shine theory). Showing interest in other people's content can help you too.

**Use the Hashtag System**

Just like Tik Tok, hashtags are an important part of Instagram. It is the middleman between you and the right audience. It's the lowest building block, especially when you're just starting out.

If you think using heaps of hashtags, including ones that do not correlate with your niche, will help, you might be wrong. It would be misusing the hashtag system, and that leads you to a direct road to the bad side of Instagram because they do, in fact, notice those who try abusing the algorithm. And not to mention, you are not gaining anything by trying to show it to people who have no interest in your niche.

The maximum quantity of hashtags you are allowed to use is 30 per post, and yes, use all those 30. Try writing those hashtags in the first comment rather than in the caption, so it looks a bit more well put together.

Perhaps not all hashtags that you assume are nice would be suitable for your own use. It is why every last one of you would want to verify to see whether the material is important to your subject.

When deciding whether a hashtag is right for your post, there are two key considerations to have a look at Niche and Dimension.

Never use only the most famous and vague hashtags, thinking you would be able to reach a larger crowd because you won't. You'll just be a hidden needle in a haystack. An invisible need at that. Why?

Because they aren't specific enough, and a lot of popular influencers already use those so you wouldn't be too noticed yet.

Please make sure you have certain hashtags that you use in every post (with fewer follows) so that you can be noticed by at least one familiar audience (needless to say, they need to be your target audience too).

It would be best if you would be able to find a middle ground between hashtags that not one soul has ever heard of before and hashtags that everyone knows about. Both would reward you little. Try hashtags that have about 90,000-900,000 post range.

## Sorry, But Buying Is NOT the Way to Go

You can purchase double-taps or follows in due to despair just to see whether a lift is what they needed to get moving all along. But while this may make you appear popular to random people; it couldn't be farther from the facts.

Finally, they consider giving up both as a waste of time on Instagram and stop bringing in any considerable effort to expand, since they just do not see what else there is to do. Don't purchase likes, fans, and also, don't try the old trick of interaction pods.

Yes, even Instagram notices it if you buy followers/likes/views. Not only Instagram but also your followers. Which makes things a lot worse. And so, you won't gain any kind of income from that.

## Using Highlights

Utilize the highlights feature and make/or find suitable cover photos for each to maintain consistency. It is making a profile that's pleasing to the eye and fitting for your niche and target audience.

## 4.4: Seeing is Believing

You may think this is all talk and no action, so let's drive that notion away by looking at a few of the many influencers on Instagram.

Notice the overall layout of this account. The username and profile instantly tell the users what the account is about.

Just the username would do this for us too but @wedarkacademia further described what it was about as well as threw in a bit of personality to the description as well as handles for other social platforms.

Their posts are consistent and related to one another. See the Highlights categorized neatly too.

@wedarkacademia Via Instagram

Responses like these encourage so much growth and engagement amongst the target audience.

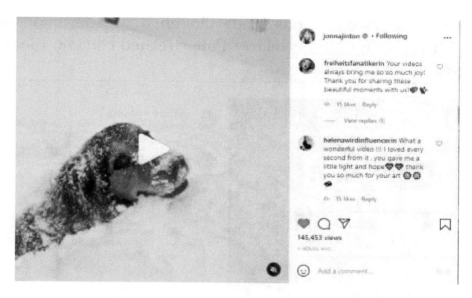

@jonnajinton Via Instagram

@madeyemoodswing interacting with their audience. Their username being humorous and instantly getting the attention of Harry Potter fans who understand the reference.

Drawing in users of various kinds though if @madeyemoodswing doesn't involve any kind of Harry Potter related content, those fans may lose interest.

@madeyemoodswing Via Instagram

Jonna Jinton, blogging her art, photography and life on Instagram whilst also mentioning that she works on another platform (YouTube). Her posts are coherent and in sync with nature and mostly winter in her home country.

Her description and highlights are simple and straight to the point which a lot of users would find convenient and contemporary.

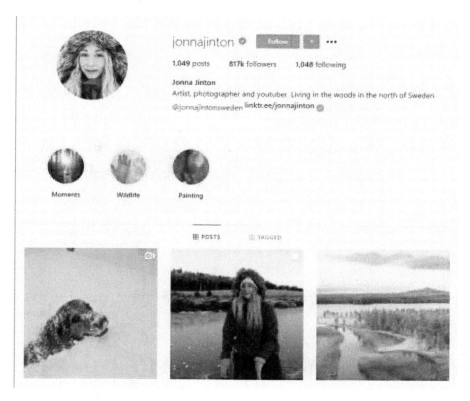

@jonnajinton Via Instagram

# CHAPTER V: Ideas for Newbies

## 5.1: Idea Generation

There is not much to implement without ideas, and since the implementation is the secret to progress, creative ideas are required to enable some sort of change. It is clear that thoughts alone are not going to make creativity possible, since you need to be able to construct a structured mechanism to handle such innovations. The concept is not only about producing lots of it but also about bringing care to the nature of it.

It's not easy to create grade A content 24/7. Often people find it difficult to break out of their usual routine and habits when thinking about working on something new. In order to get out of the negative spiral, you need to glance at the development of creativity altogether and incorporate a few of the most key factors, strategies, and procedures that could be used more routinely to produce fresh concepts.

Perhaps you need original thoughts so a new possibility can be thoroughly explored?

Maybe you are trying to find a new way of solving a creativity barrier, or are you hoping for a decent answer to the dilemma?

**Why does it matter?**

Generating ideas is the outcome of creating complex, tangible, or conceptual theories. It's at the top of the funnel for concept organization, which works on seeking potential alternatives to true or suspected challenges and possibilities.

Ideas are, as stated, the very first move into change. Fresh theories rely on you progressing as independent individuals. From the point of view of a person, whether you feel stuck with a job or otherwise unable to resolve that one dilemma, fresh solutions will motivate you to push ahead.

The aim of fresh concepts is to reinforce the manner in which you work, irrespective of your priorities or the kinds of things you're searching for.

To fuel productivity and improve nature on a broader scale, societies rely on creativity. Creativity improves emerging innovations and enterprises. They are providing creators with more opportunities.

**How do you do it?**

Chances are, you brainstorm. However, it's been found that brainstorming requires more time and tends to fewer ideas as of planning, logging, and managing the meeting would take a lot more time than it should. While there are certain approaches to boost the quality of brainstorming, it's preferred if brainstorming isn't your first thought.

Nevertheless, certain methods are worth taking a look at. As you're searching for various kinds of ideas, it is beneficial to have methods in mind that help in developing them. Several of these concept development approaches may be used for further productive brainstorming and another creativity type.

## 5.2: The Techniques

**Challenging proposals**

This concept is when you bring an issue or opportunity into view due to the possibility of innovatively solving it. It can let you make a certain doubt about your content and aim it at your audience to get more ideas and useful opinions after you have identified what you intend to gain from it.

These idea challenges come in handy, especially when you're looking to engage a large audience of up to 10000. When you plan an idea challenge, pre-define the outcomes you'd like, the niche, followers, subscribers, etc. Make sure you keep track of the time with this technique to make sure it's working.

**Similarities**

You can use data and statistics from previous posts or videos on social media platforms to improve on ideas for another piece of content; this is thinking simultaneously. It is the simplest way of generating fresh content as it's often experimented with and succeeded.

In Example, YouTuber's making reaction videos continually but of various kinds of content.

**SCAMPER**

This method applies critical thinking to alter creativity, which is already present—adjusting open-source ideas to improve and agree on the best answer.

1. Substitution – Your old content being substituted with others to gain improvement.

2. Combining- Merging two or more ideas into one master idea for your content.

3. Adapting- Evaluates the options to make a method more versatile and works on the design, system, or principle alongside other related gradual changes.

4. Modification- From a broader context, changing not only the concept but also changing the concept looks at the challenge or potential and tries to change the outcomes.

5. Improvising by putting to another use- Searching for opportunities to use the concept or current content for some other reason and, if applicable to other areas of your profile or channel, analyzes the potential advantages.

6. Elimination- This technique studies all the possibilities, and if you find more than one fragment was removed.

7. Reversal- The emphasis of this procedure is to reverse the order of factors that can be swapped of your idea.

This technique was originated from the idea of brainstorming, but it applies to your thinking technique too. If you make generating ideas a daily activity by a series of trivial things, you could have a decent chance of winning the main breakthrough. Occasionally all it takes is really to reflect on what you already have. Sometimes, creators want to worry about the next remarkable thing being discovered. It is easy to overlook that the endless gradual changes are the aspects that can have a difference in the medium haul while creating fresh concepts. As a baseline, utilizing your existing theories or methods will explain a lot in relation to your present content, and that is what the SCAMPER strategy is really about.

## Reverse Psychology

This method will make you challenge your content-related perceptions. Reverse thinking comes in handy when you feel you are trapped in the traditional mentality, and it appears to be impossible to come up with such unique ideas. It helps in checking our routinely-habits as the answer to finding more content isn't always a straight-to-the-point road. You consider the possibilities of what the opposite would do for your profile or channel, even if you end up thinking of the most peculiar of solutions.

## 5.3: Once You've Got It

### Organizing Ideas

Once you've got all those ideas down, planning and organizing them can be difficult if you don't know where to start. Creators need to collect this creativity as soon as it comes to them instead of using it as soon as it comes up.

Jotting down all your ideas in a notebook or on your phone can be helpful, and most people do this as it's only for personal use. But if you wish for other people's opinions on the matter to know their judgment, this could be a hassle. Not to worry though, there are things like idea management tools to aid you with that.

### Management

A concept tool for effective functions as the foundation of the method of idea planning. This is how you can assemble the ideas, analyze them, debate, prioritize them, take account of their success, and the overall course of the operations of your idea generation.

Since concept planning is such a huge subject and famous influencers or public figures are likely to have loads of suggestions, it often makes perfect sense for most influencers or creators to use a designated idea management system.

It is just as productive to handle ideas with a designated method as the underlying mechanism at the back end. You could create a mechanism that makes it a lot easier to produce and refine fresh concepts and create ideas a persistent practice. The methods that are too confusing can infuriate people, so try not to make things too difficult.

## 5.4: Winning at Creativity

### The Appropriate Crowd

It is necessary to include the right individuals in the equation for the content to be as efficient as possible. Start engaging all influencers who know about the content creation and are sincerely involved in you making a difference.

Ensure your community is the target audience and well educated on the topic if the aim is to involve a wider community of users to produce ideas.

### Determine Your Objective

Aim to collect as much relevant data as possible about the content you wish to make before you begin to understand the source. Define what you understand about it by now and what data is still required.

Though it sounds simple, the further you can clearly explain your actual idea, the greater the odds of producing practical ideas are.

**Limits to Keep an Eye Out For.**

It can impede imagination to convey that every idea is a valid idea, so ensure the aims are ambitious and precise enough. One approach to get some of the viewers' genuinely innovative thoughts is to set limits.

If the ultimate aim is to cut prices, suggestions such as investing truly little on content would certainly come to mind when you want to save up. The thoughts you get, though, would vary greatly if you ask yourself: "How could I save 50% on expenses and create unique and engaging content?".

**Deduction**

The goal of creating original approaches is to improve what is already present as well as to produce something new.

From a different angle, coming up with entirely novel solutions will help you tackle your creativity block. It helps you to widen the spectrum of thoughts beyond the present style of learning, which inevitably leads to much more ideas.

Sometimes, creators, influencers, and public figures use current ideas or behavioral templates while attempting to get started on a social media platform instead of attempting to think of the latest ideas. The concern with this technique is that it does not encourage you to pursue multiple options and limits the number of possibilities.

## 5.5: About Yourself

## Who are you?

Create a clip of yourself being introduced. Who are you, what are you doing? On your YouTube channel, Tik Tok, or Instagram profile, what should viewers hope to see? How frequently do you upload photos or videos? Create videos to let them know exactly what they should expect, inviting viewers to your channel or page. Aim to give a convincing argument for audiences to click on the subscribe button on YouTube and follow on Instagram or Tik Tok.

## Vlogging

Making Vlogs can be informative, fun, intimate, anything you would like to create of it, much like traditional writing. Almost all influencers and public figures may use material from vlogs to involve fans and expand their communities.

## A Day in Your Life

YouTubers love to walk through The Day in your Life videos from another's perspective. Once you wake up the next morning and lead audiences to a normal day in your schedule, start filming.

Matt D'Avella Via YouTube

## Behind-the-curtain Content

Showcase to the viewers what's going on at the back end of your Instagram account, YouTube channel, or Tik Tok account. With this famous video style, let your audience see behind the curtains. You can display your room, your house, your workplace, your city, anywhere else you enjoy.

## 20 Questions

You could make short clips or long clips (depending on your preference or niche) playing a game of 20 questions. These questions can be personal or silly, and the best have a little bit of both. Letting your audience be closer to you is what this accomplishes.

## 'Draw My Life.'

These kinds of videos are often found on YouTube, where the creator essentially draws their life often on a whiteboard with stick figures and narrating their life so far. Of course, you decide how much or how little you wish to say about yourself. Majority 'Draw my life' videos include key events or milestones in their lives.

You can even introduce your family, background, and friends in these.

## 5.6: Trending Content Ideas

### Teach them How to Cook (or how not to)

This kind of content is often made by entertainment-focused or cooking influencers. You can make it an A grade cooking tutorial, or you could completely twist it depending on your creativity and teach people how not to cook but let them have an enjoyable time watching creators do it wrong.

For example, YouTuber 'Simply Nailogical' made a video called 'Baking a cake with Nail Polish' on 18th September 2016, which got over 5 Million views. The cake was quite inedible but still entertaining to watch to over 5 Million people.

You can make this an Instagram post, a Tik-Tok video, or a YouTube video.

## Workout Routine

As it's time to start working out, lots of folks look towards YouTube videos, quick Tik Tok hacks, or Instagram posts/IGTV videos for specific fitness routines, as well as how to do those workouts. Both common subjects are exercise, stretching, or shape footage.

## Understanding the Complicated Mess

Informative and aurally captivating means of presenting data and figures that could otherwise be dull or difficult to grasp is infographics related content. Content that helps your audience's day a little easier. Every genre of content has specific things that not everyone understands, so try finding the most commonly found problem in yours and present content on that!

## Reviewing other People's Products

One of the most common kinds of information on these social media platforms is product reviews. Before deciding to buy, thousands of viewers check out this insightful content. Tech gadgets and make-up items are common themes, but reviews can be sought for all types of goods.

For example, YouTuber Marques Brownlee's Niche is tech gadgets, and a majority, maybe even all, of his video's reviews on really expensive gadgets so often people who think about buying a new phone or the PS5 watch his videos to see his opinion on it. His video called 'PlayStation 5 Review: NextGen Gaming!' received almost 6 Million views!

You can make review videos on any and every genre of content! Games, movies, books, food, universities, perfumes, songs, shows, even countries! So, search for things you can review in your niche.

## Comedy Videos

In the event that you need to turn into a web sensation, an entertaining video may very well assist you with getting there. A sizable number of the most mainstream recordings on YouTube, Instagram, and Tik Tok ended up in such a state since this sort of content made watchers chuckle or laugh.

## Pranks

Viewers love watching tricks. Pull a trick on somebody (innocuous tricks, please) and share the outcomes on your social media platforms.

Tricks have not been altogether contemplated; however, scientists have discovered that individuals find being deceived an extremely aversive encounter. Trick based humor can be coldblooded or kind, cherished or detested; however, it's not straightforward.

## Furry Creatures Content

Dogs, little cats, child elephants, the Internet loves charming/interesting creature recordings are considerably more popular than recordings of human children. So, if you have a pet, share it with the world! Everyone loves animals.

## Music Videos

Singing a song cover, and original, or even lip-syncing is always a fun sight to see. Indeed, even late-night TV gets in on the good times. Pick a mainstream tune and give it a shot!

If you have a bad voice, don't worry; try making it hilarious by a funny parody where you impress the audience with clever and witty lyrics rather than your vocals.

## Fact Check

What are some myths that are commonly believed by the vast majority regarding your niche? Compile all the misconceptions and make a post or video on the matter. Show emotion and teach your audience the stereotypes believed about your niche by the public.

As the internet is filled with so much information, a fair share of it is fake news, so spreading awareness about it would be intriguing for your audience (as long as you stay on topic).

Often people are found spreading rumors without even knowing they are rumors and not facts, so content that addresses the rumors is an interesting concept for anyone.

Needless to say, double-check whether the information you are giving your audience is proven with evidence to be right. Or else those mistakes can decrease your followers/subscribers quick.

Write a catchy caption or thumbnail with a question that quickly catches their interest. For example, '10 Myths you probably believed about professional cooks' or '6 reasons why you should not believe every thing you're told'.

## Speed-run

Can you play games as fast as humanely possible? Finish your make-up in under 2 minutes? Or maybe you can make a 3-course meal in under an hour? Show off those skills on social media!

Speed-runs are commonly found on gaming channels so viewers can quickly experience a gameplay without having to play it themselves due to the cost of the game or less time of time.

## Time-slip

@jonnajinton Via Instagram on April 17th , 2020

Time-lapse is a method where the casings of the video are caught at a far slower speed than expected. Traffic, mists, and the sunrise all will, in general, be well-known time-slip by subjects. The outcome is frequently hypnotizing.

Some creators make time-lapses of their artwork to show progress quickly as an art piece can take at least a few hours.

## Shopping/Mail Hauls

This type of video is particularly well known with style vloggers and beauty. After an outing to the shopping center, flaunt your take piece by piece. From the freshest iPhone to an in-vogue membership box or the most trending toy, individuals love to watch others open boxes. So next time you do another package, don't simply tear into it; make sure you are recording first!

You could even give out your address and your audience would send you mail. Often YouTubers make mail opening videos reviewing all the heartfelt gifts their watchers send them.

## Go Live

Why trust that the recap will show individuals what's happened? Take your watchers to the occasion with you by live-streaming to your Instagram Live, Tik Tok Live, or YouTube Live. Even after the session is over, the stream would still be accessible online.

You can schedule a certain day for every week in which you go live and make sure you let everyone know through all your social media platforms, so they are aware and wait for you to go live.

## What Most Do

A substantial number of the top Instagrammers are singers, sports brands, actors, footballers, models, and of course, Instagram themselves. The most famous YouTuber channels are often among the genre of trailer channels, singers, gamers, kids show, hack tutorial channels, and so on. Tik Tokers are often found to be comedians, musicians, artists, etc.

The best content? Ones that are so good that people feel the need to see it on other platforms too, Tik Tok video compilations on YouTube, and Tik Tok videos on Instagram, Live videos on Instagram recorded and put-on YouTube. The type of content that is put across various platforms are the ones that have gone viral or loved enough that users wish to see it almost everywhere.

# Conclusion

First things first, it would be beneficial if you ask yourself, what do you have to offer? Why would people want to watch your videos? What are they getting out of the time they spent on your video?

Is it educational? Hilarious? Scary? Relaxing? Silly? Helpful? Inspiring or motivational? Perhaps very random, either way, would your target audience enjoy or show any interest in it?

Maintain originality- the charm of social media is that you can express your thoughts and add a little more to *you*, so to speak. You can grow on YouTube, Tik Tok, and Instagram, only if you have something no one else has to give out. The basic rule to starting a business, 'what's so special about you?' or 'what do you have that no one else does?'. Write down all that comes to mind when answering these questions.

You can not copy peoples' ideas, only your own significant expression of those ideas into your videos, posts, stories, etc. However, if your content seems to be matching someone else's a little too much, change it up, brainstorm a little about what you could do to make it unique, and choose the best one. And be certain you aren't tuning out any other possibilities due to your fears.

Honesty- be honest about your opinions and where you stand. This can be a random video about car reviews or your opinion on white supremacy; it need not matter. Maybe you feel like changing your genre after a long time, but you're afraid of losing the number of followers/subscribers you've gotten so far. Your fear is valid, but you can't force yourself to put out content on something you have no more interest in anymore because you followers/subscriber will notice eventually, and they'll just fade out on their own. So, try being honest, raw, and authentic from the start.

However, being honest does not amount to being insensitive. You're trying to be the person people look up to or look forward to viewing when they're having a difficult day, so try to fill those expectations without disregarding your bad days, of course. Ending things on a positive note and be accepting of the honest truth your followers/subscribers/viewers offer in return.

Humility- Try not to overthink each comment they make because what seems like an hour of thought to you was probably not more than five minutes to them. When you start noticing your growth, don't become egotistic about it, or the people that put you where you are today will leave as fast as they came. Nobody likes a showoff.

Setting boundaries- deciding where you draw the line between your public and personal life is vital. You don't need to broadcast every minute detail about your personal life to the entire world, and you need to value the privacy of the people close to you if you wish for the same.

Motivation- find that mechanism that triggers, leads, and retains your aiming habits. Whether it be intrinsic or extrinsic motivation, keep a daily reminder for it, so you keep that drive and motivation to continue working hard. Grabbing a coffee, chocolate bar, reading, or some inspirational quote is what puts you in a nice mood and sparks wisdom, do it every day.

The physical, internal, cultural, and mental factors which trigger action are involved in motivation. Introjected motivation is when you are driven to work out of the guilt of procrastination or laziness. Identified motivation is when you know you have got work to do, yet you haven't determined anything in regard to it. Try to avoid introjected and identified motivation as it originates from a negative space.

Don't give up if you feel like you are not getting enough growth, stay consistent and keep at it no matter what. If you still feel like there has been no effect, try going over the points again and make sure you keep track of how you have been doing by statistically analyzing yourself.

Soon enough, you will catch yourself with 10,000 followers/subscribers on YouTube, Instagram, and Tik Tok. It is more or less a smooth ride from there. Good Luck!

# Short Stays Real Estate with No (or Low) Money Down

*The 7+1 Creative Strategies to Create Passive Income from Home Using the AirBnb Business Model in 2021*

**By**

**The Golden Inner Circle**

# Contents

# Introduction

If you are a forward-focused person, you can dream of leaving the profession to enjoy a retirement life that is simpler, or you might even consider early retirement. But a dream is only a wish without a plan. You need to contemplate passive income to put a few wheels on the dream. There are also plenty of different options for passive income and rationales of how to build it. Passive income is the money you collect that doesn't cause you to do a lot of "active" work in order to continue to earn it. In essence, you may do much of the work in advance and do some extra effort to earn an income. For instance, to keep the money flowing, if you develop an online course, you only need to update the content. Likewise, passive income strategies like renting out property and/or building a blog can take some effort to get up and running, but while you sleep, they would eventually earn you cash. You've already heard the word, "make money when you're sleeping." This is the main attraction that allows individuals to generate passive income. Even when you're not working, you can develop something (a course, a blog, e-book, videos, and/or an online store) which generates income. Or you can own something that helps you to earn passive income (property or stocks).

So why do you need to build passive income?

In the presence of a full-time job, your salary is your biggest income tool, a tool that usually requires your active involvement. Even if you enjoy your career, you wouldn't mind making some additional money without the tears, blood, sweat, and time commitment of another job. If you lose your job or want to generate an extra source of income when you are no longer productive or if you outlive your retirement fund, developing a passive income will improve your wealth-building strategy, create the opportunity to retire early, and save you from a total loss of income.

And how much money can passive income generate?

Generally, passive income won't make you wealthy overnight, so ignore those get-rich-quick schemes you've read about. But, over the long term, consistent, profitable passive income strategies will produce some serious money. Depending on the income stream, we're talking about anything from two to three thousand dollars to thousands of dollars.

Some people like to think of investing when we mention "passive income" because, with the least amount of effort, it can yield the greatest returns. But you should think about your retirement plan & passive income as two distinct subjects. The entire premise behind the long-term investment is to produce retirement income. If your fund options are good and they offer a match, you want to make sure you invest in your company retirement plan, like that of a 401(k). These are great choices for establishing a powerful pension plan, but before a certain age, you will face taxes as well as penalties for every withdrawal. You need to let your money grow only for the long term with retirement planning and not touch it. However, a form of low-effort income which can be accessed at any time should be passive income. After you are debt-free and have some cash left, one way to build passive income is by buying real estate and leasing it out to tenants. Rental property may be a fantastic source of additional income, but it is not the most passive option because, unless you employ a property management company, you will have to put a lot of effort and time into maintaining the property. You need to be in charge of your property if you go on the rental property route. Pay off your own home first before you buy a rental property, and buy your investment property with cash. You must not go into debt in order to purchase property for rent. You could develop something like an informative blog and/or a YouTube tutorial series to be able to generate online traffic if you have a bright idea that appeals to a particular audience. You might sell commercial space on your blog or ad spots on your channel if your content is engaging and it sees ample regular traffic. You can sit back, relax, and reap sources of passive income after you put in the heavy lifting. The list of ideas for passive income could go on indefinitely. Never go for any passive income strategies that promise a fast return or require large sums of money upfront. Your other financial targets would be sabotaged by them. In this book, we will present ideas that are steady, profitable, and trustworthy.

# CHAPTER 1: Understand Income and Importance of Passive Income

There are three main categories of income:

Active income

Portfolio income

Passive income

## 1.1 Active Income

Active income alludes to money made as a result of the provision of service. Examples of active income are wages, tips, salaries, fees, and income from companies in which there is material involvement. The owner must meet the criteria for "material participation," which is based on hours worked or other factors, in order for income from a company to be considered active rather than passive. The most popular example of active income is income earned in the form of a paycheck from an employer. "Money from business activities is deemed "active" for the self-employed or someone else with an ownership interest in a corporation if it meets the criteria of material participation by the Internal Revenue Service (IRS). That implies one of the following is valid, at least:

- The taxpayer works during the year in the corporation for 500 or more hours.
- The taxpayer performs the majority of the company's work.
- Over the year, the taxpayer works for more than 100 hours in the company and no other employee works more hours than the taxpayer.

However, income earned is treated as passive income if someone earns income from a company in which they do not actively participate. Meanwhile, portfolio income is income from investments, like dividends and capital gains. Depending on the legislation at the time, these various forms of income can be taxed differently. At present, for instance, portfolio income is taxed at lower rates than active income.

**Example of active income from a business**

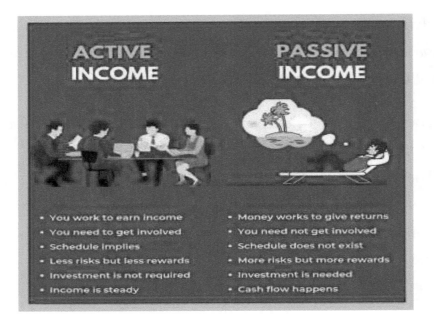

John and Laura are not married to each other. They have a 50% interest in an online business. John performs the majority of the day-to-day work in the business. Therefore, his income is considered active by the IRS. On the other, Laura helps with the marketing activities. She, however, works less than 100 hours a year in the business. It is for this very reason that her income from the business is considered passive income by the IRS. The material participation rule was established to prevent individuals that do not actively participate in a business from using it to generate tax losses which they, otherwise, could have written off against their active income.

## 1.2 Portfolio Income

Income from the portfolio is money received from investments, interest, dividends, and capital gains. Portfolio income streams are often known to be dividends received from investment properties. It is one of three main income groups. Active income and passive income are the others. Most income from the portfolio enjoys favorable tax treatment. Dividends and capital gains are charged at a much lower rate as compared to active income. Furthermore, portfolio income is not subject to Medicare or Social Security taxes. Income from the portfolio contains dividends, interest, and capital gains. Compared to active or passive income, portfolio income typically enjoys favorable tax treatment. Money from the portfolio is not subject to withholding from Social Security or Medicaid. One way to maximize portfolio income is to invest in an ETF that purchases dividend-paying stocks. Income from the portfolio does not come from passive investments. Moreover, portfolio income is not received from daily business activity. It is earned because of dividends, taxes, and capital gains or interest paid on loans. For tax purposes, the categories of income are important. Passive income losses can not necessarily be offset against portfolio or active income.

## Ways to Increase Portfolio Income

Following ways can be employed for increasing portfolio income:

## Purchase High-Paying Dividend Stocks

Investors can enhance their portfolio income by purchasing stocks that pay above-average dividends. Dividends can be paid directly to the shareholder. Moreover, dividends can also be used to buy additional shares in the company.

## Purchase Dividend Exchange-Traded Funds

A cost-effective way to maximize portfolio income is to buy ETFs that explicitly track high-paying dividend stocks. For example, the FTSE High Dividend Yield Index is tracked by the Vanguard High Dividend Yield ETF. There are 396 stocks that have high dividend yields and are included in the index. For other dividend ETF options, the selection criteria concentrate on how many consecutive years the company has paid a dividend and/or on companies that have a history of raising their annual dividend payments.

## Write Options

An investor can write call options against their stock holdings to enhance his portfolio income.

## 1.3 Passive Income

Passive income are earnings that come from a limited partnership, rental property, or another enterprise in which an entity is not actively engaged, such as a silent investor. Proponents of passive income tend to be boosters of the working lifestyle of a work-from-home and/or be-your-own-boss. Colloquially, it has been used on the part of the person receiving it to describe money being earned periodically with little or no effort. When used as a technical term, passive income is defined by the IRS as either "net rental income" or "income from an enterprise in which the taxpayer does not participate materially" and may include self-charged interest in some cases. Passive income is a source of income that may require some initial effort or investment but continues to generate payments in the future. Examples are music and book royalties and house rent payments. Passive income is the return on savings accounts. Passive income is created by a limited partnership in which a person owns a share of a company but does not engage in its functioning. Passive income consists of earnings generated from rental property, a limited partnership, or some other enterprise in which a person does not engage actively. Usually, taxes are charged on passive income. Portfolio income is perceived by a few analysts as passive income, and interest and dividends will also be considered as passive income. In order to earn and maintain, passive income needs little to no effort. When an earner puts in one of those little efforts to produce income, it is called progressive passive income. In many ways, a passive income investment can make an investor's life easier. This is true when a hands-off strategy is followed. Examples of passive income investment strategies include - Peer-to-Peer Lending, Real Estate, Dividend Stocks, and Index Funds. These four choices suggest different risk and diversification levels. As with any kind of financial investment, calculating the anticipated returns in relation to a passive income opportunity versus the loss potential is important. The main types of passive activities are explained below:

Cash flows from property income, including cash flows from a property or from any piece of real estate, capital gains, rent through resource ownership such as rental income, and in the form of interest from financial asset ownership.

Trade or business-related activities in which an individual does not engage in a company's operations other than investing during the year.

Royalties, that is, payments initiated by one corporation (the licensee) to another firm/person (the licensor) for the right to use the intellectual property of the latter (music, video, book).

## Standards for Material Participation

The standards for material participation include:

- Five hundred plus more hours toward an activity or a business from which you are earning
- If the participation for that tax year has been "substantially all."
- Up to 100 hours of commitment and at least as much as every other person involved in the operation
- Material involvement in at least five of the past 10 tax years
- For personal services initiatives, material engagement at any point in three previous tax years

According to the IRS, there are two passive activity categories. Rentals, including equipment and real estate, are the first type; and businesses are the second type, where the individual does not engage materially on a daily, continuous and significant basis.

## Examples of passive activities

The following are considered passive activities:

- Equipment leasing
- Limited partnerships
- Partnerships, S-Corporations, and LLCs where the individuals do not materially participate
- Rental real estate (some exceptions apply)

- Sole proprietorship or farm where the individual does not materially participate

## 1.4 Taxing of passive income

There are various forms of passive income, ranging from capital gains and dividends. Then the question arises whether the passive income is taxable or not. The brief response is, yes. Tax rates can differ depending on how long the assets are kept, the amount of benefit gained, and/or net income on each form of passive income.

### Short-Term Passive Income Tax Rates

For assets retained for a year or less, short-term gains apply and are taxed as ordinary income. In other words, at the same rate as your income tax, short-term capital gains are taxed. The prevailing tax rates for short-term gains are as follows: 10 percent, 12 percent, 22 percent, 24 percent, 32 percent, 35, and 37 percent.

### Long-Term Passive Income Tax Rates

Long-term capital gains (assets that are held for more than one year) are taxed at three rates: zero percent, fifteen percent, and twenty percent, based on your income bracket.

### Taxing of real estate income

With lower tax rates, investing in real estate and high yield rental assets is now even more advantageous for individuals. The authorized business income deduction is now a twenty percent deduction on the taxable income while buying and holding real estate. This deduction of 20 percent now requires investors to subtract a portion of the real estate investment holdings, which may lead to a higher ROI.

## 1.5 Why Passive Income Beats Earned Income

income Earned is the income that you earn when you work the job full-time or run a business. Notice that, in most instances, "running business" doesn't require rent real estate corporate. Money gained from royalties, rents, & stakes in the limited partnerships is passive income. Income from the portfolio is the income from interest, dividends, and stock sales capital gains. Earned income would be subject to heavy taxation at all levels. Earned money should be utilized to rapidly create wealth, but your wealth must be transferred into the portfolio and passive income pools in order to reduce your tax position. Earned incomes are subject to FICA taxation and the full marginal income tax rate. There are undoubtedly ways of minimizing tax liability, such as operating an S-earned Corporation's revenue, investing in the firm and currently earning deductible expenditures, etc., but high marginal tax rates would also be subject to net income. The issue with earned money is that you still have to spend more cash in order to minimize tax liability. Passive incomes from the rental property aren't subject to the high operational tax rates. Rental property income is privileged by amortization and depreciation and contributes to a much lesser effective rate of tax.

Let's assume, for instance, you now own a rental property, which nets 10,000 dollars before the depreciation & amortization. Let's just say that $8,000 is the total amount of depreciation and amortization. It leaves with a taxable revenue of $2,000. You can pay a tax equivalent to 740 dollars if you fall in the 37 percent tax bracket. Yet you see an effective rate tax of just 7.4 percent as we equate the $740 with the amount raised ($10,000). If you made the same 10,000 dollars in the earned income, in order to minimize the amount available to tax, you would need to expend more. Otherwise, with $10,000 into taxable income, you'd pay $3,700, meaning you're in 37 percent tax brackets. With the rental real-estate, every year, you don't have to be paying for depreciation. It's a ghostly cost which you have to claim. That's why, from a tax standpoint, passive income knocks out earned income.

## 1.6 Reasons Why Passive Income Is So Important

It's no wonder passive income's, and for a good cause, one of the most thought about, sought after aspects of personal finance. Passive income will have an incredibly positive effect on only about any financial situation, from creating vast wealth to avoiding a paycheck-to-paycheck lifestyle. But that poses the question: why does passive income matter so much? In short, passive income's essential because in financial life, it provides flexibility, prosperity, and independence. In addition, because your time & resources do not limit passive income, it may have a beneficial and important impact on the ability to build wealth. Passive income, in different words, is 1 of the easiest ways to upgrade the financial condition. But if that's not compelling enough, we've listed the top reasons why passive income's important.

## Improved financial stability

One of the most significant milestones you will hit on the road to prosperity is monitory stability. In different words, even if you really can see your financial position and realize, with certainty, that you're capable of coping with a powerful financial storm, so then you're on a very stable path. If you may count on the money rolling inside without having to fight for every cent of it, even more than that, so financial security is just a nearby corner. More money which comes in more you can be secure and comfortable in the finances. It helps you in relaxing, look at the bigger picture, & make smarter financial decisions because you don't have to grind for every dollar you earn, which, in turn, increases your financial health. This is a magnificent little cycle & one of key reasons why passive income is playing such a major role in personal finance.

## Less reliance on a paycheck

The discomfort that comes with living paycheck to paycheck is not comparable by any means. And if it is your case, then one of the best moves you can take is to add a bit of the passive income in your life. There is no secret in that sometimes it may get a bit stressful as you trade time for dollars. And the more you will distance yourself from a focus on the next paycheck, the lighter it can be in your life. One of the greatest advantages of passive income is avoiding the paycheck-to-paycheck lifestyle.

## It's easier to achieve your goals

Did you ever say to yourself, " only If I made extra money, then I could accomplish my monetary goals much more quickly...”? Well, that's just another explanation why the passive income's so awesome. It doesn't what financial targets you're trying to attain; you can accomplish your goals much quicker if you build certain passive income sources that enable you to make money all the time of day.

## More freedom to pursue your passions

You will unexpectedly find yourself with the opportunity to pursue your passions or, for that matter, your ideal job, along the same line as avoiding the paycheck to the paycheck lifestyle, while you get some of the passive income flowing through the bank account. Remember that it's easy to end up trapped in a position you can't bear when you focus on the active income to make ends meet. It is tough enough to leave a career. But it is particularly tough to leave a job if you don't have sufficient money to pay the rent that is due in two weeks. On the other hand, you have the opportunity to do the things you really want to do when you have a stable stream of passive income running into the finances of yours. Passive income, to put plainly, offers you choices. & with those choices, independence comes.

## Location independence

Likewise, in many ways, passive income encourages you to live and working from anywhere you like. Since you don't have to work constantly to earn a passive income, so you don't have to be working from a particular position either. You could tour the world if you like, as far as you earn passive income sufficient to support your lifestyle. And plenty of people do.

## Early retirement

Retirement is, to some degree, for many people, that may only be done later in life. Although, if you're building any passive income sources, retirement may not be far away as you thought. Really, if you love the thought of retirement at a young age, so then your primary financial priority should be passive income. If it means creating a company that operates even without you needing to be present there, participating in real estate, or a mix of few different sources of income, if you desire to stop working at a young age, passive income is necessary.

## More financial margin

more financial margins you will build in life, better off you will be in personal finance. In different words, the more distance you've between the expenditures & your income, the better it will get for financial life. And when you produce a constant stream of the passive income per month, it becomes much simpler to build the financial margin. Let's say, for instance, that your monthly gross expenditures increase up to 3,000 dollars. Now, if you're earning $4,000 inactive household revenue, then the monthly margin is $1,000. Yeah, that's not bad. However, if you add an additional $2,000 in passive monthly income in to the mix, life just got a lot better.

## Reduced stress

There's one unity between all, after everything we've spoken about so far. It's plain; passive revenue has a distinctive way to reduce the financial burden. A passive income life is considerably less difficult than a life deprived of it. Because your financial security, margin, independence, and too much more are improved by passive income, it's only logical that it will help alleviate your financial burden. So, if financial condition makes you feel a little tightened around the collar, you may just want to give passive income a little more priority.

## It's exciting

Passive income is not constrained by the effort and time that you can put into it. In different words, at all the hours of night and day, passive income can be earned, including while you are sleeping. Yet, at the same time, making money is incredibly thrilling. There's nothing like waking up in the morning thinking that you've won a few hundred bucks while you're sleeping. And the more you are enthusiastic about the financial condition, the more probable you are to continue to improve it.

# CHAPTER 2:  Passive income ideas to help you make money in 2021

Passive income may be a wonderful way of helping you produce more cash flow, & global upheaval created primarily by the pandemic is evidence of the importance of having many income sources. Passive income lets you cross the gap whether you unexpectedly become jobless or even whether you willingly take the time from work away with the pandemic tossing the working condition of most people into disarray. You might get the cash rolling in from passive income even while you follow your primary career, or if maybe you can build up a good passive income pool, you may need a little to kickback. Anyway, you are granted additional protection from passive income. And if you are concerned about being capable of saving enough money to reach your retirement objectives, accumulating capital through passive income also is a tactic that could be appealing to you. Regular earnings from a party other than the employer or the contractor are counted as passive income. IRS (Internal Revenues Service) notes that passive revenue will come from 2 sources: a company or a rental property in which one is not directly participating, such as paying book royalty or dividends on securities. Most individuals agree that passive income's about getting more for nothing. It's got get-wealthy-quick charm, but it also includes work in the end. What you offer is work upfront. You may do any or all the job upfront in practice, but the passive income also requires some extra labor along the way too. To keep the passive dollars flowing, you might have to save your merchandise updated or well-maintained rental property. But if you're dedicated to the approach, it could be a perfect way to make income, and by the way, you'll build some more financial stability for yourself.

## 2.1 How many streams of income should you have?

"When it comes to generating revenue sources, there is no "one size fits all" advice. How many revenue streams you have can depend on where you are financially and what your potential financial targets are? But it is a decent beginning to get at least a handful. "With multiple lines in the sea, you'll attract more fish. Rental assets, revenue-producing shares, and company ventures are a perfect way to diversify your income stream, in addition to the earned income produced by your human capital. You'll want to make sure, of course, that bringing work into a new passive income stream would not cause you to lose sight of the other sources. So, you want your efforts to be aligned and make sure you pick the right options for your time.

## 2.2 Passive income ideas for building wealth

So, if you're considering building a passive income source, look at these techniques and absorb what this takes to succeed with them, whereas still recognizing the dangers involved with each strategy.

## 2.3 Selling information products

One common passive income approach is to produce information products, such as e-books, or video or audio lessons, and then kick back while cash rolls inside from product sale. Via platforms such as Skillshare, Udemy, and Coursera, courses could be distributed & sold. Otherwise, you may think of a "freemium model"-making a free content follow-up and only charging for the more comprehensive details or for the ones who wish to learn more. Language teachers or

/ & stock-picking guidance, for instance, can use the model. Free material serves as a demonstration of talents and can draw those who want to be going to the next stage. You may use advertising (or sponsor) to make your revenue as the third alternative for this concept while offering information or material on a free forum like YouTube to a growing audience. Take the love of music or video games, for instance, and transform it into the content.

## Opportunity

The Information products will have an outstanding revenue stream, so after the initial time outlay, you quickly make money.

## Risk

development of this product typically requires a huge amount of effort. And it needs to be good in order to make great money off it. There isn't space out there for trash. If you wish to be competitive, you must create a strong base, advertise your products & prepare for other products. Unless you get very lucky, one product isn't business. Generating more outstanding products is the easiest way to market an established good. You could create a strong income stream once you understand the business model.

## 2.4 Rental income

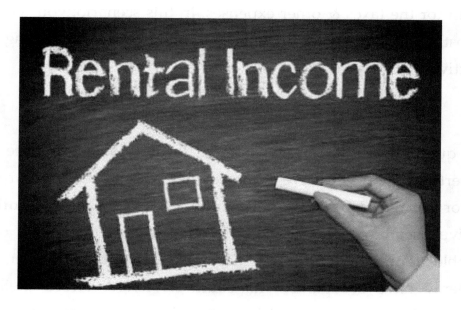

A successful way of earning passive income is to invest in rental properties. But more work is always needed than people expect. You could risk your money if you do not take the time to know how to create a profitable venture.

## Opportunity

If you want to earn the passive incomes from the rental properties, then you must determine three things:

- Financial risk of owning property.
- Property's total expenses and costs.
- How much profit you need on investment.

For example, suppose your objective is to make $10,000 in a year in the rental income. At the same time, your property has monthly mortgages of 2,000 dollars and charges another 300 dollars in one month for the taxes & other expenses. In this scenario, you will have to cost 3,133 dollars in the monthly rent for accomplishing your objective.

## Risk

few questions should be considered: Is there a marketplace for a property? How if you have a homeowner who pays off the property late or harms it? Suppose you cannot rent the property out? The passive income could be significantly impacted by any of the variables. And pandemic also has raised new threats. You could suddenly have occupants who could no longer afford their rent because of the economic crisis, although you may already have a mortgage of your own to be paying. Or, if earnings fall, you couldn't be capable of renting out homes for as far as you did before. So, to secure yourself, you'll want to consider these threats and have a contingency plan in place.

## 2.5 Affiliate marketing

However, with affiliate advertising, website owners, "influencers" on social media or blogs support the goods of third parties by including a link to the product on the forum or the social media network. The best-known associate partner maybe Amazon, but Awin, ShareASale and eBay, are all among the bigger brands. And for those watching to develop a following and sell goods, TikTok and Instagram have become major websites. To attract attention to the blog or else steer people to goods and services which they may like, you might also start growing an email list.

## Opportunity

The site owner receives a fee if visitors click on the link and make a transaction from a third-party associate. The commission may vary from 3-7 %, so it would obviously need substantial traffic to the site to produce serious revenue. But you could be able to make some serious coin if you may expand the following or even have a more profitable niche (like tech, fitness, or financial services). Affiliate advertising is deemed passive, and, in principle, only by adding a link to your social media platform or website, you will gain money. In fact, if you cannot draw readers to the site to tap on the link and purchase anything, you won't earn anything.

## Risk

You'll have to be taking time to develop content and generate traffic if you're just starting out. Building a following will take important time, and you'll need to discover the best formula to reach the crowd, a task that could take a while on its own. Worse, the audience might be likely to fly to the next famous influencer, topic, or social media site after you've expended all that energy.

## 2.6 Flip retail products

Make use of online sales sites like Amazon or eBay, and offer goods you find nowhere at prices of cut-rate. You will arbitrage the difference between the prices between your purchase & selling, and you will be able to create a following of the people who monitor your transactions.

## Opportunity

The price disparities between what you'll find & what average customer will be capable of finding would encourage you to take advantage of them. If you've contact that may help you obtain affordable goods that some other individuals can locate, this might work extremely well. Or you might be capable of uncovering useful products which others have completely missed.

## Risk

Although deals can happen online at any moment, you'll probably have to rush to find a reputable source of goods to help keep this strategy passive. And you're just going to have to know the competition so that you don't buy at a price that's too much. Otherwise, in order to market, you can finish up with goods that nobody needs. Moreover, you may be forced to slash the price drastically in order to make the product worthwhile for the buyers.

## 2.7 Peer-to-peer lending

Peer-to- peer (or P2P) loan's personal loan supports by the intermediary of third-party like LendingClub or Prosper between you & borrower. Funding Circle that targets firms & has greater borrowing caps, and Payout, which targets better collateral losses, are other players.

## Opportunity

You generate income as a lender from interest payments made on loans. Yet, you face the possibility of default because the loan is insecure, implying you might end up with nothing. You must do two things to cut the risk:

By paying smaller sums on different loans, diversify the lending portfolio. Minimum investment for each credit is $25 at Prosper.com and LendingClub.

To make educated choices, evaluate old data on the prospective borrowers.

### Risk

It takes time to learn the lending metrics of P2P because it's not completely passive, and you'll want to vet your prospective borrowers closely because you ought to pay particular attention to payments earned when you're engaging in several loans. If you intend to create profits, whatever you make for interest can be reinvested. Economic recessions may also make the high-yielding personal loans more likely to default candidates because if the COVID-19 manages to harm the economy at higher than historical rates, these loans will go bad.

## 2.8 Dividend stocks

The Shareholders in companies with dividend-yielding securities receive a payout from the company at regular intervals. The Companies pay the cash dividend out of the earnings on a quarterly basis, and what you need to be doing is to own stock. Per-share of stock, dividends are funded, meaning the more shares that you hold, the larger your compensation.

### Opportunity

Since stock income is not linked to any operation other than the actual financial investment, it may be one of the most passive ways of money-making to own dividend-yielding securities. In your bank account, the money will simply be deposited.

## Risk

Choosing the correct stocks is a tricky aspect. Without carefully researching company issuing stock, too many novices leap into the market. You have to study the website of each organization and be acquainted with their financial statements. 2 to 3 weeks you can spend researching each venture. That said, without wasting a massive amount of time analyzing firms, there are some ways to participate in the stocks dividend-yielding. ETFs, or Exchange-traded fund, are strongly recommended for income generation. ETFs are hedge vehicles containing collateral such as equity, commodities & bonds but trading like stocks. The ETFs are an excellent alternative for novices because, due to much lower prices than mutual funds, they are easier to understand, affordable, highly liquid, and offer much higher potential returns. Another key risk's that the stocks or the ETFs will decrease dramatically over short periods of time, particularly in times of volatility, such as when the financial markets were shocked by the Coronavirus crisis in 2020. Economic uncertainty may also cause certain firms to fully cut the dividends, while the diversified funds can experience less of a pinch.

## 2.9 Create an app

Creating an app may be a method to invest time in advance and then enjoy rewards over time. Your software may be a game or one that allows smartphone users to execute any feature that is difficult to do. Users download it once the application is public, & you can generate revenue.

## Opportunity

There's a big upside to an app if you can create something that captures your audience's fancy. You'll think about how it's best to generate revenue. You could run in-application advertisements, for example, or else make users pay a small fee to use the app. You'll definitely add incremental improvements to keep the product current and popular as the app gains attention or you get feedback.

## Risk

Perhaps the greatest risk here's that you spend your time unprofitably. You have no financial drawback here if you contribute little to no money to the project (and/or money which you'd have spent otherwise, for instance, on hardware). It's a competitive market, though, and genuinely popular applications must give consumers a persuasive benefit of experience. If your app gathers some data, you would also want to ensure that it is in accordance with privacy rules, which vary across the globe.

## 2.10 REITs

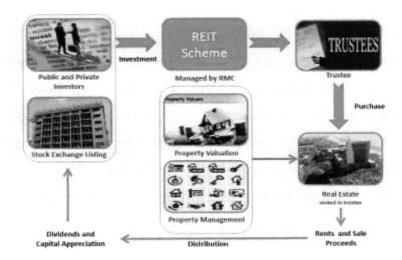

For a corporation that owns and manages real assets, REIT is a real estate investment trust, which is a fancy word. REITs have a special legal arrangement such that although they pass over any of their income to owners, they pay no or little corporate income tax.

## Opportunity

In the stock exchange, you can purchase REITs much as every other business or dividend stock. You're going to earn whatever the REITs payout as a payout, and the strongest REITs have an annual record of growing their dividend, meaning over time, you might have an increasing supply of dividends. Specific REITs could be more expensive, like dividend stocks, than buying an ETF composed of hundreds of REIT stocks. Fund offers instant diversification, which is inherently much better than owning specific stocks & you can always earn a good return.

## Risk

You'll have to be capable of selecting good REITs, much like dividend stocks, that means you'll have to evaluate any of the firms you might purchase, which indeed is a time-taking process. Also, while it is a passive activity, if you do not know what you're doing, you might lose a lot of money. And neither are REIT dividends safe from difficult economic times. If REIT does not produce enough income, this would possibly have to slash or totally remove its dividend. So just when you want it, most of the passive income could get hit.

## 2.11 A bond ladder

bond ladder's sequence of bonds maturing over a number of years at various periods. The phased maturities help you to reduce the risk of reinvestment, which is a risk of locking up your cash as bonds offer interest rates that are too low.

## Opportunity

bond ladder's a traditional passive investment that for decades has attracted near-retirees and retirees. You will sit back to collect the interest payments, and you "extend the ladder," transferring the principle into different package of bonds as the bond matures. For starters, you could start off with one year, three years, five years, and seven years of bonds. In the year that 1st bond matures, you have two years, four years, and six years of bonds left. You may use proceeds from the newly aged bond to purchase another one year or roll out an eight-year bond with a longer-term, for example.

## Risk

Bond ladder reduces one of the big dangers of purchasing bonds, the possibility that you may have to purchase a new bond as the bond develops when the interest rates will not be attractive. Bonds, too, come with the other risks. Although the federal government backs Treasury bonds, corporate bonds aren't, meaning you could risk your principal. And to diversify the exposure & eliminate the risk of someone bond harming your total portfolio, you'll want to buy multiple bonds. Many investors move to bond the ETFs because of these issues, which include a diversified fund of bonds that you may put up on a ladder, removing the possibility that a single bond will harm your returns.

## 2.12 Invest in a high-yield CD or savings account

Investing in an online bank's high-yield deposit certificate (CD) or savings account will help you to produce passive income and get one of the country best interest rates as well. In order to make money, you won't even have to leave home.

## Opportunity

You'll want to do a fast check of the nation's great CD rates or the top savings accounts to make the most of your CD. Going to the online bank instead of the local bank is typically far more advantageous since you will be able to pick the highest rate available in the region. And if the financial firm is backed by the FDIC, you will also receive a fixed return of principal of up to 250,000 dollars.

## Risk

Your principal is secure as far as the bank is backed by FDIC and under limits. So, it is just as secure a return as you'll find to invest in a CD or savings account. Nevertheless, though the accounts are secure, these days, they return even less than before. And with Federal

Reserve aiming at 2% inflation, the least in the short run, you're going to miss out on inflation. A savings account or CD can, though, yield less than keeping your cash in cash or in a non-interest paying checking account where you will earn about zero.

## 2.13 Buy Property

Real estate can be a decent way to make a passive income, depending on where you invest and when. There has been a rapid growth in the value of property in common cities such as Toronto-44 percent in Canada alone in the last five years. You will find some lower-cost properties by purchasing pre-construction condos, which will rise in value by the time it is eventually completed, enabling you to sell the property once it is complete for a profit. Like for all investments, it can be dangerous, so if you're new to the market, it's better to talk to a real estate agent to help you purchase the correct investment property.

## 2.14 Rent out your home short-term through Airbnb

This simple approach takes advantage of space that you don't need anyway, and converts it into an opportunity to make some money.

Whether you're leaving for summer and/or have to be outside of the town for some time, or maybe even you want to fly, try renting your present space out while you're gone.

## Opportunity

On a variety of websites, including Airbnb, you may list space and set rental conditions yourself. With limited additional work, you'll receive a check for efforts, particularly if you rent to a tenant who might be in place for a couple of months.

## Risk

You do not have a lot of financial downsides here, but it's a gamble that's atypical of the most passive investors to let strangers stay in your house. Tenants can, for instance, even deface or ruin your property or steal valuables even.

## 2.15 Air BnB Business as a Passive income Strategy

Airbnb is an online website for selling and renting urban homes. It ties hosts and travellers and promotes the rental process without owning any rooms on its own. Moreover, it cultivates a cooperative economy by allowing private flats to be leased by property owners. Airbnb is an internet platform which links individuals that wish to rent the homes to an individual in that area who are searching for a room. It currently surrounds more than 100 thousand cities in the world and 220 countries. The name of the business derives from the "air mattress B and B." Engaging in Airbnb is a way for hosts to gain some money from their home, but with the possibility that it may be damaged by the visitor. The benefit could be comparatively cheap lodging for visitors, but with the possibility that property wouldn't be as advisable as the listing has made it look. For less than the cost of a hotel bed, travellers may also book an Airbnb. The traveler's biggest concern is that the property could not live up to its listing. The primary concern for hosts is that their property may be badly damaged by guests.

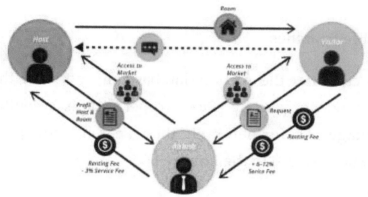

## The Advantages of Airbnb

It offers the following advantages:

## Wide Selection

Airbnb hosts list several different categories of properties on the Airbnb website, like single rooms, a suite of rooms, moored yachts, , whole homes, studios, houseboats, even castles.

## Free Listings

In order to list the assets, hosts don't have to be paying. Listings may contain written descriptions, captioned photographs, and user profiles so prospective visitors can have the knowledge about hosts a little better.

## Hosts Can Set Their Own Price

It is the host's prerogative to decide how much to charge per night, per week, or /and per month.

## Customizable Searches

The Guests can filter the Airbnb database and not only through date & location, however also by price, property type, amenities, and the host's language. To further limit their search, they may also add keywords (such asclose to the Louvre').

## Additional Services

Airbnb has increased its services to include events and restaurants in recent years. In addition to a list of available hotels for the dates they expect to visit, individuals searching by the venue can see a list of opportunities provided by nearby Airbnb hosts, like classes and sightseeing. Restaurant listings also contain Airbnb hosts' reviews.

## Protections for Guests and Hosts

As a protection for customers, before transferring the funds to the host, Airbnb keeps the guest's payment for 24 hours following check-in. For guests, Airbnb's Host Guarantee program "provides security for up to $1,000,000 in damage to covered property in eligible countries in the rare incident of guest damage."

## The disadvantages of Airbnb

It has the following demerits:

## What You See May Not Be What You Get

Booking Airbnb accommodation is not like booking a space with a big hotel chain, where you have a fair promise that the property will be as described. Individual hosts, though some may be more truthful than others, create their own listings. Previous visitors, however, often post updates about their experiences, which may offer a more critical perspective. To make sure the listing is correct, review the reports of other guests who have stayed at the Airbnb house.

## Potential Damage

The greater concern for hosts is potential that their property will be damaged. Although most stays go without incident, when the Airbnb hosts assumed they were renting to a peaceful household, there are reports of entire houses being trashed by thousands of partygoers. Some insurance is offered by Airbnb's Host Guarantee program, mentioned above, but it does not cover anything, like cash, rare artwork, jewellery, and pets. Also, hosts whose homes are destroyed can experience significant inconvenience.

## Added Fees

A number of extra charges are imposed by Airbnb (just like, of course, hotels and other lodging providers). To cover Airbnb's customer care and other programs, travelers pay a guest management fee of 0 percent to 20 percent on top of the reservation fee. Prices are shown in the currency that the customer chooses, provided it is sponsored by

Airbnb. Banks or issuers of credit cards can, where applicable, add fees. And though listings are free, to cover the cost of handling the transaction, Airbnb charges a service fee of at least 3 percent for each reservation.

## It Isn't Legal Everywhere

Would-be hosts need to review their municipal zoning codes before listing their properties on Airbnb to make sure it is legal to rent their properties. To receive special permits or licenses, hosts may also be required.

## 2.16 Advertise on your car

By merely driving your car across town, you can be able to raise some additional income. Contact a specialized advertisement firm to determine your commuting patterns, like when and how many miles you drive. The firm will "wrap" your car with the ads at no cost to you if you're a match with one of their advertisers. Newer vehicles are being searched by agencies, and drivers should have a clear driving record.

## Opportunity

If you're still putting in the miles anyway, though you may have to get out and drive, then this is a perfect way to earn hundreds every month at little to no added expense. It is reasonable to pay drivers by the mile.

## Risk

Be extra cautious about locating a reputable operation to work with if this idea seems good. In this space, many fraudsters set up schemes to try to bilk you out of thousands.

## 2.17 Invest in Stocks

When you look at the wealthiest people in the world, it's pretty fair to conclude that their deep, endless savings accounts are a result of their major investment in stocks. Warren Buffett reads 500 pages a day, but he doesn't read your usual mystery novel. He reviews the annual corporate reports. He better knows whether or not a company is doing well by reviewing annual reports each day, which helps him improve his decision to invest in stocks. While the act of investing in stocks is very passive, the analysis that goes into it is active. Nevertheless, investing in shares will help you gain passive income that goes well beyond what your value is worth at your 9 to 5 work. So, if you enjoy reading about the success of different firms, consider this passive income approach.

## 2.18 Make Your Car Work for You

Driving is another everyday practice that you can translate into passive income. When you're just walking around, why not pick up a commuter or two to run errands? Uber can help you make money by taking people to their designated destination by driving your vehicle. You may also put ads on your vehicle to collect cash as you drive around. When your car is not used while you're on holiday, driving, or just during a normal workday, it will still make money. You will make thousands of dollars with an app like Getaround by renting out your car if you're not using it. Plus, drivers of Getaround vehicles get the best parking spaces in town, a $50 monthly rental credit on any vehicle they want, and one million U.S. dollars in primary insurance coverage.

## 2.19 Sell your Videos

We live in a day and age where video content fascinates hundreds and thousands of humans. You would want to take out your phone and hit the record if you still find yourself in the middle of drama and excitement. To allow you to make some passive income, you can sell stored content. Why? It is because the video can be sold to a news site. And you can make some recurring income for weeks, months, and maybe even years if the video takes off. Of course, being at cultural gatherings such as marches, rallies, and festivals is the best way to get in on the action. You'll find ways for your material to be sold anywhere there's controversy. And corporations will pay you to make viral videos along with providing a share of total earnings if you are successful at creating engaging content.

## 2.20 Create YouTube Videos

The passive income source that just keeps on giving is YouTube. You'll find that you can make a regular income from your YouTube channel, from funded videos to ad sales. Creating videos on a regular basis for a long time is the key to creating a profitable YouTube channel.  If you stick with it in the long run, you will finally start reaping the benefits of passive income.

## 2.21 Write an eBook

In 2009 and 2010, e-books came onto the scene and are now a hugely successful content medium. While they first became popular a few years ago, to this day, there is still a very decent chunk of individuals who make passive income from writing e-books. It's an insanely dynamic business, of course. Yet, you might find yourself with a nice slice of the profits if your writing chops are stellar. You could build a fanbase of loyal readers by designing how-to e-books on famous niches and marketing them.

## 2.22 Sell Digital Products

You can make digital goods if you're trying to create your own products rather than selling someone else's. You can sell your digital goods online using Shopify. From e-books, educational classes, PDFs, custom graphic templates, stock images, or some other digital goods, digital products will contain anything. Selling these items is the epitome of passive income, and with immediate updates, the whole operation can be streamlined on Shopify.

## Car Wash

Car wash is a perfect way to earn a semi-passive income. Although a car wash will need daily cleaning, it is something you can either contract out or do once a week. We are talking about the very simple car wash that is cinderblocks, a pressure washer, and the powered coin, as a side note. It's certainly a corporation vs. a passive income stream if you're trying to run a drive-through car wash.

## 2.23 CPC Ads (Cost Per Click)

You get really paid whenever anyone clicks on your link and signs up for something or orders something through affiliate ads. On the other hand, show advertisements charges depend on the volume of traffic and eyeballs that you receive on their ads. On the other hand, for CPC advertisements, also known as "cost per click" ads, anytime someone clicks on an ad, you get paid no matter what they do after that. You don't have to hope or pray that they're buying anything or signed up for something. Any single click takes money into your account with the bank. Does that mean that all day long you can go to your own website and click on ads? It is not realistic since the corporation will inevitably find out what you are doing and cut you off. With all that in mind, it should not be a part of your plan here to click on your own ads. Instead, aim to build up traffic so that more and more viewers every day see the ads.

## 2.24 Minimize your taxes on passive income

A passive income may be a wonderful side-income generation strategy, but you can still create a tax burden for your effort. But by setting yourself up as a business and building a savings portfolio, you can reduce the tax bite and plan for your future, too. However, this solution will not work with all these passive strategies because to qualify. You will have to be a legal organization.

Register with the IRS to make your company receive a tax identification number.

Then call a broker, such as Charles Schwab or Fidelity, who will open a self-employed retirement account.

Determine the type of savings account that will fit well for your needs.

# CHAPTER 3: Airbnb Offers The Best Passive Income Generation Strategy

rental vacation industry is rising quickly. It is real quick indeed as a matter of fact. The sector is currently generating 57,669 million dollars in sales, according to recent analysis reports from Statista.com. The revenue is awaited to grow to a market value of 74,005 million dollars by 2023 and is projected to see an average growth rate of 6.4 percent. This data illustrates just how broad & robust the holiday rental management industry is. And you should expect demand for Airbnb property management to pursue to grow over the coming years with the growth of Airbnb rental properties in recent years. Therefore, if one day you are aiming to become a manager of Airbnb property, now is a great time to be entering the business. But how are you able to get started? We will supply you with what you have to know regarding how to be an Airbnb vacation rental property manager. We're going to teach you what this takes to handle rental Airbnb properties, particular instruments you're going to be needing before you start, and stop points for the beginners for achieving successful property management. So, without further ado, over here are all six steps to beginning an Airbnb property management career in real estate.

## 3.1 Understand the Vacation Rental Industry

Just like some other business, without learning at least the fundamentals of this area, you can't succeed. However, no formal qualification is necessary to become an Airbnb property manager, and many find success with the only diploma of high school in this profession. Thorough knowledge of how the holiday rental industry

& Airbnb run is what you need to have. So, if you don't already have it, having this information now is the 1st step to being the manager of the Airbnb properties. Ideally, as Airbnb hosts yourself, you should have some experience. If you've already hosted your rental property on Airbnb, run it yourself, you can show to potential buyers which you know exactly what you are doing. Furthermore, this will allow you to be prepared better to predict challenges, recognize potentially troublesome travelers, and cope with common issues. But if you don't have the experience, through online guides and classes, you can empower yourself about the rental vacation industry & how Airbnb works. There are plenty of those out there that can help you create a good base on which you have to learn. For instance, you may take marketing coursework to know how to extend your scope and get bookings more and business courses to know how to manage a company, keep records, & file tax. As an Airbnb property manager, it'll help you improve your creditability. Before you start, another significant point to learn is where the Airbnb hosts invest in rentals for the short-term. You'll know the place to find customers looking for management support with this detail.

## 3.2 Create a Maintenance Management System

Managing rental of short-term rentals ensures that you'll get visitors checking in & out repeatedly. One of many duties of the property managers, of course, is to review property before visitors visit & after they depart. Every now & then, operators of holiday rentals must also conduct repairs to ensure that the properties are in perfect shape. This is vital to ensure the happiness of both your customer and guests. For instance, imagine having visitors who had parties and had rental property trashed before leaving. Nobody with such a situation is going to be happy to step into a rental. As a consequence, before addressing the issue, the manager of Airbnb property can never leave the maintenance as an afterthought or even wait for the property owner to receive several inquiries. In addition, to offer high-quality care on their behalf, great short-term property rental operators often work alongside a dependable maintenance team. Your staff should include, among others, plumbers, house cleaners, and electricians. For any check-in, these entities will ensure that Airbnb assets you handle are tip to top.

## 3.3 Put Together a Vacation Rental Marketing Strategy

The most significant tasks of property managers are promoting and selling holiday rentals to attract prospective visitors. Today, there are millions of listings on Airbnb & more rental sites for the short-term, which is creating rivalry among the Airbnb hosts. It is why one of the first things potential users would like to know is how you're going to get reservations and increase their occupancy rates for Airbnb. As a consequence, you must have a basic comprehension of tactics and methods for property marketing. Therefore, having a marketing campaign that will draw Airbnb visitors to the holiday rentals you run is the next step towards being Airbnb properties manager. Start by writing an enticing listing that will maximize the probability of retaining a high rate of occupancy & a positive flow of cash. To make rental properties under your management stand out, think about investing in advanced photography & videography facilities, also branding services. Moreover, selling holiday rentals suggests that you have to go outside the listing platform. It is why active rental managers of Airbnb use social media and also SEO to meet the target tenant audience. If you don't know how it works, before you begin handling rentals in the short term, we strongly suggest that you begin to read about real estate marketing.

## 3.4 Invest in Property Management Tools

You can handle them with hard work and a few spreadsheets as you become manager of Airbnb property for the first time when you have only some rental properties underneath your belt. This becomes difficult, though, as you continue to add more assets to manage. How are thirty check-ins & cleanings going to be done in 1 day? At an early point, it is best to begin thinking about it so that you're planning yourself & your company for success and expansion. Using real estate management of property software that allows to automate & remain structured is the best approach for this.

In order to operate their businesses more effectively, modern holiday rental property supervisors rely a lot on technology. There are several high-tech solutions that make it easy to handle Airbnb rental, from the smart lock to invoicing, pricing, and the guest screening software systems. You will even find holiday rental apps which will synchronize schedules and handle multiple Airbnb profiles for free from different platforms. Not only does the use of such instruments make your life more effective as a manager of real estate properties, but they can also give you the strategic edge to keep rising. Mashboard, for instance, is a software that lets managers of Airbnb property connect with their customers and find the right properties for those to expand their business.

## 3.5 Outline Your Guest Management Strategy

Amazing client care is one of the abilities that any manager of real estate property wants to provide when handling both conventional and holiday rentals. It is how effective operators of Airbnb assets set themselves away from the audience. A good selling point, particularly for Airbnb travelers, is customer service that goes beyond and beyond. Getting a guest engagement plan ensures that during their visit, the services can be open to visitors and their demands at whatever time. Expect the short-term visitors to have to inquire or inquire over something. You must be capable of responding in a timely way to such unannounced requests. How can you treat a case, for instance, where the visitor has misplaced keys to a holiday rental and can't get in? There will be a contingency in it and other cases for a successful Airbnb property manager. In addition, to manage communication with visitors, managers of top-performing properties also have automation tech systems in place. Airbnb guests really enjoy great customer service & show this by posting favorable feedback. This, in essence, helps to get more bookings & boost cash flow, that will surely make the customers happier. As you could see, one of the most critical skills for good management of Airbnb property is definitely customer service, so don't consider it as an afterthought.

## 3.6 Set a Reasonable (But Competitive) Price

To become a manager of Airbnb property, the only thing you need is a pricing plan. Usually, the holiday rental manager takes a percentage cut from the real host's secured rental fee. A selection of online outlets recommends anywhere from ten to twenty-five percent. At the same time, others believe that more consumers would be drawn by charging the lowest price; that isn't the case. Customers base their options on the quality o facilities rendered by property managers-not dependent on costs. Thus, providing the lowest price means that you don't have top-tier facilities for owners of Airbnb property. You need to take several factors into account in order to fix the correct price. First of all, as stated, is what kind of services you are providing. Naturally, for something that you don't sell, you do not charge. Look at experience instead, what distinctive points of selling you may give, and set rate accordingly. The local economy and what the other rental property (short-term) managers in the area charge, the seasonal demands, also current events, you will need to remember. Ultimately, you need to set a fair price which you are sure will be getting you back that your service is worth.

## 3.7 How an Airbnb Business Works

Nearly everyone has listened to Airbnb or has used it. It is the platform for online home rentals that helps hosts renting vacant private short-term accommodation from a single room to whole homes. Airbnb launched in 2007 & has expanded exponentially to have listings in further than 65 thousand cities in the world with more than three million available properties. Here is how to start a sustainable Airbnb company if you have sufficient rental space and are searching for additional revenue. Through uploading photographs and details of the room for rent, the first move is to be a host on Airbnb and register the home. When an Airbnb property's listed, travelers searching for a room in the host area will access it. Guests may use a number of requirements to check for Airbnb listings, like:

- Availability dates
- Destination
- No. Of rooms, such as bedrooms and washrooms
- Price
- Host language
- Amenities such as hot tub, breakfast, pets allowed, and etc.
- Facilities like air conditioning, parking,etc.

Prior to booking the chosen space through the Airbnb guest may establish a contact with hosts directly for gathering additional information through the Airbnb service of messaging.

**Access**

Along with browser access, Airbnb offers mobile applications for Android and Apple IOS devices.

**Security**

For security purposes, the hosts are expected to provide Airbnb with appropriate identification. Travelers should post the reviews of hotels to create a trustworthy group (and the hosts may review the guests). The Reviews aren't anonymous.

## Guest Services

Airbnb offers a stable payment platform for the guest's calmness of mind, and fees to the hosts are deferred until 24 hr after the arrival of the guest. In the event that any difficulties are faced during the renting time, Airbnb has a 24-hour hotline for the guest.

## Fees

Host sets the price for lodging. Moreover, Airbnb charges under-mentioned fees:

Host: Three % transaction payment fee

Guest: six to twelve % booking fee

The Hosts can also ask for a security deposit & could well charge a cleaning fee.

## Taxes

Airbnb could apply provincial, state, or city taxes for guest bookings depending on the jurisdiction.

## Travelers Prefer Airbnb Rentals

One of the best things about operating an Airbnb company is that, for several reasons, travelers choose Airbnb over motels, hotels, or hostels:

Cost: Usually, Airbnb rent is much inexpensive than a similar hotel room. In certain instances, an entire house may be rented through Airbnb for the cost of a single suite of the hotel, depending on the location.

Living locally: Living the life of a local person is the key advantage of the Airbnb service. Most guests of Airbnb choose to stay inside the community and explore the destination way the locals do, instead of renting a generic hotel room.

Privacy: customers of Airbnb are not continuously surrounded by visitors and workers at the hotel.

Peace & quiet: the Airbnb rents are usually more secure and do not suffer from loud hotel events, such as guest exits early in the morning, young children, maid service, and traffic.

Witness what you get already: Unlike a hotel where you can see a snapshot of similar rooms on their Airbnb page at best, you get full images and explanations of the real premises.

Diversity: From yachts and boathouses to castles and lighthouses, Airbnb has an immense variety of available accommodations.

Home comforts: Airbnb has a homey atmosphere of a real living space instead of generic hotel spaces (few have resident pets even). Kitchens allow the guests to cook their own food if they desire to save money on outside dining or have dietary issues.

Friends or Family: Through Airbnb, you may save a lot of money by renting a whole apartment/ house/condo rather than the multiple rooms of a hotel for family and friends.

## Is Renting Your Space Permissible or Advisable?

Ensure you're legally permitted to be an Airbnb host into jurisdiction before you plan to start an Airbnb business, & you're prepared to respect local laws & regulations. Depending on the state/ city or regional rules, municipal laws governing the hosting of paid visitors will vary greatly; they are absolutely banned in some areas whilst they're subject to occupancy tax in others if space is condominium or apartment, check to view if it is allowed to sub-let the premises. There are also regulations in place for apartment landlords & condominium societies to prohibit an owner from renting the units out as Airbnb rooms. Renting your apartment out without the knowledge of your landlord will have you evicted. Neighborhood ties are also a significant concern. In the area, a few inconsiderate or loud Airbnb guests will easily turn you in a pariah. If none of the challenges are insurmountable, it could be an outstanding opportunity of home-found business to become an Airbnb host.

## Are You Committed to Becoming a Host

There are a variety of additional concerns to remember prior to making a definitive decision to host Airbnb:

Would you like to start a business? Then Starting an Airbnb company is like establishing any business- that you need enthusiasm, entrepreneurial spirit, & the ability to make the required effort, starting off with doing relevant background analysis and developing business plans.

Do you've energy? It could take a great amount of time to be a landlord, particularly for the short-term rents. You'll have to:

- Manage reservations and reply to interactions with prospective tenants.
- Plan to meet the guests to give out or receive keys
- ensure the property, including fresh linen, breakfast supplies, is cleaned properly and ready for the arrival of the guest (if applicable)
- Fix some property maintenance problems such as plumbing and pest control, electrical & appliance repair
- Be accessible to the visitors on a 24 into 7 basis if the property has any problems.

Demand: The deciding factor in the popularity & price of rented accommodation is visitor demand. The highest places for rental returns are:

 sought-after tourist destinations with high hotel rates (famous neighborhood ranks higher on the Airbnb searches)

situated Centrally, close to visitor attractions, shops & public transport,

Featuring panoramic views and facilities like parking, balconies, etc.

Seasonality: Demand for the property in the northern hemisphere will definitely drop drastically in winters (unless you're renting a ski chalet). In comparison, rental accommodation demand in colder southern locations (like Arizona) decreases dramatically in summers.

What are the marketing aims? Are you trying to earn a little cash or create a stable income on the side? The financial portion of the business plan must show target market analysis and reasonable forecasts of your property's future rental income. The income from the Airbnb contract depends upon:

Before you start thinking about leaving your job & making a living through running an Airbnb company, make sure that by seeing rental prices & booking regularity for comparing Airbnb listings of your area, you carefully examine the revenue potential of your property.

Extra costs: In addition to booking fees paid by Airbnb, there are extra costs involved with Airbnb hosting, including:

Insurance: Standard insurance plans for homeowners do not include the use of the property for commercial uses, including renting on Airbnb. Airbnb has a free host compensation insurance policy in Canada, U.K., U.S., and many other nations, offering up to 1 million dollars in guarantees against personal harm or property loss. If your place is not protected by Airbnb policies, please contact your insurance provider to see if there is sufficient coverage.

Business Licenses: Airbnb hosts are being required by more & more cities to hold a business license.

Repair and Cleaning: You want to keep rental properties in top condition all the time in order to keep your Airbnb host ranking at a high standard, which includes extensive cleaning during guest stays and daily repairs. The charges will contribute to your expenses if you have to sub-contract cleaning and repair duties.

**Listing and Pricing Your Property on Airbnb**

Accurately describe the place and make this stand out. Note that Airbnb is an online marketplace & you have to be thinking like a realtor to make listing stick out from the competition in order to optimize guest interest in your house. Start by looking at the same Airbnb listings inside the region and consider the amenities/features and prices listed. If this works, make a spreadsheet. The definition of your listing must be precise, comprehensive, complete, and highlight, which makes it special. Comprehensively define the facilities and functionality of your room also as any regulations or preferences of visitors. Providing high-quality photographs of the room is incredibly necessary. Airbnb has specialist availability of photography service in certain places if you are unable to do this yourself.. You don't want visitors to be upset because the room isn't as advertised or you've exaggerated amenities. Note that the guest rankings would be partially dependent on the accuracy of your listing description.

**Price Your Listing Competitively**

You should also get an idea of how to market your listing from your analysis of similar listings. It needs to be competitively priced to keep the property consistently booked (and increase profits).

**Improving Your Host Ranking**

Higher the property pops up in rankings, the more probable it's to be chosen by visitors, so having good rankings of Airbnb is crucial to the success of Airbnb business. Airbnb rankings are like internet search rankings. And by building confidence and offering a fantastic experience to your visitors, you will boost your rankings.

**Build Trust**

Airbnb community's based on trust and guests would be searching for hosts with contact information, credentials, and favorable feedback.

## Verification

For the new hosts, verification is highly essential: change your profile and include other details like the email address, phone number, Facebook profile, and etc. For giving prospective visitors some confidence that you're a reliable host.

## References

You should post the references from colleagues, co-workers, relatives, business partners, etc., to build more trust. For the other Airbnb users, you may even write references.

### Provide Great Customer Service

Like any entrepreneur would tell you, the cornerstone of any successful business is customer care, and becoming an Airbnb host has no difference. Positive ratings, better search scores, and more bookings reward hosts of Airbnb who have the best experience of the guest. The hosts with the most popular are:

## Responsive

The Hosts that can not be bothered for responding in a timely manner (or at some) to inquiries are a big turnoff for visitors. In reality, Airbnb keeps track and rates your replies to guests accordingly. With higher search rankings and improved bookings, the host who has the highest ratings of response is awarded. At all times, Airbnb mobile application will help you to keep connected. All the time when visitors are present, be available through phone and check up with them on extended trips and see if there's something more you may do to maximize the services.

## Update Their Calendars Regularly

Keeping your calendar current, also enhancing the guest experience, boosts the Airbnb rankings of search.

## Fix All Problems quickly

When a guest mentions problems like leaky taps or a burned-out lightbulb, it should be repaired promptly and render an apology to the guest. Sure ways to boost the guest rankings is to provide five-star service.

## Act on Their Reviews

Fix the issue and benefit from the failures if a visitor writes a critical review. React to complaints all the time in a respectful way.

## 3.8 The Bottom Line

In real estate, there are many ways of earning profits. The growing success in the U.S. housing sector of Airbnb and other short-term rentals has created opportunities not just for real estate developers but also for property managers. Today, there is a great demand for vacation rental managers, and industry analysts expect that over the coming years, there will be national growth. Therefore, imagine being an Airbnb property manager if you're looking for a profitable means of generating passive income.

# Conclusion

In a nutshell, passive income is money that comes at regular intervals without having to invest a large amount of work into generating it. By blogging, one method of producing passive income may be achieved. If you've figured out how to produce content that attracts sufficient traffic to the host advertising, you can make a product that your customers would want to purchase. From a basic e-book to a sophisticated app that produces sales for several years after it is released, passive income could be anything. Similarly, people have a lot of things, and they still look for cheap places to store this. What might be simpler than asking people to pay you for storing their things? An investment on a large-scale in purchasing storage facilities (with the cash) or anything simple like offering the basement or the shed might entail creating passive income by offering storage. All you'll need is to make sure their goods are clean and stable. You will make money by selling them to others against such charges if you've any things that you don't use at all times, which others will love to borrow. As rental items, useful items such as a tractor, trailer, kayak, trampoline, or your own lawn even may give you passive income. With the support of platforms like Airbnb, this also involves renting spare rooms out in your home. Upload the pictures of items, fix a date, and tell the world they're ready for the rent on your favorite social networking site. The reason why it is necessary to have passive income is that it will help increase your financial consistency. The more passive income you make, the easier it becomes to be consistent with your financial life, from consistently saving to consistently spending to consistently donating. One of the strongest and most relevant aspects of a sound financial condition is passive income. It is beneficial for you in several ways, from enhancing your financial health to reducing your financial burden.

# The Golden Ratio Trading Algorithm

*Discover the 9+1 Bulletproof Strategies that Helped 113 Dead Broke People Get Out of Debt*

**By**

**LEAONARD BLANCO**

# Table of content:

# Introduction:

Defining your corporate plan lets you make the best of your opportunities so you can accomplish your objectives. A successful business plan may be the difference between living and flourishing.

Some companies grow to a stage where the entrepreneur can no longer manage it themselves. Now is a perfect opportunity to start dreaming about a plan that can lead the company to accomplish its goals, e.g. by encouraging people to make choices. Getting a well specified approach to achieve your company goals will also help you clarify your plan to your staff, networks, sponsors, consultants, borrowers, accountants and investors. It's vital for moves like finding finance.

Overall, the effect of a successful plan is that you remain efficient over the long term, stop making typical errors, and stay ahead of the market. A plan provides a common understanding of your goal, making everybody in the company appreciate what you're working for. It will support you:

- Prioritise work

- Make the correct decisions

- Say 'no' to distractions

- Make the best of your place in the marketplace.

When you're experiencing loads of rivalry, developing a plan involves recognizing your benefit and your optimal place in the business. Then you should schedule things to reach you there. In this guide you can find lots of things to focus on so now it's up to you how well you select certain strategies and incorporate them in your business.

Working on a plan will help you discover your keys to progress, and set a course to follow towards reaching your goals. It may also help you grow into new goods or services. Without a consistent business plan, you might make choices that clash with each other, or end up in a bad financial and competitive role.

# Chapter 1: Become a YouTuber

Until you even make a video that has viral value (making videos is not incredibly difficult if you enjoy what you do), you have to develop a platform that sticks out. It is also accurate that the videos you produce are the chemical X that will make your channel highlight. However, I have noticed that building a killer channel before releasing the first video is crucial. Let me also figure out that we shall not discuss how to build a channel; what we shall discuss is how to create your channel and make it stand out. Here are the ideas you need to accomplish this:

Create and design your brand

We will not cover, as I have indicated, how to create a channel. I should point out, however, that if you have a Google email and comment account or like YouTube videos, chances are, you already have a channel. It is important to note that your YouTube brand is at the heart of the channel you create. This is what's going to prompt viewers to sign up for your channel. What this means is that the proper attention it deserves must be given to your channel's name. The name of your channel should be memorable and relevant to the content you're going to share with your subscribers and the world. For example, you might create a channel under the name 'beauty within if you want to create how-to-make videos.

If you don't know how to build a channel, here is the link to the portal for creating a channel.

Exude professionalism

You will notice one outstanding thing, which is the quality of video and interactions if you take a second to wade through all the videos that attract many views and comments on YouTube. This simply implies that you have to be professional to create a killer channel and video that draws in millions of views. You need to be skilled in your presentation, how you make the video, and in particular, the technology you use to shoot the video. This means that you can use your iPhone (not recommended) if you do not have a video camera, but make sure to keep the phone as steady as possible. In addition, the audio on your video should be of excellent quality. It also suggests that you should seriously consider adding subtitles to your video if you are not a native English speaker or have an accent. I can guarantee that your channel will never come close to the status of stardom if your videos are out of focus. Visit some of the more popular channels to find out what is professional by YouTube standards and emulate their video presentation.

Create a video response

Despite the fact that they could generate high-quality sharable material, most YouTubers fail to get their channel noticed. This leaves the uploader with only the possibility that his or her channel may be found by anyone with a broad following. Here's a trick to make sure your channel is out there more easily. The trick is to produce a video answer to a famous video of high quality. In addition, to guarantee that other individuals click through to your platform without actually caring who you are, make your answers either informative or extremely divisive. Video answers that are divisive, fascinating, surprising, or informative can also guarantee you a few subscribers who believe your perspective or design appeals to them. On the other side, even though you don't receive viewers, the chances are good that a couple of your videos would be viewed by anyone who clicks through to your site. Using video responses is a caveat; make sure you do not attempt this trick until there are some really good quality, interesting videos on your channel.

Bait the crowd with reviews

The first thing you probably do anytime you want to purchase an object is to head over to Google to look for ratings. Video analysis is the quickest and more likely to go viral. As long as you make sure that the analysis is thorough and appeals specifically to the crowd of people involved in that specific thing, it really does not matter what gadget or item you review. All of us still search for product feedback (perhaps even you); as such, build a platform that gets many views and subscribers. The endeavor to create a few highly measurable review videos of some famous devices or items is well worth it.

Channel your energy on the channel

If only every three years your favourite musician produced a song, how would that make you feel? The word is Bored! A very similar approach is taken by a YouTube channel. If your commitment to the channel waivers, all the subscribers and subscribers you have gathered will drift off to another channel that consistently offers them videos if it takes you very long to upload. Uploading doesn't stop; you need to be active on the channel, interact with viewers, respond to their comments, and just make sure they feel appreciated and connected to you. If you do seem to keep your audience's interests at heart, they will move on by constantly interacting and uploading videos.

Key point/action step

To develop the mindset and routine necessary for creating an outstanding YouTube channel, fall into the habit of logging onto the site daily, watching a few videos and commenting on those that interest you. This is especially important because it will fuel your idea machinery and push you to create videos that people like.

How to Apply What You've Learned?

I am aware of the fact that too much information can work against you at times; the same applies to your journey for YouTube stardom. To help you out, I have decided that all we have learned will be summarized into an actionable plan that you can easily follow. Let it get to us.

### *Fuelling your idea tanks*

Draw your ideas on YouTube from other videos that are doing well. I can guarantee you that there are other YouTubers in the field, regardless of which field or category you intend to upload to. Visit their channels, view their videos, and take away the best practices from their videos. Watch how they make their videos, voice-overs, etc., and then find out if you can replicate their style but add a flare of personality.

Viral does not come easy.

It is not easy, as stated earlier, to create viral videos. Sadly, to create viral videos, there is no trick or outright blueprint. There is only one definite way, on the other hand, to ensure that your videos are near perfection and closer to viral, and that is practice. Practice using various cameras, different lighting, and even different angles to create videos. You increase your video creation abilities when you employ this tactic. Make sure you don't look back in simple terms and say, 'I should have shot that angle differently.'

SEO plays a very central role

We looked at the numerous variables leading to the YouTube and Google rankings. Optimizing the video and platform is key to this rating. This suggests that to make the video rank higher, you have to read what you can about keywords and how to use them efficiently. Fortunately, the internet is full of tools you can use for SEO and keywords. You don't even have to use paying keyword queries since Google's free keyword analytics service works best.

Engagements make all the difference.

Through commenting, enjoying, and uploading their footage, you must actively connect with other YouTubers to push traffic to your channel and posts. When you create video responses to widely famous videos, this is particularly successful. In addition, commitment ensures that you have to interact with YouTube regularly by making and sharing videos as much as possible.

# Chapter 2: Create an Instagram channel

### *What is Instagram?*

According to Wikipedia, Instagram is an online mobile video sharing, social networking, and mobile photo-sharing service that allows different users to take videos and photos and then share them on different social networking platforms like Flickr, Tumblr, Twitter, and Facebook. As you can see from the description, it is a mobile app for smartphones and is available on Windows mobile, iOS and Android.

With the app, you can add captions and filters to your photos, get likes, and increase followers tremendously. You can also follow friends or whoever else you like to get their pictures on your Instagram feed.

If you are awfully talented in taking amazing pictures or want to turn your many followers into customers, there are many ways you can begin to earn money on Instagram.

### *A brief history of Instagram*

Instagram was officially launched around 2010 and three years later became one of the largest and most engaging social networks. It's no wonder why Mark Zuckerberg, the Facebook CEO and founder, bought this photo-sharing app for a whopping amount of 1 billion dollars from its rightful founders (Mike Krieger and Kevin Systrom). Most people thought he was crazy. At the time of purchase, Instagram had only 13 employees had less than 22 million active users and no website. It has since grown so fast to currently have more than 300 million active users, definitely more than Twitter or Pinterest and over 100 employees. In fact, according to recent research, people are spending more time on Instagram than on Twitter or

Facebook. It's the fastest growing social platform in the world, and its future is very bright. Just as it has upgraded Facebook's balance sheet, it can upgrade your income. Instagram's social feeds and easy-to-use editing tools make everyone capable of creating and sharing nice edited pictures today. It has empowered people in unexpected ways, even those who don't bare Bieber, Hilton or Kardashian names. You can use it to share your interests, for instance, skateboarding, art, and other experiences, or just share your photos or videos and make money for such a simple effort. Many big companies are now using this platform to reach out to customers worldwide, and their sales have skyrocketed. Companies like Puma are even hiring Instagrammers with massive, profound, and engaging followings at more than $5000 a day to capture photos that display the respective company products.

Key Point

With over 300 million Instagram users, anything is possible. Think of it as a large billboard in a large intersection where over 300 million people frequent, and you will discover that this is an immensely big number of people. So, whatever it is that you might want to do, whether to gain in popularity or to make money, the potential is limitless.

## Basic Tips for Making Money on Instagram

Like many people out there are doing, you can turn this so-called hobby to be a money minting cash cow by following the basic guidelines given below;

### *Build a follower base*

Getting people to follow you is the first step to making money with Instagram. Without a very minimum of a few thousand followers, it will be hard for you to convince any brands to sponsor your posts. Even with the over 300 million users, it doesn't mean that being on Instagram automatically qualifies you to have access to this large number of users; you must strive to get a fraction of this number to follow you. Just like any other product, before you start making sales, you need a market, and this is your followers. Here is how:

1) Increase followers; Take all the time you need to expand on the number of your account followers by interacting with your followers and posting unique photos. You will learn more about this in the next chapter of this book.

2) Use hashtags to attract more people. For every photo you take, make sure that it has at least three hashtags that can add to your viewers. The hashtags should speak about the photo but should be broad enough to show up in numerous searches. Don't worry! You will learn more about hashtags later in this book.

### *Upload quality images*

1) Master your craft; the fact of the matter is that if your photos aren't so good, people will not be willing to buy them. This may mean many different things to different people, but you need to take quality pictures if you want to end up selling them.

2) Use different cameras; avoid limiting yourself to your phone's camera. With Instagram, you can upload photos taken using other devices; all you need is to transfer them to your phone first.

Get yourself a nice camera and notice the significant difference in the quality of photos you take.

## *Set Up Your Store*

Without an online store, you are almost doomed. You can't sell your photos via Instagram directly, so you have to set up an alternative way that people can buy your pictures. Here are some ways you can go about this.

1) Hire a store service; you can sell your photos directly through Services like Twenty20 and soon through their site. You get 20% of the sale, and they handle the printing and shipping for you.

If you want to avoid dealing with printing and shipping orders, this can be useful.

2) Get your own store; you can use your personal website to set up your own online store. You will definitely get more money than you would if you used a hired service, although you will have to take care of orders, as well as shipping and printing the images. For each image you upload to sell on Instagram, it should have a caption containing a link to its store page regardless of which method you use to set up your storefront. So that the link doesn't take up the whole caption space, use Tiny URL or Bit.ly to shorten the address. Take advantage of apps such as 'Hash Bag,' which automatically identifies and posts any items that have the hashtag '#forsale' on your Instagram account to their respective market.

### Market your Products

After you gain followers and therefore in a good position to approach and convince any company, do this:

1) Contact companies; you need to explain and convince your target companies how you can help increase awareness for their brand through your Instagram account. Show them how often you update your Instagram feed and give details on the number of followers you have. Carry some sample shots to display and illustrate you know how to take clear, artistic pictures which can shed some positiveness to their product. Services such as Popular Pays and QuickShouts can connect you with companies, which hire aspiring Instagram marketers.

2) Work out a contract. You need to have a clear written contract indicating matters such as the expected number of pictures you are supposed to take and bonuses for the improved number of followers, if any. To protect yourself from being underpaid by the company you are marketing for, sign a contract.

3) Take quality pictures of the service or product. For sure, you wouldn't like to upload a mediocre or bad photo of a product you are supposed to be marketing. For you to keep the contracts coming in the future, you need to play your role as an ambassador for a given product effectively and uphold the expected standards.

You are free to add some personal touches to the photo, and in fact, you should. You don't want your followers to feel as if this is just one of those advertisements they would spam so easily if they weren't following you. Your followers need to relate to your image on a personal level.

### Turn your many followers into Customers

1) Point followers to your blog or site; you should have a link to your company's or personal website or blog always on your Instagram profile. As you continue to gain more random viewers or followers, traffic to your site will also increase. Emphasize your skills. You can showcase your abilities and talents on Instagram, including fashion, web development, photography, and several other fields. Update your current projects and latest work on your Instagram feed always. Remember to use hashtags to attract potential buyers to your image.

2) Take your product's photos. If you run a business that deals with physical items like vehicles, cupcakes or whatever, one of the best ways to advertise your merchandise to new people are through Instagram. Take photos of some of your latest products, then make sure you use hashtags to entice more followers. Some hashtag examples include the product name and use, your company name or slogan. If you have a store page, make sure you link to the product's image comments. Remember to submit the nicest photos you got of the product and avoid those low-quality cameras at all costs.

### *Offer Brand Takeovers*

You can earn some good money by doing an "Instagram takeover" as a substitute for sharing sponsored posts on your own account. It's exactly what it sounds like and is all about posting photos on another person's Instagram account. Either you can get temporary access to the person's or company's account, or you can be asked to supply photos, additional descriptions and hashtags to them. This works especially well for travel accounts, "We supply 5-7 amazing images to a company or tourism board and they feature our photos showcasing how we see the destination," says Bouskill, an Instagrammer.

### *Sell Your Account*

You can sell your account for profit once you have a tremendously successful account. You can even get a six-digit for selling accounts that have 500,000 to a million followers.

Key point

Stay active on Instagram to get as many followers as you can, upload quality images of what you are selling, set up an online store, market your great skills to companies, and then turn your devoted followers to customers. Do "brand take over" or sell your account if you please. Don't forget to put the links and the hashtags on your Instagram images or comments. When you do that, you can watch your bank account swell in due time.

How to Post Memorable Content

You need to create posts that will stick in people's minds for a while. Here are some ways you can do this:

### *Take unique and interesting photos.*

This may seem so obvious, but simply taking good pictures is one of the best ways to get followers on Instagram. Instagram is flooded with pictures of people's cats and meals, so have well-shot photos to set yourself apart. Let the pictures you take related to your audience fully. People are hesitant to follow you if you always post images they can't relate to. It doesn't have to be a "perfect" photo to be good. Good photos are more human, and any imperfections make them more so.

Put a boundary on "selfies." You can post some 'selfies' on Instagram, but don't let them dominate your account. Your followers don't want to see you but rather want to see your photos. You can seem narcissistic if you post constant selfies, and this can put off many followers. Sad as it may be, there is an exception to this if you are very attractive. Posting attractive pictures of your gorgeous self can drive many followers to your account. Still, don't let this take over your content!

### *Post Every Day*

You need to have a new post every day and post reasonable several times if possible. Your presence must be felt all the time. With this, your follower's list will grow every day.

### *Add filters*

Instagram became so popular because of the filter options. These filters fine-tune the colour of your photos and give them a more "real" feel. There is a variety of filters available on Instagram, so feel free to try out several until you identify the one that works well with your photo. Don't use the same filters too often, or your images will start to seem too similar.

#nofilter is a popular hashtag on Instagram; if the picture is too striking to even need a filter, use it!

### Place captions on every photo

You will be amazed at how fast you can turn an okay photo into a remarkable one with a good caption. Your viewers' attention is grabbed by using a caption. The more people you make smile or laugh using a caption, the more you'll retain them as followers. Cute captions or jokes are particularly trendy.

### Utilize apps for extended editing control

While you can slightly edit images on Instagram, there are many apps for both Android and iOS that can provide a lot more tools. Use these apps to darken, brighten, crop, add effects, text, and so much more.

Popular editing apps are Afterlight, Photo Editor by Aviary, Bokehful and Overgram.

### Create collages

A fabulous way to show a collection of images or progression is to make a collage to post on Instagram. You can do this using several apps, including InstaCollage, PicStitch and InstaPicFrame.

### Post your photos at a good time

Since Instagram is an extremely popular service, your followers' feeds are probably constantly updated. Post your photos at the right time for them to be seen by as many people as possible. Make sure you post photos in the morning and after the end of normal work hours. Instagram photos normally stay around a person's feed for 4 hours so if you want your followers to actually see your images, avoid posting them in the middle of the night.

### Most Beautiful Photos

Not only do you need to post consistently, but you also need to post beautiful images, which are instrumental to increasing your Instagram followers. You can even be featured in media houses for outstanding photos. You need to inspire people through your photos and not shock them out of your account.

### Avoid Posting All Your Photos at Once

The necessity to post photos regularly does not mean you post all the photos you have taken at one go. If you want to post more than one photo a day, make sure they are spread out in the day. Share one photo every three to four hours. You don't want to make your followers oversaturated with images-keep them yearning for more. Don't just dump all of your photos at the risk of making your followers start passing over them.

### Pick up an Insta-Style

Like most successful Instagrammers, you need to develop a signature style for your photos.

Whichever technique or filter you choose, make sure your photos stand out from the crowd.

# Chapter 3: Make money through binary options

What are the options?

Options are financial securities that give the consumer the opportunity, but not the responsibility, on or before a certain date, to purchase or sell an underlying financial commodity at a certain amount. Just as you know, with specified terms and conditions, options are like every other financial asset or instrument. It is important to note that options are not assets themselves, but their values are derived from other financial assets such as stocks, hence the name derivatives.

Two styles of choices are primarily available; call and place. Call options grant you the opportunity to purchase an underlying one at a given price on or around a specific date in the future, but not the responsibility. Call investors are betting that the value of the commodity will grow in the future and thereby allow them the ability to make market profits.

On the other side, placing options gives the customer an opportunity, but not the duty, to sell an underlying commodity during a specified time at a specific amount. Placement buyers conclude that rates are expected to collapse in the immediate term.

Why options trading?

Options have been branded as some of the riskiest investment ventures. However, over the past decades, participants in the options market have tremendously grown. Why would an investment vehicle think to be so risky to gain such popularity? There are several benefits that are attributed to this, but let us shift focus on the two main reasons why people use options hedging and speculation.

## 1. Speculation

Speculation is better understood if thought of as betting on the price of an underlying asset. People base their beliefs on what the security price will be in the future as the market adjusts itself and make a bet on the predicted market movement. The use of options for speculation is what makes options a risky venture. You not only have to be accurate in determining the direction of the market movements but also the timing and size of such movements. Let's say you predict that the price of Microsoft stocks will likely rise in the next three months; you can buy the call option, which will enable you to buy the stocks at a lower price and sell them at a higher price. If the market moves in your favor, you can make substantial gains. However, if the market movements do not favor you, you lose 100% of your investments (options price).

## 2. Hedging

Options can be an insurance policy for your investments. You can use options to hedge your investments against a downturn. For example, if you assume you wish to take advantage of the upside of technology stocks like Microsoft, you can buy a put option and take advantage of the upside keeping the stocks safeguarded against any downturn.

Key point/action step

Investing is all about determining the kind of investor you are and the goals you hope to achieve in investing. When investing in options, you have two main reasons for investing; to either hedge or speculate. It is important that you determine your reason for investing in order to invest wisely.

Types of binary options

There are many types of binary options available to you as an investor. Interestingly, the most common types of binary options not only confuse new traders but also experienced ones. I will go slow just to ensure that you get this information clear.

## 1. Digital binary options

Under this, we have call/put and up/down options.

Call options: You place a call option if you believe that the price will rise above the entry price.

Put options: You use this if you believe that the price will not rise above the entry price.

With up/down options, you only need to predict the direction of the price movements when you entered the market. Will it move *up/down?*

## 2. Touch binary options

These types of binary options come with predefined rates needed to win the trade as opposed to the trading participant just predicting the direction of the price movement. Here, you predict a level of decrease or increase it will reach (touch) and the level it will not reach (no touch). Please note that these types of binary options only trade when the market is closed, mostly during weekends. If the market touches or passes the specific level by 1700GMT on Monday, you get your returns. No-touch pays when the level defined is not reached.

## 3. 60 seconds option

Are you the type that gets excited by quick rewards? Perhaps this is your best bet. This option expires in 60 seconds. With this, it is easy to predict price movements. Basically, I usually recommend this option for traders who wish to profit quickly from a trending market.

## 4. Boundary options

This is sometimes also called range options. It differs from digital options in that two-level supper, and lower are defined. The asset must stay inside this boundary for a trader to receive any payout. This method is ideal for stable markets when trading inside the boundaries and volatile markets when trading outside the defined boundaries.

Key point/action step

As you have seen in this chapter, there are different types of binary options that you can invest in; hence, it is important to choose wisely. My advice would be to start small with binary options that are easy, for instance, the boundary options that give you more leeway when it comes to anticipating price movements. However, it is up to you to choose the most suitable option to trade-in depending on the returns you are looking for. If you are the adrenaline junkie kind of investor, then the 60-second option is most suitable for you.

# Chapter 4: Social media advertising

There are a great many ways to earn money through social media. What we'll discuss for this chapter are the more straightforward methods of making money from your social media accounts.

More than 50% of all internet users all over the world go online for social media. This goes without saying that websites like Facebook and Twitter are huge opportunities for advertising and marketing, and many have taken advantage of the situation by allowing people to earn by displaying advertisements on their profiles.

This is especially profitable for people who have large networks and can be considered 'influencers.' Influencers are those who have a great number of followers and therefore have more powerful recommendations.

Earning can work in several ways. Once you display a Facebook ad, you can earn when someone clicks on the link, makes a purchase and leaves their mobile number or email address.

One can also go for paid tweets such as SponsoredTweets.com. As the name suggests, you get paid when your followers click on promotional links via Twitter.

Pros: Displaying Facebook ads can give you around two cents per click, depending on your arrangement with the advertiser. Sponsored tweets can earn you $6 for one tweet for 2000 followers and can reach up to $1000 for those with a massive following. Given the amount of time that you actually spend on your social media accounts, the rate is fair enough.

A good thing about displaying ads is that you are totally in control of the content that you wish to display. This is also an opportunity to help your followers by making quality recommendations while earning at the same time.

Cons: What seems to work for social media ads can also work against it. Most people really don't like ads, and so coming up with advertising links that are catchy enough to warrant attention may be tricky. Too much hard selling can also turn off some of your followers. It may not be as effective for people who have not yet established a large network of followers.

Social media advertising can be a very lucrative venture; however, it also highly depends on the extent of your social network.

# Chapter 5: Stock trading

If you find yourself with more saved cash and an appetite for risk, stock trading may be a good venture for you. To describe it simply, stock trading involves buying shares of certain companies for a particular price, then selling them afterward for a profit when the value of these companies rises.

While it does sound easy, comprehensive research must be done before one engages in stock trading as it's not uncommon for people to lose their hard-earned money when the economy stumbles, and the prices of companies suddenly crash. Smarter traders can get profits of as much as 600% in three years, but this is backed by long years of experience and the 'feel' of the stock market.

Here are a couple of tips to earn extra money from stock trading.

Be in it for the long haul. Patience has always been a virtue, and the same holds true for stock trading. You will need to learn to apply the "buy at the low and sell at the high" law, and it requires a lot of patience to keep yourself from buying just because everyone else is buying because chances are the price maybe a little too high, and it will affect your profits.

You also cannot expect a 30% profit right away in your first year of trading, as it may take five years for you to truly realize your profits.

Buy great companies. One of the things that make stock trading a hit is a fact that your earnings depend on how well your company performs. That being said, a great deal of research must be done on a company before you decide to buy a piece of it. Does it have a good management team? Does it have years of experience to show for its stability? How profitable is it? Many experienced investors say that you should only buy a company that you truly know about for you to understand how it will be affected by key events.

Diversify. Another good tip is to not keep your eggs in the same basket. Do not focus all your investment on a single company to keep yourself from crashing with it when unexpected events take place. It is always a good practice to invest in various industries to create a buffer for your investments.

# Chapter 6: Blogging and freelance writing

Blogging

Blogging is one of the most common platforms for web content on the internet and can be done by almost anyone. It is a form of social networking that allows you to create your own comprehensive content where you can showcase whatever you wish.

Blogspot and WordPress are some of the leading blog posts where people can sign up for free, and it allows anyone to publish their content online. If you have a knack for writing, this one is for you. You can post a wide array of content, from blow by blow accounts of how your day went, reviews of the latest movie you watched, opinions about current events, social commentary, book reviews, advice for mothers, shared experiences about pets and many more. Writing can be done for self-expression or to share experiences that you believe can help other people.

As fun as it sounds, establishing a blog isn't a walk in the park because you will need time and commitment to update it with quality content to keep readers coming back. Junk content that is simply copied from other web pages will easily be disregarded as plagiarized content and will not help the reputation of your site. It is also recommended to find a niche topic that you can focus on so as to target a specific brand of readers and establish a regular following.

A golden rule for web content: quality is king. If your readers find that your website offers something that they cannot easily find with other webpages, they will keep coming back. More readers mean a better reputation for your blog and, therefore, higher potential earnings.

Earning through blogging can be done by leasing your webpage space to advertisers, by writing sponsored reviews or blog posts about particular companies, or by selling actual products.

When you gain a following, people keep coming back to your page. The more traffic you get, the more attractive your page becomes to advertisers because they would want to take advantage of your page views and use it for advertising their product.

Using this concept, various sites offer bloggers the ability to display advertising banners on their webpage and get paid for them. There are hundreds of sites that offer these services, and some of the most popular are Infolinks, SiteScout (formerly Adbrite), and Clicksor.

You can get paid from $0.01 to $2 per click, depending on the value of the banner. The more traffic you get, the higher chances of people clicking on the banner link, and therefore the more money you get.

Other companies pay for impressions, meaning visitors really don't need to click on the ad for you to earn; they simply have to 'see' it. This has much lower payout rates but is also more convenient to use. Bloggers strategize on the placement of their ads to come up with more clicks and more impressions.

Google AdSense is one of the leading providers of blog advertising. They are the most popular; they provide the highest payouts but are also the strictest. It is recommended that you purchase a top-level domain (www.ebook.com instead of www.ebook.blogspot.com) for them to approve your request. They also go for top-notch quality as all pages with traces of plagiarism or copied content are immediately disqualified. They also strictly screen the nature of content that they approve to ensure that it only provides quality information for potential readers. If one passes through the rigorous screening of AdSense and keeps working on improving their blog quality and traffic, they can expect earnings of $0.15 to $15 per click, with most getting up to $48 for 1000 visits, the highest among all advertisers.

For those who have established a reputation with their blog—if you are a mom known for providing valuable baby-care advice, a girl known for fabulous taste in clothing, or a guy popular among bloggers for keenly observing gadget updates—some companies may want to bank on your influence in the blogosphere by sending you free products to review or by asking you to create a write up about their brand for a fee.

This can be a tricky line to tread, however, as some readers may get 'turned-off' when they find that you are being paid by companies to make positive reviews. A good way to work around this is by providing 'full-disclosure' to your readers by telling them if a particular post was sponsored by a brand. You may also want to keep your tone from getting too patronizing to keep your blogger's integrity intact. This way, the trust system between you and your reader is maintained. Another great thing about blogging is that the manner in which you create your posts and how you build your reputation is entirely up to you. Therefore, anything that happens is really under your responsibility.

Another great way to monetize your blog is by selling products. You may have some handmade crafts that others may find useful or a friend who knows a great supplier of accessories and clothing. Instead of renting an actual physical store, you can just post your goodies on your blog, advertise them on your social networking sites and receive orders from people. Selling with this method normally involves having the products delivered to your customers, so make sure that you also know the procedure for shipment.

A lot of people have earned a living by selling online products and relying on social media and word of mouth for their advertising. It's a pretty hassle-free method because your online space is mostly free, and you invest in your product and seller reputation alone.

Blogging is a great way to earn money online, but it takes passion and commitment to keep it going because the internet is flooded by all types of bloggers, and sometimes it takes a special flair to stand out.

Blogging is not as easy as it seems, but if you've got what it takes, it can also be the most rewarding.

Freelance Writing

Freelance writing is another way to earn online through the power of the pen—or in this case, the keyboard. Several bloggers venture to freelance writing and vice versa, while a lot of them actually juggle being both. The key difference between blogging and freelance writing is that with the former, you are in full control of the layout and content, and you write for your readers on your terms. Freelance writing, on the other hand, is pretty much like outsourcing your talent for their purpose, and therefore all articles are written on the client's terms.

It may be easier or harder, depending on which side of the fence you're on. But freelance writing will definitely give you a more reliable stream of income once you've got the hang of it. Beginners can start on sites like Odesk.com or Elance.com, where potential clients and freelancers can meet to discuss terms and gain an interface for communication. The more experienced ones eventually gain contacts of their own and can get projects for higher rates.

Articles can range from a simple 400-word description of products or 30-word description of hotels to 4000-word essays or long sets of blog posts. Formatting and tone of writing can also vary, which will require flexibility and good writing skills. A strong command of grammar and spelling is a basic requirement, along with the ability to consistently meet deadlines. This also includes the patience required for hours and hours of research.

Freelance writing can be as demanding as a day job or even more. However, it still allows you to manage your own time and decide which projects to accept and which to set aside for a later time, as long as you meet the expectations of your client.

Beginners can earn about $30 to $50 an hour, while the more serious ones can earn as much as $80 for an hour and even $2000 for a month.

While these sound like really good money, one must be aware that the life of a freelance writer is anything but easy. Here are a few tips that one should bear in mind when aspiring to become a freelance writer.

Get ready for rejections. Because of the increasing level of competitiveness that this industry requires, one must be ready to experience multiple rejections of their articles. Remember that they are not rejecting you as a person, only your work. Only when you are able to resist taking rejections personally will you be able to hope to make a living out of freelance writing.

Keep your reputation clean. Your reputation as a freelancer can either make or break you. Being able to consistently submit deadlines, work according to your agreement with the client and provide quality work are sure-fire ways to boost your chances of being referred to new clients.

Socialize. Go out, meet people and socialize. This is another way to develop networks and attract potential clients. Learn to market yourself.

Set your goals. Are you content with making $1000 a month, or would you like to earn $2000 or more? Set your goals according to your family situation; if you find that you can get a lot of more than 8 hours a day for freelance writing and that you would like to earn a significantly larger amount, then you should go for higher-paying clients and better writing gigs.

Seek help. Hundreds of websites are available for freelance writers who would like to improve their craft or would like to get the hang of the technical matters involved in the trade. Take advantage of these groups in order to meet fellow writers and keep yourself motivated.

# Chapter 7: E-book publishing

If you are a book lover or enthusiast, at one point in your life, you may have dreamed of publishing your own book and being a world-renowned author. You might have sniggered at the thought back then because getting published seemed too far-fetched and ambitious. What if you learned that you can now be a full-fledged author of your own book for real?

The landscape for book-reading had changed quickly since 2012 when e-books outsold hardbound covers for the first time. More and more people have been turning to e-books because of their easy accessibility and portability. In no time, self-published authors gained popularity as well. Digital publishers are making it unbelievably easy for people to publish their own books, and many are taking advantage of this opportunity. Several authors are finding themselves easily selling a thousand e-books a month and are definitely outselling their hardbound counterparts.

If you have an idea sitting in the dark corners of your mind for quite some time, now is the best time to write that e-book, and who knows, it might just give you your first million! Here's a rundown of how:

Write. There's an initial draft that is basically your brain spilled over pages of chaos, a review draft that finally organizes your thought and develops what you really want to say, and the polished editorial draft ready for publishing.

This is, of course, the most important part of the process because, without publish-worthy content, your book will not sell a dime. Focus your thoughts and define your goal straight up—would you like to entertain, inform or inspire?

Formatting. This involves making use of the digital publisher format for your e-book and coming up with a cover. The design of the cover is critical for people to take an interest in your eBook. Take note that it also must be attractive even as a thumbnail because that's how your eBook will initially be presented.

A lot of self-published authors try to design their own covers with awful results. It is recommended to hire a professional cover designer to create a more polished look for your book. If you're going to earn thousands of dollars from it, you might as well invest, right?

Publish and Promote. Head over to your digital publisher, login to your account and follow the pre-defined steps to publish your e-book. You must have your tax info ready for royalties and legality purposes.

Pricing is a very important aspect. Most e-books are priced at $2.99 to $9.99. However, it is found that most readers buy e-books in the $2.99 to $5.99 price range. Price it too high, and no one will buy it, but if you price it too low, you may not gain enough profit.

There are many digital publishers out there like Nook, iBook's, and Smashwords; however, they have already established themselves as one of the most credible sites for online transactions. The intensive feedback system is top of its class, and they help to extend the reach of your book even to people who have no idea who you are.

Promoting the book is critical to the success of your e-book because no one will buy it if they don't understand that it exists. Make extensive use of social media, offer incentives for every purchase, or advertise it in online forums and blogs. Take advantage of the digital nature of e-books to spread awareness. It may take a lot of work, but it's definitely worth it.

Publishing e-books is a great way to leave a legacy on your passion or expertise. Now is the best time to do it!

# Chapter 8: Make your own video games

Your Debut into The World of Making Video Games

I am very tempted to tell you that the video game industry is a gold mine waiting for you to prospect, and indeed, it is. I am also tempted to tell you that video game creation is only a success story only for big game companies, but alas, I will not. Why? Because I would be telling you a lie. In the interconnected technology-driven world, which is where we live, anyone, and I mean anyone, can create a video game.

Do not get me wrong; I am not necessarily proclaiming video game creation success to all. I am merely stating the fact that thousands of people across the globe have been able to make their own games. Here is another fact; long gone are the days when video games had only two platforms: computers and gaming consoles. Today, with the advent of mobile technology, video gaming has gone mobile. With 98% of the world's population being owners of a mobile phone, it is only right that the video game industry would take advantage of this. Again, today, there are more mobile phone-based games than there are computers or gaming consoles in the world. What does this mean?

It means that the fruits are ready for the picking and that the pickings are in plenty. It means that if there ever were a time to get into video games production, now would be it. Contrary to popular belief and media hype, you do not need to be a geek with 'mad' coding or programming skills to create a video game (this does help, though). Anyone, even you, can create a video game. All that you require to create a game today is a bit of know-how, a lot of passion, and tons of patience. I am not promising that your video game will be an overnight sensation. I am also not promising that the journey will be easy. In fact, it may be very hard. What I promise you is that by the time we are through, you will be in a better position to create video games and well on your way to making some money from your video game creations.

Key point/action step

Although it is possible to make your own video games, you need creativity, passion, and patience if you are to become a success story.

After writing up your concept, hashing it out, and reflecting on it, it is time to fuel that enthusiasm train. Unless you are a serious video game creator with a few thousand dollars to fork out and some experience in pro programming, Unreal 4 Engine is not for you, albeit being one of the best video game creation engines. For the rest of us, who do not want to start from scratch, neither do some serious coding, we must rely on the help of software. Fortunately, the web is full of free and premium video game creation software. What I have found is that in a world of choice, most people are unsure of what to choose. It is important to point out that most of the software available each has different features, merits, and demerits. Your choice of software is entirely dependent on your game creation needs and level of expertise. I must also point out that you can do much using the available software that we will discuss shortly.

Before we move on to that, you are probably wondering why you should use an engine. Why not program the game by hand. I can give you a couple of reasons. However, I shall give you just one substantial reason. Engines provide a host of developmental tools, which aid and simplify the creation process. Furthermore, they are time efficient and less complex compared to hand programming. An engine also makes it easier to manipulate your AI (artificial intelligence), sound, and graphics.

Before I give you that list of software, I have to point out that some software is best suited for 2D graphics while others work best for 3D graphics. Above all, and regardless of your engine choice, most engines do come with tutorials to guide you in usage and creation. Here are the engines you can try to use.

### Game maker: Platform-Windows and Mac OS X

The game maker engine is a product from YOYO games. It is a comprehensive engine well suited to help you create beautiful games without necessarily being a programming whiz kid. However, the program does require some getting used to (learning curve). Fortunately, the program does have a tutorial, manual, and a very vibrant user base and community ready and willing to provide you with answers to pressing questions. Unfortunately, only the light version, which does not allow for more robust features such as export, is free. For the premium version, you may have to pay up upwards of $500. Additionally, I have found the engine interface to be a bit lacking in terms of design. One of the more outstanding features of the software, both the free version and the premium version, is that you can port your game to different operating systems such as android, iOS, desktop, and HTML 5 (Web) with no basic knowledge of scripting or coding. This makes it an outstanding tool for a beginner.

### Construct 2: Platform- Windows

If you liked Game Maker, then you will most definitely like Construct 2. Like Game Maker, construct 2 is also a premium engine that comes with its own user base, tutorials, manuals, and active community. Unlike Game Maker, construct 2 does not offer a free version. Instead, they offer a free 30-day trial of the full engine. Because the engine base is HTML 5, it is the best alternative to web animation tools such as Adobe Flash or Java. Using this engine, you can create beautiful 2D games that you can easily port to Windows, Linux, and Mac PCs, as well as Firefox Marketplace, Chrome Web Store, and the iOS and Android app stores. This means your games can be available on many different platforms. Unlike Game Maker, construct 2 has an appealing and robust user interface. Additionally, the engine has an in-built event system that allows you to instantly program actions and movements. The premium software costs about $120. However, if you want to use the commercial package of the engine, you will have to pay $400.

### Stencyl: Platform- Linux/OS X/Windows

Stencyl is probably the most popular engine. More than 120,000 developers, with over 10,000 games published games across the globe used it. In its simple form, the engine does not require any programming skills. However, if you are tech-savvy, you can write code within the program to create more advanced features and functions. The engine has a drag-and-drop feature that adds to the easy use of the engine. Unlike all the other engines we have looked at thus far, Stencyl is not an all-out by. Instead, it works on a subscription basis; a $200 annual subscription basis; the $200 is for the most expensive (and comprehensive) package.

The engine offers cheaper discounts for students and game design experimenters. Because of the subscription nature of the engine, developers tout it as the easiest way to make some quick money (this means that the engine is commercially driven), rather than it being a fun way to experiment with video game designing. This does not mean that once you create your game, you have to submit it to them for sponsorship (which they offer)!

### Flixel: Platform-Open source

Flixel is an open-source video game creation engine. This means that regardless of how you intend to use it (for commercial or personal purposes), it is completely free. This engine is very versatile. You can use it to create a wide range of 2D vector animations. The software itself runs on the backbone of ActionScript 3, an object-oriented programming language. ActionScript 3 adds a wide range of development tools to the program. These tools allow you to customize the engine. If you are looking to create filmstrip games or 'epic' 2D animation with side-scrollers, this is the 'it' engine. However, I have to point out that despite its versatility, Flixel cannot handle 3D modelling. On the other hand, I also have to point out that the tile-maps at your disposal in the engine are fulfilling and intuitive. Additionally, the engine has a plethora of camera functions; the in-built save game function and the pathfinding design all make this software one worth trying. Because the software is open–source, it has a bit of a C-style programming learning curve. I must point out that this should not stop you from using the engine. Why not? Because the open-source nature of the platform also means it has a wide user base and a thriving community.

### Unity: Platform- OS X/Linux/Windows

If your aim is to make outstanding 3D video games on a budget, Unity is the choice for you. Unity is an outstanding fully-fledged design/development suite. The engine has a free version for personal use. However, for the commercial version, you must pay $1,500, i.e., if your aim is to create commercially viable games. Let not the money worry you, as the free version of the engine is something to behold too. The software, even the free version, can port to up to 10 different platforms, not limited to mobile and desktop. It is also capable of delivering crispy clear video and audio.

Key point/action step

Regardless of which engine/software you opt for, you will need to familiarize yourself with it fully if you really want to derive the most benefits. Therefore, I recommend you create your video game with a starter mentality. Additionally, if there are functions you are not sure of, turn to the online user community. They (community members) have a wealth of knowledge and are always willing to share

How to Publish and Market Your Indie Video Game

With more and more developers publishing games out to a hungry lot of gamers, generating downloads and sales for your games is harder than it has ever been. Do not despair; here are some tips to publish your game and get it noticed.

### Publishing your game

Like any other store in the category of apps, your best chance for success in publishing your app is variety. Depending on the platform of your indie game, submit it to as many stores as you can find. This will ensure that more people get a chance to view or download it. Additionally, when publishing your video game, make sure that you fill out every single detail.

When you visit a store for submission, there is usually a game heading (what most of us call Meta tag), a game description, and an overview. Make sure to fill out all the fields. Also, make sure that you fill everything out correctly using keyword-rich sentences. What do I mean? If you are filling out the heading of your game, make sure it is something relevant to the scope of your game. If you are filling the description and overview field, view it as a marketing platform. It is your chance to tell users why they should download or purchase your game and what makes it different. Publishing your game is very standard and uncomplicated.

A key point you must note and a mistake that many developers make is that they fail to post their game in the right category within the store. If your game is a racing game, make sure you specify the category to increase your chances of discovery.

### Marketing your game

Marketing your game is more difficult than it sounds. Moreover, it is the single most important thing to do if you are not creating video games for the fun of it. Therefore, you must create a marketing plan. A video game marketing plan is no different from any other product-marketing plan. You must set out well-defined goals and timelines by which you want to achieve those goals. You must also set out a marketing budget and resources (time, workforce etc.). If you do not have the money to hire someone to market the game for you, here are a few things you can do to enhance your total download and sales revenue.

*Use social media-* Social media is a vibrant marketplace that may have a great positive effect on the total sale and download of your game. If you have many friends on social media, share the game with them first and ask them to share the game with others. This is especially effective if the game is a free version. If your video game has a price tag on it, share the link to the video game with all your friends and ask them to download it. Additionally, social media also has very many developer groups. Join a few of them and contribute to topics. When you have racked up some points, tell the members that you just developed a game and you would love their support. In most cases, programmers are supportive of each other, and you will get some sales.

***Use Forums-*** Forums are also another way to drive up your sales and downloads. They are especially effective because they provide a dedicated user base. For example, if your game is a racing one, you can join a developer's forum that caters to the racing niche. Here, you will find many people willing to download and try your game.

***Create a website-*** This is very critical to your marketing. Most users will often time visit the website of a game they want to buy before they download it. They do this so that they can get more information on the game. Additionally, owning a website dedicated to your game sends a message of professionalism. Additionally, a website gives you more play with keywords and search engine optimization. This can be a gold mine for download and potential sales.

Key point/action step

If you are developing a video game for fun, you can simply publish your game and wait for users to try it. However, if you are doing it for a piece of the $97 billion, you must invest some money into marketing.

# Chapter 9: Web industry freelancing and art of domain flipping

With almost all stores and transactions now going online, there is a great demand for people who are able to deal with the more technical aspects to securing their online presence. Web professionals are quite like the carpenters, civil engineers and architects of the online world. And so, if you have a good command of this field and would like to earn extra online, here are a couple of things you can do:

Create tutorials. There are a lot of web enthusiasts who would love to learn how to set up a website, create a good blog design or deal with servers. One can set up a blog and provide quality and targeted tutorials and earn by blog advertising, or readers can also pay a fee for your expertise. Just make sure that people get what they pay for. Earnings can range from $50 to $150.

Design web pages and blogs. The design of a website goes beyond what it 'looks like' but also deals with the interface and ease of navigation. It takes technical knowledge to correctly configure these. You can offer these services to aspiring bloggers or start-up companies.

Selling templates, patterns and icons. If you have a great eye for design and love tinkering with patterns and graphics, you can put up some of your designs for sale. Sites like Theme forest allow you to post your original works, and interested users can buy them directly from the site. This is a great way to produce passive income from your creativity.

Keep in mind, though, that coming up with profitable designs takes years of experience to pull off as it involves an intricate play of shapes, colours and lines.

Finding bugs. In an era of increasing cybercrime, larger companies realize the value of fool-proof software that can prevent hackers from taking advantage of their efforts. Because of this, they offer a hefty amount of cash for people who find vulnerabilities in their codes.

James Forshaw was rewarded $100,000 by Microsoft in 2013 for finding a potential security flaw in one of their software. Bugcrowd is a community of similar people specializing in finding coding glitches. It's pretty much positive reinforcement for people who have incredible skills in order to put their talents to good use instead of resorting to hacking.

The Art of Domain Flipping

Think of 'domains' as addresses to a house. This refers to the site address of your webpage, like www.ilovethisebook.com, for example. However, to get this address for yourself, you will have to buy it from a web host and domain providers so you could own it. This prevents someone else from the opposite side of the world from putting up a page named www.ilovethisebook.com because that domain name is already yours.

So, what if you have gotten so successful and realized that you would like to rename your site to www.ilovethisebooksomuch.com? You will have to buy this domain again and leave your former webpage address to expire. This will allow the happy lady from the opposite side of the world to finally own a website named www.ilovethisebook.com.

Domain flippers work in between these transactions to make profits. You can go through a list of the unregistered domain in sites like GoDaddy and look out for expired domain names that may be of great value for someone you know. You can purchase www.ilovethisebook.com for about $70, then send an email to a happy lady who would gladly pay you $200 for it. Bravo! The profit is made!

The key in earning through this method is being observant of current trends and insightful for things that may spark interest among people, purchasing domains while their value is still low, then selling it at a great price when you find it most profitable.

It definitely involves risk as you may encounter having to sell domains for zero profit. However, the rewards you get in the process may make this worth a try.

# Chapter 10: Some other ideas

Turn Passion to Profit

" What do you really want to do?"

This is one of the most daunting life questions that hit us some time in our teenage years and stretches up until forever. Some people find the answer sooner, and others never really find out. Circumstances often lead us to do things that we'd rather not, and necessity tells us that we cannot always do what we want because the cool things don't always bring food to the table.

What if life finally granted you the opportunity to work on what you've always wanted?

The internet is a world without boundaries. It finds value in the smallest of things, reward your grandest efforts and grants you the possibility of reaching out to all corners of the earth. What may not work in your town may be a hit on a city that is miles away from you. This is a stellar opportunity to finally explore what you've always wanted, feed it to the world wide web and even earn from it! All in the comforts of your home!

Many people have followed their passion and have now gone on to become professional artists, writers, consultants and the like. Do not hesitate to explore your own.

Get Paid for Your Reviews

Do you remember spending a whole day debating with girlfriends on the phone on which makeup was better or what brand of shampoo was the best? Looks like you can actually earn from it!

Again, it all boils down to marketing and advertising. Companies would love to know what you think of their product and are willing to pay you for your opinion.

Vindale Research is an online shopping site that pays you for posting reviews about items that you have bought from their site. You can expect to get paid up to $75 both for answering reviews and surveys on their site. You can make withdrawals via PayPal to ensure the security of your information.

Other websites pay you to review other items like User Testing for website interface reviews ($10 per review), Shvoong for reviews about newspapers, academic papers, books and random articles (payout depends on revenue of the product).

Review Stream is another popular pay-for-review website that pays $2 for every review on hot topics and also gives additional points when people rate up to your review.

There are a great many legitimate sites that offer payment for each review you give their products; now, isn't that a better way to spend all that energy raving or ranting about various consumer products?

Pay-for-review is another targeted approach for earning extra money. It is a great feedback system that the common consumer can use to reach out to retail companies in order to improve the very products we use.

Getting paid for sharing what you think about your latest purchase seems to be a neat idea, yes?

The Era of Mobile Apps

The smartphone and tablet market are now saturated with apps of all shapes and sizes. While smartphone designs and capabilities are all the craze right now, mobile apps are quickly catching up because they allow you to use your phone for several functionalities that the manufacturer wasn't able to include.

There's an app that measures your heart rate, an app that reads your horoscope for the day, an app that gives directions, an app that plays dice and not to mentions the gazillions of games that are available both in Android's Playstore and I phone's Appstore. The most successful of apps are known to be earning thousands of bucks per month out of user purchases, and believe it or not, Candy Crush is actually earning $947,000 every day. Incredible!

What attracts a lot of people is that it is open to everyone with the right number of tools and knowledge. In spite of the saturated market, people still love to create something that others can use or have fun with, quite similar to publishing e-books. And there's always that hope of being the next viral thing and waking up a millionaire the next day. Remember Flappy Bird?

Creating a mobile app entails a complicated web of wireframing, data integration, user-interface development and design, server-side logic and user management, among others. But the bottom line is to create an app that can delight, entertain or be greatly useful for specific applications.

The interface of the app must be designed in an appealing and engaging manner following the modern laws of design and user-friendliness. It has to be comprehensively tested and refined with zero to minimal bugs.

Android will let your apps launch untested in the Playstore, while iPhone requires all apps to undergo a review process that takes about a week. Once it's out there, your apps will be tested through user reviews and purchases.

One thing that developers forget, though, is to advertise their apps. This is essential if you really want to earn.

Bookkeeping

Another technical skill that could be put to use is bookkeeping. This basically entails keeping a clean record of all the cash flow details of a particular company or individual. This includes keeping track of all invoices, receipts, earnings and payables. This is gaining increasing momentum in several countries because more and more entrepreneurs are trying to enter businesses without knowing how to streamline their cash flow. This is critical to businesses because it allows you to keep track of your collectibles and your deadlines. Unmanaged finances will only cost a business more money and a bad reputation in the future.

This type of industry is good for people who don't get bored with numbers, have an eye for detail and the integrity to keep records clean. Various online courses are now being offered for people who would like to get the hang of the industry, but one may require a couple of years of actual training before gaining enough reputation to work as an independent bookkeeper.

Armed with sufficient storage, reliable accounting software, and a great ability to organize, bookkeeping can be a great work-at-home job for people. The average bookkeeper earns $25 to $40 per hour but can also increase depending on workload and location.

Adding tax preparation services can also increase your value as a bookkeeper, and so does an accounting background. Having business cards and referrals from former satisfied clients will also boost your reputation.

Pay-to-Click Sites (PTC)

Clixsense, Probux, Neobux and Fusebux are some of the most trusted online sites when it comes to pay-to-click industries. This is by far the easiest way to earn money on the internet. It basically starts with you clicking the "Register now" button and signing up for their services; then, you start to familiarize yourself with the website interface while earning. It will not require you to pay upon registration though some of them may require an optional 'investment' for you to grow your earnings faster, although you'll do just fine even without availing of this option.

The main mechanism of earning is by clicking and watching 30-second ads and quickly moving on to the next, depending on how much you intend to earn.

Pros: This is the easiest way to earn on the internet; no experience or necessary skill sets are required, and you decide how much time you are willing to allot. They also design the site and advertisements well enough to keep you engaged and entertained during the whole session.

The product also has a community forum where users can share ideas and help in navigating the site, which makes it all the more legitimate because you are confident that other people are really using and getting paid with it.

These companies also make use of PayPal, Payza, Perfect Money, SolidTrust Pay, and Ego Pay, which allow users to receive their payment without really revealing too much financial information.

Cons: In as much as they provide the easiest ways to earn money, they also have the lowest rates of payment. Clixsense has one of the highest payouts, which is $0.02 per click.

These sites also have a minimum payout threshold, meaning you have to accumulate a certain amount before you are able to withdraw to your account. Clixsense has a minimum payout level of $10, which means you'll have to click through the ads 500 times before you are able to withdraw. That's about four and a half hours of viewing ads! As you see, it may take a long while before you are really able to withdraw a substantial amount.

Other sites offer a smaller payout threshold like Neobux that only requires $2, and Probux, for only $5. However, the rate per click is also lower.

Earning PTC ads is a great idea only when you intend for this to be an additional activity while browsing the internet. You'll also need to be extra patient with it because it will take a while before you are able to really earn.

Value in the Smallest Efforts

Companies spend a great bulk of their budget on advertising and will go to great lengths just to extend their brand reach and to understand how their consumers perceive their products. This concept has driven an online industry that allows people to earn dollars by doing very simple tasks like clicking links, answering surveys, viewing advertisements and the like.

Many people are flocking to this kind of industry because of the promise of earning with very little effort.

As attractive as it is, this type of industry is also one of the most prone to abuse and scams and must therefore be examined carefully before getting involved. If you feel like the pay is way too large for the equivalent effort required, follow your gut feel and check if it is a scam.

Nevertheless, there are legitimate companies who really use these methods as part of their advertising, and it's a great deal for people who want to earn extra bucks for a couple of minutes. If you can spend a whole hour watching cat videos, then the idea of answering a 15-minute survey for five dollars shouldn't be a bad idea, yes?

No effort is too small for the internet. Everything has value.

# Conclusion:

To conclude, business valuation, if done correctly, can work in your favor. That is also true for the intended buyer. Business valuation can be done in-house or through the help of certified public accountants and business valuators.

It is also very important to discuss matters about selling your business with people around you (business partners, workmates and family members) to help you cement the idea. Once a business changes hands, it is permanent until the current owner decides to sell again.

Placing value on your business and eventually selling it off is the culmination of all the years, tears and hard work of building the business and running its day-to-day operations. Some business owners are anxious about separating themselves from their own businesses. In the end, through proper business valuation, you will be able to see your business as it is. It is just an income-generating machine that you built and developed.

Remember that although this book provides you with the basic knowledge on how to place a value on your business' worth, the need for professional business valuators and certified public accountants are still necessary. The practical knowledge that they possess concerning this aspect of the business is one gained through constantly perfecting their craft.

This book aims to open your eyes to what goes behind the scenes during these transactions and help you understand the business valuation process. The simple action steps provided in each chapter and subchapters are there for you to perform on your own business.

Finally, it is imperative that you are keen on the details of your own business and are meticulous about keeping records. These records will help you find the true value of your business.

# The Complete Startup Crash Course

*How Digital Entrepreneurs Use Continuous Innovation to Create Radically Successful Businesses and How You Can Copy Them*

## By

## The Golden Inner Circle

# Table of Contents

# Introduction

An entrepreneur is a clever fellow who wants to create an enterprise in circumstances of intense complexity. More than often, a company's priorities don't always fit the ways people need or want a service or product. New products and new projects stall at some stage or don't live up to their full potential. It is where the Lean Startup model comes in. The core philosophy behind the Lean Startup model, which is an evolution of astute businessmen's management style, promotes an atmosphere that allows new concepts to thrive while finding ways to reduce waste. Sometimes as challenging as it may be, the only way ahead might be to ditch what you have and start again from scratch. In stagnation or unfavorable economic conditions, we all are advised to do something for less. All of you must be well aware of the idea of having to do a great many things with little money along with reinventing ourselves or our systems to cater to the ever-changing needs of our consumers. Astute entrepreneurs have insight plus know means and strategies of evaluating success.

Additionally, they can determine the next steps of action, find shortcomings, and make commensurate changes to change with the changing circumstances and atmosphere to develop and further innovate. It is generally accepted that hard work and determination, combined with historical predictors, are automatic performance measures. However, the future is uncertain, and the old methods of working are just not applicable. The management of the previous century does not work with the instability of today's economy. Frustrated with conventional strategies and approaches to entrepreneurship, the creative entrepreneurs begin looking for other ideas to bring to the test. They all have come up with the Lean Startup model that focuses on innovation and getting to know customers' needs and habits to create a better product or service. It focuses on the correct process, that is, to work better and not simply harder to solve difficult circumstances. Whether it is a start-up of tech, small businesses, or a project inside a big corporation, Launching a new organization has long been a hit-or-the-miss proposition. According to the decades-old formula, you always write a marketing strategy, pitch this to the investors, build a team, launch a product, & start to sell it as much as you possibly can. & somewhere in the chain of events, you will inevitably suffer fatal failure. Most of the time, the odds aren't in your favor. A recent study by Harvard Business School reveals that 75 percent of all start-ups crash. But lately, the important countervailing factor has arisen, one which can make the task of beginning a business less dangerous. It's a technique called the "leaned start-up," & it encourages experimentation over the elaborate organizing, customer input over intuition, & iterative designs over conventional "big designs upfront" expansion. While methodology's only a few years old, and its constructs like "minimum viable product" & "pivoting"— have rapidly taken hold in the start-up community, & business schools have already started modifying the curricula to explain them. The lean start-up movement is changing traditional thinking around entrepreneurship. Newest ventures of every sort try to boost the chances of survival by pursuing the ideals of struggling quickly and learning quickly. Despite methods name, some of the greatest payoffs can be earned by the major corporations that embrace it in the long run. This book shall explore in deep as to how digital entrepreneurs utilize continuous creativity to build fundamentally profitable companies and how you can imitate them.

# CHAPTER 1: Lean Start-up

lean start-up is a strategy used on behalf of an established business to create new companies or launch a new product. Method of lean start-up advocates the development of products that customers have already shown they want so that as quick as product's launched, a market will already exist. It is in contrast to creating a brand and then hoping the demand would emerge. Developers of Product can measure consumers' interest in a product & determine how the product may need to be clarified by employing lean start-up principles. The process is referred to as validated learning & can be used to prevent unnecessary usage of the resources in the creation & development of products. If innovation is likely to be failed by lean start-ups, it'll fail cheaply and quickly instead of gradually & expensively, thence the word "fail-fast." Lean start-up's example of customers dictating the type of goods that the respective markets deliver, instead of deciding what products they would be provided.

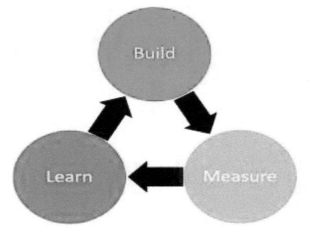

Lean Start-ups vs. the Traditional Businesses

When it comes to hiring, the lean entrepreneurship approach often differentiates itself from the conventional company model. Lean start-ups attract employees who can adapt, learn, and work efficiently, whereas conventional firms recruit employees based on knowledge and expertise. Lean start-ups employ multiple financial recording metrics also; they concentrate on the customer acquisition expenses, lifetime consumer value, client churn rate, & how viral the product maybe, instead of relying on revenue statements, balance sheets, and cash flow statements.

Requirements for the Lean Startup

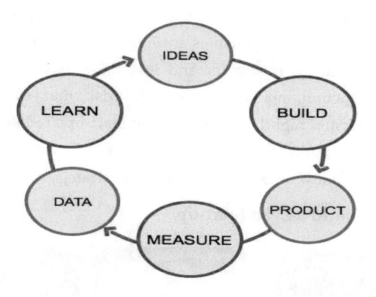

Experimentation is perceived by the lean start-up approach to be extra valuable than comprehensive planning. A waste of time is viewed as five years of business plans designed on unknowns, and consumer response is paramount. Instead of the business models, Lean start-ups use business concepts focused on assumptions that are easily checked. Before proceeding, data doesn't have to be completed; it only has to be more than enough. The start-up easily changes to limit the losses & return to the production of goods consumers want when customers do not respond. Failure is generally regarded as the rule. Following this strategy, entrepreneurs validate their theories by engaging with prospective consumers, investors, & partners to evaluate their responses to product specifications, packaging, delivery, and customer retention. With the data, entrepreneurs make tiny changes to goods called iterations, and big adjustments known as pivots fix any major issues. To best suit the current target consumer, this testing process could result in exchanging target customers or altering the product. A problem that must be addressed is first defined by the lean start-up method. It then produces the minimum workable product or smallest product type that enables entrepreneurs to offer prospective buyers. This strategy is simpler and less risky than checking final product production, and decreasing the risk that start-ups face reduces their usual high failure rate. Lean start-ups redefine start-up as an enterprise aiming for scalable growth models, not the one that is determined to follow an established business strategy.

## 1.1 Learn to build a Lean Start-up

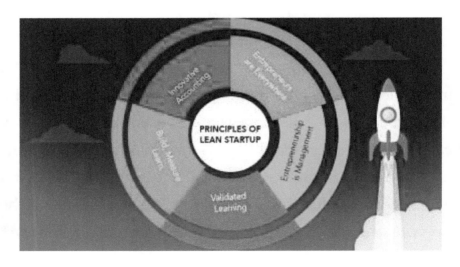

Do you know the 75 percent of all start-ups usually fail? You're likely to encounter obstacles, difficulties, and roadblocks of all sorts, no matter which type of company you're beginning to build. You could spend years on one business idea to fail if you've followed the conventional start-up formula of drafting a business plan, setting up to the investors, developing your product, & selling it. The Lean Startup Methodology is an inexpensive, fast, and less risky technique to carry your business concept to the market. Launching some form of business has always been risky. "Instead of using more traditional methods, the main distinction between building lean start-ups with Lean Start-ups Methodology is that entrepreneurs must ask themselves that "Should the products be built? "instead of "Can the products be built? It is about identifying a problem, validating the question, and creating a product that can fix the problem to create a lean start-up. When you create a lean start-up, you need to ensure that your product is consistently checked and verified, so your product's in the customer's hands as quick as possible. Subsequently, Lean Startups Methodology would help you optimize business growth. To begin creating a lean start-up, here are three moves entrepreneurs may take: Find, Execute, & Validate it.

Find the Business Idea

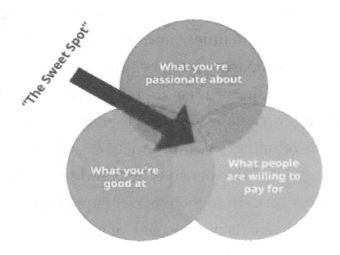

the big question is not: "could this be built?" or "Should this be built?" "It puts us in an extraordinary historical moment: the success of collective imaginations depends on our future prosperity. It's important to determine whether the product can fix is significant enough for clients to choose to buy it while selecting a company concept to pursue using the Lean Startup Approach. It can be easy to find a business idea, so it's essential to pay attention to the challenges people face daily. For the product to gain momentum, clients must be aggressively looking for solutions to a problem. It is time to execute the project after you settle on a business idea.

Execute the Business Idea

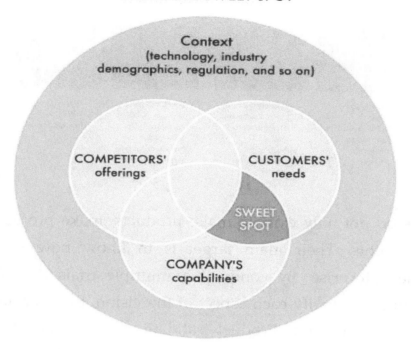

STRATEGIC SWEET SPOT

Next, you can create minimum viable products (MVP). MVP is a version of a product you plan to create, allowing the team to quickly gather as much knowledge as possible on your prospective consumers and their input on the product. Any Lean Start-up Philosophy advocates recommend that you take the "Kickstarter Approach" for your product, i.e., start selling the product before it's completed to build market value and drive demand in the product while collecting funds for the Lean Startup. It's time to validate the business plan once the business ideas are executed.

Validate the Business idea

## 4 STEPS FOR IDEA VALIDATION

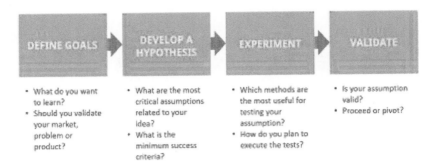

| DEFINE GOALS | DEVELOP A HYPOTHESIS | EXPERIMENT | VALIDATE |
|---|---|---|---|
| • What do you want to learn?<br>• Should you validate your market, problem or product? | • What are the most critical assumptions related to your idea?<br>• What is the minimum success criteria? | • Which methods are the most useful for testing your assumption?<br>• How do you plan to execute the tests? | • Is your assumption valid?<br>• Proceed or pivot? |

Start-ups do not only exist to make products, make profits, or even support clients. Their main target is to know how to create a profitable enterprise. By conducting multiple trials that allow the entrepreneurs to verify each aspect of the vision, this learning can be scientifically validated. Product validation's a crucial step in the development of profitable Lean Start-ups. In this phase, in the real world, it's time to play with the business idea. Early adopter or otherwise, test the MVP with actual consumers in the industry to see whether the product is feasible and to gain knowledge that you could study. Use this knowledge to determine if you can continue building your product, modifying the product, or pivoting your market plan. If the findings are mainly good from checking MVP in the marketplace, continue to develop your products using your initial approach while integrating tester input. If the outcomes of marketplace MVP research are favorable and unfavorable, tweak the product or business plan to make the product ideally suited to your consumers' desires and needs. If the findings are mainly disappointing from checking MVP in the industry, it's time for pivoting your product & business plan. To adapt vision to suit the desires and the needs of the clients would entail a radical change in your technique and work. Under certain circumstances, mainly unfavorable reviews would indicate that Lean Startup can fully quit the marketplace.

Why should one build a Lean Start-up?

Start-up's different way of seeing at the growth of innovative and new products, all at the same time highlighting rapid iteration & customer insights, huge vision & great ambition. Building a lean start-up is an ideal opportunity for entrepreneurs who need to start an inexpensive company and easily bring them to market. Building lean start-up essentially shortens product creation times and means that developers build products through experimentation & validated learning that satisfy consumer needs.

Example of Lean Startup

For instance, a healthy meal delivery service that targets busy, single twenty-somethings in the urban areas could learn that thirty-something wealthy mothers of newborns in the suburbs have a better market. The business could then alter its delivery schedule & the types of foods it serves to provide new mothers with optimal nutrition. It could also add options for spouses or partners & other children in the household for meals. The lean start-up approach is not intended to be used solely by start-ups. In developing countries where electricity is unreliable, companies such as General Electric have used the technique to develop a new battery for cell phone companies.

# CHAPTER 2: Importance of Market Research

The method of evaluating a new product or service's feasibility through surveys carried out directly with prospective consumers is market research. Market analysis helps an organization discover the target market & collect customers' views and the other inputs on product or service participation. This form of research may be performed in-house through the organization itself or a 3rd party company specialising in market analysis. Through polls, product testing, & focus groups, it can be achieved. Usually, research subjects are compensated with the samples of goods or/and paid nominal stipends for the time. Market analysis is a vital aspect of new products or service's research and development (R&D).

The company uses market testing by engaging individuals with a prospective buyer to test its feasibility or service.

Companies will find out the target customers through market analysis and get customer reviews and input quickly.

This form of research may be performed in-house through the organization itself or an independent company specializing in the market analysis.

The study includes surveys, testing of products, & focus groups.

## 2.1 Develop an understanding of the Market Research

Figure 2.8  Proper Definition of the Marketing Research Problem

The market research aims to examine the market related to certain products or services to decide how the audience receives them. It will include the compilation of information for the market segmentation & product differentiation purposes that could be used to target promotional campaigns and assess what attributes are perceived as a concern by the customer. To complete the process of market analysis, an organization must participate in plenty of activities. Based on the business area being investigated, it needs to collect information. To assess the existence of certain trends or the related data point that it can use in decision-making, the organization needs to evaluate and understand the resulting data. Market research's a vital instrument for helping businesses identify what buyers expect, produce goods that people can use, & maintain a strategic edge over other businesses in their sector.

## 2.2 Collection of information through Market Research

The market analysis contains a mixture of the primary information, meaning what the organization or a person recruited by a company has collected, & secondary pieces of information, or what outside source has collected.

## Primary Information

The Primary data is either compiled by the organization or gathered by an individual or a business contracted to do analysis. Generally speaking, this kind of knowledge falls into two categories: exploratory &/or specific research. Exploratory analysis is a less formal choice that works by many open-ended inquiries, resulting in the presentation of questions or challenges that might need to be answered by the enterprise. The relevant study seeks the solutions to questions previously understood that are mostly called to light by exploratory researches.

## Secondary Information

Secondary data is data that has already been obtained from an external agency. It could include the demographic statistic from federal census results, research studies by trade groups, or research provided by the other organization working within the same business area.

Example of Market Research

Often firms use market analysis to evaluate potential ideas or gather customer knowledge on what types of products or the services they like and do not have at present. For instance, to test the feasibility of a product or service, a company considering going into the business might perform market research. If consumer interest is confirmed by market research, the company can proceed with the business plan confidently. If not, to make changes to the product to get it in line with consumer expectations, the organization should use market analysis findings.

Components of Market Research

The research of market involves the gathering of information about:

customers – for developing a customer profile

industry & market environment – for understanding factors that are external to the business

competitors – for developing competitor profiles.

**Learn to research the industry and market environment**

the business & market factors analysis will concentrate on knowledge regarding any legal, political, social, economic, and cultural problems or developments that may impact your organization. This external analysis will then be used to obtain knowledge about the composition of the target market, market differences, emerging market patterns, and where the new market prospects may lie. Research on the industry and business outlook could cover:

- Market size & trends
- Business regulations
- Marketing channels
- Market demographics (for example, age, gender, income)
- Sociographic (for example, beliefs & attitudes, lifestyle factors, interests).

## Sources that can be used for collecting the data

- Pertinent business & industry associations
- Online trade journal
- Newspapers
- Council businesses support service
- Print media
- Television
- Industry expos along with trade shows

Regional councils & relevant state governmental departments (which is depending upon the industry)

consumer lists or Commercially sold marketing

search engines for Internet

## Research the customers

To collect the relevant information about who your clients or future customers are, & what, where, when & how they shop, you can use consumer analysis.

Customer analysis will also provide you with useful insights into your consumers' perceptions towards your organization and your goods and services.

Research on customers may cover:

- Needs & expectations
- Social & lifestyle trends
- Attitude towards you
- Customer demographics (like age, income, gender)
- Attitudes towards your opponents.

**Sources for researching customers**

- Focus groups
- surveys & questionnaires for staff and customers
- Observations of the customer behavior
- Personal interviews
- Feedback on points-of-sale
- Sales staff
- Phone surveys
- Social media
- Development offices for local business (local council & independent)

**Research the competitors**

Your study into competitors will obtain data on current and future competitors. You will use your rival's data to gain knowledge such as the existing business advantages of your competitor, shortcomings in their sales tactics, & how their consumers view their goods and services. Analysis of competitors may cover:

- Present turnover & market shares
- Pricing structures and policies
- Products & services
- Branding, marketing, advertising

## Sources for researching competitors

- Competitor marketing & advertising material, the price-lists
- Past clients
- Suppliers
- Official offices like licensing bodies
- Business directories
- Competitor stores, pages on social media, and websites
- Complaints blogs & chat sites
- Competitor print & lists of electronic mailing
- Personal & staff observations

# CHAPTER 3: Digital Entrepreneurship

It is important to academic study to consider the conditions and reasons that promote digital entrepreneurship (DE) and to direct market practice and public policies aimed at promoting this development, given its positive impacts on job development and economic growth. Digital entrepreneurship is a concept that determines how entrepreneurship can evolve as digital technology begins to disrupt industry and culture. Digital entrepreneurship illustrates trends in the practice, philosophy, and curriculum of entrepreneurs. In a modern world, digital entrepreneurship encompasses everything new and distinct about entrepreneurship, including:

- New ways of locating customers for entrepreneurial ventures
- Innovative ways of designing and offering products and services
- Unconventional ways of generating revenue and reducing cost
- Identification of fresh opportunities to collaborate with platforms and partners
- New sources of opportunity, risk, and competitive advantage

Digital entrepreneurship opens up new opportunities on a realistic basis for someone dreaming about being an entrepreneur. Some possibilities are more technical, but many others are within reach for someone who learns the fundamental skills of digital entrepreneurship. Such specific skills include looking online for potential clients, prototyping new business concepts, and improving data-based business ideas. Digital entrepreneurship is all about new ways of thinking about entrepreneurship itself and learning new technological skills, which is another way of suggesting that it introduces new entrepreneurship theories. New questions about the policy, chance, and risk are opened up by digital entrepreneurship. Digital entrepreneurship unlocks new opportunities in terms of education to train the future generation of entrepreneurs. 'Doing it' is the perfect way to practice entrepreneurship and draw on the learning. In the normal world, beginning the latest company or releasing a new product is expensive and dangerous for beginners. Not only does the modern world reduce the hurdles to beginning something new, but it provides a range of routes to growth. Educationally, it's such a different environment from case studies, simulations, and business plans. There is also controversy over the precise concept of digital entrepreneurship, partly because it is early and partly because it is changing. What is fresh in digital entrepreneurship can change over time as digital technology progresses. Maybe one day, any business projects will be born digital,' and digital entrepreneurship will cease to exist as a separate topic. However, today, there is a strong need to help educate entrepreneurs for the modern world and offer a new route to entrepreneurship to more individuals.

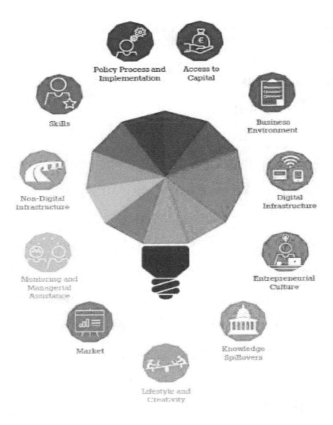

## Simple Types of Digital Business Ideas

Digital marketers don't have a good sense of what is possible at the very beginning. It is advised that they begin with one of five basic forms to help beginners conceive of new digital business ideas:

A business offering knowledge on every specialized topic

It is possible to raise revenue through advertising, referrals, sponsorship, or merchandise

A neighborhood enterprise, hosting a vibrant and helpful discussion on every specialized topic

The sales opportunities are close to the industry of information

An online marketplace that markets goods or services

The objects may be tangible or digital

A matchmaker corporation that puts together two sets of individuals. For instance, a product or service provider (for instance, prospective babysitters) and another group who will need their services are always one group (parents looking for a babysitter). Advertising income is a probability, but with good matches, a transaction fee may also be received.

A promotional organization that draws online clients to a market that already exists

A possible revenue stream here, or advertising, is fees per client referral

An ideal new business plan can be impossible to come up with right from the start, but everyone will easily develop a realistic idea among these five options. As long as they can conceive of a subject that could attract at least a few hundred other individuals, a product or service they want to market, groups of individuals that may support each other, or some small company who could use some promotional assistance, digital entrepreneurs will launch their journey from the beginning. These five basic forms often make it easy for a digital business concept to be shared. In this case, a new business concept is:

A content provider on [your subject]

A [your subject] neighborhood business

An online shop that sells [your product or service]

A matchmaking firm that connects [service providers/group A] to [service users/group B]

The promotion of an online business [a local business]

The options are nearly infinite, and they are still evolving

Digital Entrepreneurship in the face of the Pandemic

Small firms and start-ups have been struck hardest by the recent pandemic than any other area of the economy. To survive a disaster, small firms usually have few resources. Usually, small companies still have little background in the new world of becoming creative, which is now one of their best choices for weathering the storm. In this moment of recession, a variety of digital practices can be considered by small companies. The typical guidance involves applying for federal support, staying in contact with online buyers, and beginning existing products' sales using e-commerce. These are all positive moves, but studies on digital entrepreneurship suggest some additional solutions. For small companies and start-ups, here are three extra fields of digital opportunity.

## New models for doing business

It's a smart idea to learn ways to market your current goods online but think about marketing your experience as a new online service. Many families have at least one person with increased time to develop new things or with an immediate need to discover new, more customized ways to entertain themselves. Another option is to offer digital products, such as online classes or digital how-to guides, depending on your expertise. However, digital entrepreneurship helps you pursue brand new areas of operation and offer similar new goods and services. The opportunity to pursue innovative business ideas at little or low cost is a major benefit of digital entrepreneurship. Your new digital company, for instance, may provide useful knowledge that lets customers make other buying choices. During this recession, internet traffic and investment are up and catch these emerging internet traffic sources' attention. Advertisers and marketers are involved and can pay for quality customer leads. Display advertisements, performance advertising, sponsorships, and commission fees from affiliate marketing transactions are new revenue possibilities. Another new potential for digital business is to become a matchmaker, connect individuals who need an online product or service with someone who can better provide it, and charge a purchase fee or percentage. What types of people do you meet already? During this crisis, what are their special needs? And where can you refer them to for assistance? Many of the world's major digital matchmakers, Airbnbs and Ubers, would need to be temporarily replaced by more local alternatives that fit local conditions and will be able to handle local constraints as they evolve.

Perfect the digital business process

An easy way to think about digital business is to see it as an ABC method with three steps: acquisition, behavior, and conversion. The acquisition adds new buyers through social media campaigns, search results, email, search, or social advertisement, among many other platforms to the digital sector. Behavior is what tourists do to fulfill their needs and help them reach their goals through their digital presence. Conversion is the task that each of your guests would like to do, whether it's finishing order, clicking on advertisements, calling for an appointment, or installing a menu. In each of these three critical regions, this problem is an incentive for the organization to develop its capability. Now is a perfect time to create digital marketing campaigns for the acquisition of consumers. When they are ready to buy again, this will make buyers and opportunities ready for it. By enhancing the digital consumer experience, behavior can be changed. To see which ones are more popular, improve interaction, try new features, new content, and new ways to organize and manage your online presence. Your friend, here is the analytics data supplied by your digital company. An integral digital business capability is to turn tourists into future or real customers. Use the time to try new calls to action. It would help if you also used this opportunity to tell clients to do something that would improve their engagement. Practice getting the guests to do easier things such as likes, comments, and shares. Then intensify the participation by signing up for updates and discounts, uploading their material, or scheduling a future appointment. Don't fail to remember how they all come together when you practice each of the digital business ABCs. With promises that can't be met or ambitions that you can't meet, it's easy to have new tourists. Acquire the right visitors who are happy and will convert.

Start experimenting

The freedom to innovate continuously is a key advantage of digital entrepreneurship. There are several fresh ideas to try in each part of the ABC process. Get familiar with the analytics data, which will be from Google Analytics for most digital entrepreneurs. It will provide you with reliable input on what works and what doesn't. It is still being practiced by major corporations, conducting hundreds or thousands of tests on their clients every day. If they continue to remain competitive, small firms would need to develop the skills of digital experimentation. Fortunately, the benefit of emerging start-ups is that they can hop on emerging developments that are not yet big enough to interest the big players. A crisis scenario is a hotbed of emerging developments in the quest, new hashtags, new memes, and new points for the conversation to be taken advantage of. Once digital marketers discover innovative business concepts that work with their first 100 to 1,000 visitors, it is fairly inexpensive and easy to scale up such ideas when trends take off. Be on the lookout for new 'nano trends' as these developments play out, and be ready to expand.

# CHAPTER 4: The Best Business

It doesn't need to require a big investment to start a profitable company. You can start a company without spending much capital, or even purchasing inventory, with a great business concept and the right resources. Adapting to a growing economy requires finding new, smart ways to fulfill clients' needs. To find the answer to the following important questions, you have to analyze the market:

What sorts of goods or services will fulfill the new consumer demands?

As an entrepreneur, how can your skills better fulfill those demands?

Any of the money-making, small business ideas that need very little investment are provided below.

## 4.1 Start your own online Dropshipper business

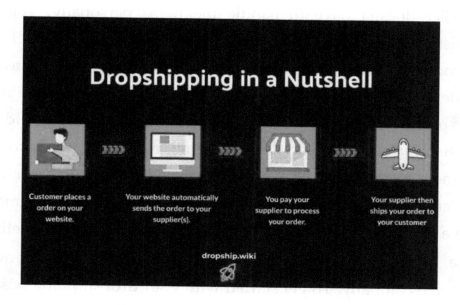

To sell online, you do not need to store inventory or spend a lot of money. You escape the expense of producing goods, handling inventory, and exporting with the dropshipping business by working with third-party vendors that do it all for you.

**How it works**

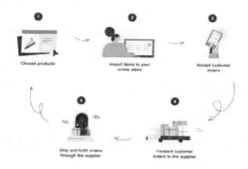

Dropshipping is a retail fulfillment technique where a retailer does not hold the items in storage that it offers. Instead, when a store sells a product using the dropshipping model, it orders the product from a third party and directly sends it to the consumer. As a consequence, the seller doesn't have to handle the items personally. The main contrast between dropshipping and the traditional retail model is that no product is held or controlled by the selling trader. Instead, to execute orders, the seller purchases inventory if appropriate from a third party, typically a wholesaler or retailer. You should start advertising your company using digital marketing tools to drive customers to your site once you're finished setting up your online store, and your site goes live. You'll get an order notice each time they make a transaction. They will complete it after the order is delivered to the supplier. You've just become the manager of your own e-commerce company. To get started with your dropshipping business, link your Wix account with Modalyst or Spocket. You can sell all kinds of great goods at your set prices after procuring products from millions of reliable suppliers. Just try to strike a balance with each sale between competitive prices and how much you earn.

**Choose products to sell**

You may need to select dropshipping items to sell before you launch your online business. Take the time for clarification of your brand and vision. To figure out what individuals are buying, do some market research. Before selling them in your store, determine the future demand, price, and profit margin of items. For an online shop, you will thrive by finding a way to stand out. Explore specialty items to source and market, and by offering a range, aim to stop placing all the eggs in one bowl. That said, to make your online store easier to browse, aim to organize your items into collections. Keep out of markets that are still saturated with stores. Take the time to set up marketing and advertising efforts to save you time and improve your revenue eventually.

## Example: Trending work from home products

Think of what customers do at home to select the right business to establish with little investment. With equipment for living room workouts, open your online fitness shop. Open an adorable store selling puppy items for professionals working from home, such as quiet pet toys. It's all about feeling at ease in your home setting during COVID-19. It is why items such as sweatshirts, leggings, hoodies, slippers, and socks selling out everywhere. The athleisure trend has a moment. While people do not dress up at home as much, with cute pajama sets or multi-use makeup for a simple beauty routine, they may also look for ways to feel and look healthy. Your customers can also opt for at-the-home beauty items, such as grooming accessories or nail kits, with salons now less available.

As remote employees and students set up shop at home, home office products are also common. You have to dream of tech devices such as lap desks, laptop stands, desk organizers, keyboards, or home storage. The market has also spiked for ergonomic desk chairs that help posture and back alignment or convenient seat cushions. But not all of this is work and no play. As consumers search for new recreation ideas, gaming items have also become popular. As people look for things to do, at-home leisure products, such as game boards, trivia, or knitting equipment, sell well. Shoppers must spend more time cooking at home with restaurants closed. It suggests a spike in sales of kitchenware as well as online food and beverage items. Parents also need childcare and work-life to be tackled. So, consider adding quiet toys and play spaces to your dropshipping company, like the car park mats. Shoppers also like to video chat or watch Netflix with friends without holding their laptops all the time. In the dropshipping shop, try offering bedside mounts and table mounts.

**Promote your online store**

When you introduce items, it's time for your shop to be advertised. It Is where a strong approach for e-commerce marketing comes into play. Allow the best of the business software for the e-commerce website. Automate your email marketing promotions and client outreach to save time. Advertise your dropshipping business on Facebook and Instagram with paid campaigns. Work with influencers to support your brands and advertise them to their followers if it's important to your company. In promoting your online dropshipping business, your SEO strategy will also play a crucial role. It suggests the development of high-quality advertising and low-budget ads to improve the search engine results' exposure. Increase the visibility of your website with keyword optimization, for example. Let's presume you're selling home clothing for comfortable work. If you include the phrases "luxury comfort wear," "work from home," or "athleisure clothing" in your web copy, when people search for those keywords, you will have a better chance of ranking on Google.

Get creative with branded products designed by you

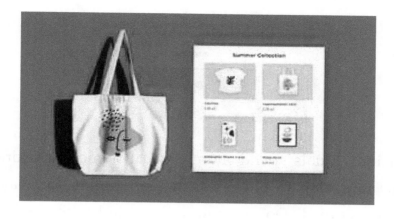

Now, let's take one step further with dropshipping. By linking Printful or Printify to your online shop, you add a personal touch with print on demand. You partner with print-on-demand businesses supplying the inventory, just like with dropshipping. Choose any customizable merchandise and introduce your creative touch, from t-shirts to phone cases, bags, and more. Go ahead and design graphics, quotations, or images to be printed on the chosen items. Start by choosing from thousands of different products to customize your online store and sell your designs. Start a business with funny quotes on a t-shirt. Add photos of your cat to Novelty Socks. Your logo or designs that match your brand create stickers — another cool option: selling goods made by you with original artwork. Yet, to market exclusive designs, you should not have to be a graphic artist. Hire and collaborate with freelance artists to create unique art for your products that are printed on-demand. You will distribute to over 90 places internationally when you receive an order. Forward your orders while managing everything from your Wix dashboard to your chosen supplier. Only think about it; shoppers would rock all over the world your exclusive creations.

Create digital video content

Now that individuals spend more time at home, by taking on new hobbies or returning to old ones, they're looking for ways to keep themselves occupied. Do you work in an industry, such as fitness, restaurants, or education, traditionally requires face-to-face interaction? Use this opportunity to create digital instruction videos, such as cooking demonstrations, workout routines, and more streamed online by people. The shutdown of schools and daycare services in 2021 means that parents have to spend a lot more time with their little ones at home. Moms and dads are searching for ways to keep their children busy, engaged, and learning. So if you are at home and temporarily out of a job, how can you apply your experience to satisfy this market demand? Especially now, family-friendly activities are always trendy. Get ahead of the competition by selling children-friendly video content. Create exercise videos for children if you're a fitness trainer.   Promote the use of child-friendly content, such as workouts or classes for baby yoga. To help parents home-school their children, post daily lessons online. With your children, you can even create an entertaining cooking show. With digital video content, there are distinct pricing models to earn money. To give customers full access to exclusive content, you may charge a monthly channel subscription. You can monetize your content based on the number of viewers if you work with video hosting platforms like YouTube. Selling or renting your videos is another option. Over a 24-48-hour cycle, viewers may download the video or watch it on your site. To give clients an idea of your product and nudge them to make a purchase, consider offering some of your content for free. Zoom, Vimeo, and YouTube can also host live streaming or webinars.

Comprehend the Supply Chain of Dropshipping

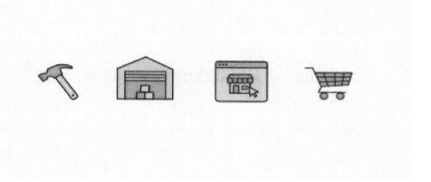

Supply chain's some fancy word that defines the journey a commodity takes to move from creation through manufacture and eventually into a customer's hands. If we are talking about suppliers of hard core chains gurus, they would insist that the supply chain stretches all towards mining products to make an object (like oil & rubber). But it's a bit intense. We do not need to be quite so specific. The three most important participants in the dropshipping supply chain must simply be understood: wholesalers, manufacturers, & retailers.

Manufacturers

Manufacturers produce the commodity, & most don't sell directly to the public. They sell bulks to wholesalers & dealers instead. The easiest way to buy goods for resale is to buy straight from the manufacturer, but most of them have minimum purchasing standards you'll desire to follow. When shipping them to consumers, you'll still need to store & re-ship goods. It's also cheaper to buy from the wholesaler for these purposes directly.

Wholesalers

Wholesalers purchase products from manufacturers in bulk, mark them up marginally and then market them to the retailers to sell them to the public. They're normally much smaller than those needed by a vendor if they have buying minimums. Wholesalers normally store goods from thousands of producers, if not a hundred, and prefer to work in a single field or drop shipping niche. Many operators are exclusively wholesalers. It means that they only sell to retailers & not direct to the general public.

Retailers

the retailer is anyone who sells the products directly to the public after adding his margin. If you are running a business that fulfills your orders through dropshipping suppliers, you are a retailer.

**Dropshipping is a service, not a role**

You will find that "drop shipper" is not one of the supply chain players. Each of the three will operate as drop shippers - manufacturer, wholesaler, and retailer. If the manufacturer is prepared to supply its supplies directly to your consumer, it's "dropshipping" for your sake. Similarly, a supermarket retailer will offer drop ship, but its price would not be as favorable as a wholesaler because the manufacturer does not buy it directly. It doesn't mean you're having bulk rates simply because someone declares to be a "drop shipper." It means that, for your sake, the company would ship goods. You desire to ensure that you deal exclusively with a reputable manufacturer or wholesaler to get the best prices.

## The order process

Let us observe how the drop shipped order is processed so that you have understood the players involved. We would follow the order put with a theoretical shop, an online seller Phone Outlet, specializing in smartphone accessories, to demonstrate. Phone Outlet dropships all its items directly from the wholesaler that we will call Wholesale Accessories. Here's a sample of what the whole ordering process could look like:

## Customer Places Order With Phone Outlet

Allen requires a case for the new smartphone and places an order through the Phone Outlet online store. A few things happen once an order has been approved:

Phone Outlet & Mr. Allen would receive an email of confirmation (likely alike) of new orders which store software automatically generates.

During the checkout process, the payment of Mr. Allen is captured and automatically placed into the bank account of Phone Outlet.

## Phone Accessory Outlet Places the Order With Its Supplier

The step is generally as artless as sending the confirmation of an email order to a sales representative at Wholesale Accessories by Phone Outlet. Wholesale Accessories has a credit card from Phone Outlet on file & will charge it for wholesale goods, including handling fees or shipping. Some sophisticated drop shippers will support XML Automatic (a normal format for stock files) orders uploading or the ability to place orders manually online. Still, email is the most common method to place orders with dropshipping vendors because it is universal & easier to use.

## Wholesale accessories ships the order

If items in the stock and wholesaler have positively charged the Phone Outlet card, the order will be boxed up and shipped directly to the customer by Wholesale Accessories. Although shipments come from the Wholesale Accessories, the name & address of the Phone Outlet would appear on the label of the return address, and the logo would appear on the invoice & packing slip. Wholesale Accessories would then email invoice & tracking numbers to the Phone Outlet once the shipment has been finalized.

Turnaround time is often quicker than you would think on dropshipped orders. In a few hours, most feature suppliers would be capable of getting the order outdoor, allowing merchants to publicize shipping on the same day when they use drop shipping suppliers.

## Phone outlet alerts the customer of shipment

When this tracking number's collected, Phone Outlet gives the customer tracking information, potentially using an email interface built into the online store interface. The order and delivery process is complete with the order delivered, the invoice received, and a customer told. The benefit (or loss) of Phone Outlet is the contrast between what this costs Mr. Allen & what this paid for wholesale accessories.

## Dropshippers are invisible

The drop shipper is invisible to the end buyer, despite its vital position in the ordering & fulfillment process. Just the Phone Outlet return address & signature would be on the shipment when the package is received. If Mr. Allen obtains the wrong case, he will call Phone Outlet, who would work with Wholesale Accessories behind scenes and get the right item shipped out. To the ultimate buyer, the wholesaler does not exist. Stocking and shipping dropshipping products is the sole responsibility. The merchant is responsible for all else — website creation, marketing, customer support.

## 4.2 How to Find and Work with Reliable Dropshipping Suppliers

One of the most popular questions ambitious entrepreneurs pose is: What is my e-commerce store's best dropshipping supplier? Supplier directory for dropshipping is a distributor database grouped by niche, market, or commodity. Many of the directories employ a few scanning mechanisms to ensure that legitimate wholesalers are suppliers listed. Many are managed by for-the profit corporations who charge a fee to use their directories. While membership folders, particularly for brainstorming the ideas, may be useful, they're by no means essential. If you already know the commodity or drop shipping niche that you need to sell, you must locate the big suppliers in the market with a little bit of searching & the techniques mentioned above. Plus, you once start dropshipping company, unless you want to locate suppliers for the other things, you would probably not need to revisit the directory. That said, the supplier directory is an easy way to scan for or/and browse a vast range of suppliers in 1 location easily and is useful for brainstorming ideas for marketing goods or entering niches. If you are short of time and ready to spend cash, a helpful tool may be supplier directories. There is a range of different suppliers and businesses for dropshipping.

**Best dropshipping suppliers**

CJdropshipping

Oberlo

CROV

DropnShop

Supplymedirect

Modalyst

To make this easier to select best drop shipping companies for specific needs, we will focus on the following factor:

Location and shipping options

So, Where do the supplier's locations exist? How much time is consumed in producing the item after the customer has put orders?

Product types

Which kinds of products they dropship?

Recommended for

And Is the particular suppliers suited for experienced or beginner dropshippers?

**Oberlo**

Shopify. The Oberlo is dropshipping the platform, making it easier to find AliExpress items to sell in the Shopify store. It is the best online drop shipping supplier directory for Shopify. The platform provides over 30 thirty of the latest dropshipping goods from vendors across the globe in 60 plus niche categories. Oberlo has free registration, beginning at 29.9 dollars a month for paid plans.

Location & shipping options

In different places around the world, Oberlo links you with suppliers. Usually, each includes many delivery solutions for the clients to send products. On each commodity page in the Oberlo app, you will find what delivery methods the supplier uses. the Popular shipping method includes:

China Post. Affordable / Free shipping expenses. Delivery could take 20 to 50 days.

AliExpress Shipping. Affordable costs of shipping. Delivery can take up to 15 days.

ePacket. Affordable / Free shipping expenses. Delivery could take 15 to 30 days.

DHL/UPS/FedEx. Express the shipping expenses. Delivery could take between five to fifteen days.

Product types

So You may find anything that includes bracelets, antiques, car parts, wedding supplies, sunglasses, furniture, and much more.

Recommended for

It's recommended for the beginner & veteran drop shipper.

## CJDropshipping

With fast delivery, it is the best dropshipping service. CJDropshipping is a marketplace that allows retailers to scale up the drop shipping business affordably. You can conveniently import goods directly from 1688 and Taobao marketplaces into the Shopify store, usually at a price lesser than on AliExpress. Along with other dropshipping applications like Oberlo, it's also a free Shopify application that you could add to the store.

Location & shipping options

To perform processing on the same-day for the store, CJDropshipping uses US-based warehouses. UPS, USPS, DHL, & FedEx work with it.

The shipping line known as CJPacket will bring goods to the US in 7 to twelve days if you are shipping from China.

Product types

Independent designers & owners of small businesses in China are home to the 1668 and Taobao marketplaces. Via CJDropshipping, there are 100s of millions of listings you may browse, & products vary from mainstream goods to difficult-to-find items & even the virtual product. If the CJDropshipping app does not have a product, you can upload a request & CJDropshipping would list this once the best source is identified.

Recommended for

The retailer who needs a 1-stop location for all the things drop shipping, including inventory procurement, order preparation, distribution, and fast shipping to United States, is highly recommended.

**SupplyMeDirect**

It is the strongest dropshipping provider for the UK, US, & European markets for private labels. SupplyMeDirect is a wholesale provider that supports the size of dropshipping business. The app provides private labeling & secure sourcing. It's a free Shopify application that you could contact twenty-four 7, supported by dedicated support staff.

Location & shipping options

The SupplyMeDirect is different. The reason is that nearly 60 percent of the stock resides in the warehouses established in the United States, the UK, Canada, & Europe. It makes shipping reliable and fast. The shipping has an average time of delivery of 4 to 7 days.

Product types

Any product from apparel to kitchenware, the toys to the accessories, & more

Recommended for

It is best for the drop shippers who intend to sell in the whole world & want fast shipping.

## CROV

For the multi-channel vendors, it is the strongest dropshipping provider. CROV links retailers from vetted lists of US vendors to a wide variety of items. It is yet another free-of-cost Shopify app to populate the store with products and automate orders.

Location & shipping options

In the 42 countries, shipping is available. Costs rely on vendors & their shipping processes, which can be found in a directory on every product detail page. To ship the domestic orders quicker, CROV has a US warehouse.

Product types

It offers extra than 35 thousand products in more than 20 other trending categories from the selected suppliers.

Recommended for

It is the best for eCommerce sellers. Especially for those who need to sell different products on Amazon, Shopify, & eBay.

## Modalyst

It is the greatest supplier of dropshipping high-tickets for US apparel. For online retailers, Modalyst is an automatic dropshipping program. It is known for delivering items that customers would enjoy from the brand names such as DSquare, Calvin Klein, Dolce, and Gabbana, & other famous brands. For any target demographic, Modalyst often features a curated collection of independent & trendy brands. The website has an official API collaboration with AliExpress Dropshipping, allowing you to access the millions of items with a Google Chrome plugin to connect to your shop with one click.

Location & shipping options

The Modalyst has the own marketplace of US manufacturers and products that can offer domestic orders free of charge between six to eight days. Also available are UK dropshipping vendors & Australian drop shippers. Businesses, except countries in South America and Africa, will ship to more than 80 countries in the world

Product types

It generally emphasizes premium and fashionable products. Modalyst is part of the Booster Program of AliExpress also, offering an infinite catalog of items for drop shippers to browse.

Recommended for

It is recommended for users of Shopify who want their shops to add exclusive items. You will also market goods using Modalysts Private Label Software with your branding. You will take advantage of any of the luxury brands and vendors that Modalysts has to sell if you chose the Pro plan.

## dropship

It is the best source of dropships for French goods. DropnShop is a dropshipping program for Shopify that provides online sales of French goods. It offers inventory from the top factories of French. It takes the requests from e-commerce partners to diversify product catalog and expand your business due to partnerships with thousands of producers. There's an availability-free plan.

Location & shipping information

To have worldwide delivery at a decent rate, DropnShop partners with numerous suppliers. Every product has different shipping information, but you may find anything you require to know on the product detail page of the app.

Product types

Would you like to sell France's best cosmetics products in your shop? With DropnShop, you may. The supplier also sells 1000s of SKUs, all 100 percent manufactured in France, across several categories, from children's toys to the hair & products of skincare.

Recommended for

It is the best for eCommerce stores. It is best, especially for those who desire to add the French product to the catalog.

Let us learn to find dropshipping suppliers

Suppliers are not always made equal, like most things in life. It is also more important to ensure that you are dealing with top-notch players in the dropshipping community. The supplier is a vital part of the dropshipping fulfillment operation.

**Before you contact suppliers**

Okay, so you've discovered a range of good suppliers & are prepared to go forward—great! Yet you would want to get all ducks in a row before you start approaching businesses.

**It would help if you were legal**

we discussed earlier, before authorizing you to register for some account, most amazing wholesalers would need confirmation that you are a legal entity. Most wholesalers report their prices to licensed consumers, but you will need to be legally authorized before seeing the type of pricing you will receive. Before contacting vendors, make sure you're lawfully integrated.

**Don't be afraid of the phone**

One of the strongest worries people have is picking up phone & making the call when it comes to vendors. It is a paralyzing prospect for many. For such problems, you may be capable of sending texts, but you'll have to pick the phone up more frequently than not to get the answers you need. The good news's that this isn't as terrifying as you would imagine. Suppliers, including novice entrepreneurs, are used to having the people calling them. You're going to get someone to answer questions who's polite and happier. Here's a trick to motivate you: just type your questions down in advance. When you have a list of already written questions for asking, it is surprising how easy it's to make the call. Great vendors for dropshipping tends to have most of the following six characteristics:

## Expert staff and industry focus

There are knowledgeable distribution agents from top-notch manufacturers who truly know the market and the product lines. It's invaluable to contact a representative with concerns, especially if you're starting a store in a niche you're not too familiar with anything.

## Dedicated support representatives

individual sales agent responsible for taking good care of yourself & any concerns you have should assign you to quality drop shippers. Problems take even longer to fix because we generally must nag the people to take care of a crisis. Getting a single interaction with a supplier allows you to locate the entity responsible for fixing your problems which is very valuable.

## Invest in technology

When there are many great suppliers with obsolete websites, suppliers that know the advantages of technology and spend extensively in it are typically a joy to deal with them. For online retailers, features like an inventory of real-time, a detailed online catalog, personalized data feeds & online searchable history of orders are pure pleasure & may help streamline the activities.

## Can take orders via email

it may seem like a small challenge, but have to call in each order or put it manually on a website makes handling orders even more time-consuming.

## Centrally located

It's helpful to use a centrally placed drop shipper in a big country like the United States since shipments can cover more than 90percent of the country within 2-3 business days. It may take an additional week for shipments to be delivered around the country where a retailer is based on one coast. Centrally placed vendors allow guaranteeing quicker turnaround times reliably, theoretically saving you cash on shipping costs.

## Organized and efficient

few vendors have qualified personnel and outstanding processes that contribute to effective and often error-less fulfillment. Every 4th order will be botched by others & make you need to rip the hair out. But without ever using it, it's impossible to tell how a professional supplier is.

While it cannot give you the full picture, it will give you a better sense of how suppliers perform by placing a few small test orders. You can see:

How to order process is done

How rapidly things ship out

And How fast this follows with monitoring details and invoice

quality of package when the product arrives

It is important to learn how to distinguish between genuine suppliers of wholesale & retail stores acting as wholesale suppliers when looking for suppliers. A real wholesaler buys straight from the producer & will usually offer you even better prices.

How to spot fake dropshipping companies

You will come across a significant number of " fake" wholesalers based on where you're looking. Unfortunately, historically, legal wholesalers are bad at selling and appear to be more difficult to find. It results in non-genuine wholesalers showing more often in searches, usually only intermediaries, so you'll need to be careful. Following dropshipping tips would help you decide whether it is a legal wholesale supplier.

**They want ongoing fees**

Real wholesalers don't charge their clients monthly fees for the luxury of doing a business & buying from them. It's usually not legitimate if a retailer asks for a monthly subscription or a service fee. It's necessary to distinguish between the suppliers and directories of suppliers here. Supplier directories are bulk supplier directories grouped by commodity categories or sector & screened to ensure suppliers' authenticity. Many directories, either 1 -time or continuous, can charge a fee, but you do not take it as an indication that the directory itself's unlawful.

## They sell to the public

You would need to register for a wholesale account to get real wholesale rates, demonstrate you are a legal entity, and be accepted before making your first order. So Any wholesale seller selling goods at "wholesale" to the general public is the only retailer offering the items at inflated rates. However, here are a few legal dropshipping charges that you would possibly encounter:

## Per-order fees

Depending on the size and complexity of the goods being dispatched, certain drop shippers would charge a dropshipping fee per shipment that can vary from 2-5 dollars or more. As the prices of packaging and delivering individual order is much greater than shipping bulk order, this is common in the industry.

## Minimum order sizes

There would be a minimum beginning order size for certain wholesalers, which is the lowest sum you may have to buy for your 1st order. They perform this to weed out window shopping vendors with questions & minor orders that will not translate into real sales and will waste their resources. If you're dropshipping, some problems may be caused. For starters, what would you might do if you have a minimum order of $500 from a supplier, but your mean order size takes about $100? Only for the privilege of making a dropshipping account do you not want to pre-order $500 of the stuff. It's best to make an offer to pay the seller $500 in advance, in this case, to create a loan with them to apply for the drop shipping orders. It helps you fulfill the retailer's minimum purchase obligation (as you are committed to buying a product at least 500 dollars in product) without having to position a single big order without accompanying any customer requests.

Tips for working with dropshipping wholesalers

It's time to start looking for vendors now you can detect a scam from the actual deal! There are a variety of different techniques that you may use, some more successful than others. In order of usefulness and choice, the ways below are enlisted, with the preferred methods enlisted first.

### Contact the manufacturer

It may be the ideal way for legal bulk vendors to be conveniently identified. Contact the manufacturer to inquire about their wholesale dealers' list if you know the product(s) you intend to dropship. To observe if they dropship and ask about setting an account up, you may then email these wholesalers. Because most wholesalers carry goods from several manufacturers within the niche, you are pursuing, and this strategy would permit you to source a range of items easily. You'll easily be able to find the leading wholesalers in that market after making few calls to leading producers in some niche.

### Use Oberlo

Oberlo helps you quickly import goods straight into the Shopify store from vendors and directly send them to your consumers, all in some clicks.

Features

Products can be imported from suppliers

Product customization

Orders are fulfilled automatically

Inventory & price automatic updates

Pricing automation

**Search using Google**

You may use Google to fetch high-quality suppliers. It is quite obvious, yet there are some factors to keep in mind:

You have to search extensively

Wholesales are not good at marketing & promotion. Furthermore, they aren't going to cover the top search results related to "wholesale suppliers for some product X." You will have to do all the research yourself.

Don't judge by their website

Wholesales are now infamous for making '90s-style websites. Although a quality site can suggest a successful supplier in some instances, many legal wholesalers have cringe-worthy website homepages. Don't let you get turned off by the bad design.

**Attend a trade show**

trade show helps you to engage in a niche with all key manufacturers & wholesalers. It's a perfect method to make friends, all in one place, and research the commodities and suppliers. It only applies if the niche &/or product has already been chosen, and it is not possible for everybody. But it's a perfect method to know vendors and the suppliers in the region if you have the time and resources to participate.

Ways to pay dropshipping suppliers and companies

A large number of suppliers shall accept payments in 1 of 2 ways:

## Credit card

Many suppliers will ask you to make the payment by credit card as you're starting. Paying with credit cards is always the better choice after you've developed a flourishing business. Not only are they easy (no requirement to constantly write checks), but lots of loyalty frequent flier/ points miles can be racked up. You will rack up a high number of sales with your credit card without requiring to pay any real out-of-the-pocket costs when you are purchasing a product for a client who has already paid for it on your website.

## Net terms

"Net terms" on invoices are the most typical method to pay the suppliers. It assumes that you have certain days for paying the retailer with the items you have ordered. So if you're on the "net 30" term, you have exactly 30 days to pay the supplier for the items from the purchase date you ordered by bank draw or check. Usually, before providing net payment terms, a supplier would make you have credit references, so it's lending you money. It is a normal procedure, but if you have to provide any documentation while paying on net terms, do not be alarmed.

Usually, before providing net payment terms, a supplier would make you have credit references, so it's lending you the money. It's a normal procedure, but if you need to provide any documentation while paying on the net terms, do not be alarmed.Bottom of Form

Top of Form

Bottom of Form

FAQs about dropshipping suppliers

Given below are some of the frequently asked questions, along with answers about the dropshipping suppliers.

**How do I find dropshipping suppliers?**

On directory vetted such as Oberlo, you can find dropshipping suppliers, colleagues' suggestions, or look the suppliers for the products for brands you like. You may also find several excellent alternatives with some research work.

**What are the best dropshipping suppliers in 2021?**

Some top suppliers for dropshipping are Worldwide Labels, Doba, SaleHoo, AliExpress, Alibaba, Wholesale Central, & CDS.

**Is dropshipping still profitable in 2021?**

In 2021, dropshipping also represents a viable market opportunity. Since you don't need to spend on the inventory or incur holding expenses, it's a sustainable business model.

**Which platform is best for dropshipping?**

Combined with the Oberlo, Shopify allows for a streamlined setup for dropshipping. On Oberlo, you can check for vendors and make items available on the branded Shopify website for sale. You make the sales, & your drop shipping supplier will do the rest.

Common questions about dropshipping

We have compiled a list of questions that could be posed by anyone planning to start a new drop shipper business.

**How much do I need to invest in starting dropshipping?**

While it is difficult to predict exact prices for any individual company, to get started, there are few things on which each drop shipping company would need to be spending money. Here's a short rundown of the critical expenditures.

**Online store**

Estimated price: ~29 dollars per month

To establish & host an online shop, you'll need to find an e-commerce site. We suggest launching a shop at Shopify. You will be capable of syncing source items with Oberlo marketplace conveniently, and you will get access to a full range of themes & free branding software so that you can quickly get your company up & running.

**Domain name**

Estimated price: $5 to 20 per year

Without the domain name, it's difficult to develop trust with clients. Although there is a range of top-leveled domains available (example,

example. co example. shop), if one is available, we recommend searching for the .com which suits the brand.

**Test orders**

Estimated price: Varies

While dropshipping helps you to have limited interference in managing your total product catalog, that you can set aside, also little of the time, cash to test the items you want to sell. You threaten listing products with too many flaws or faults if you don't, which will lead to disappointed consumers and a lot of the time wasted coping with refunds.

**Online advertising**

Estimated price: the Scales with the business; It is recommended to start budgeting with a minimum of $500

Each e-commerce organization must look for ways of reducing the average cost of acquiring a client across organic networks such as SEO, content marketing, & word of mouth. But advertising is typically an important medium for many product-based firms to start every company. Search engine marketing (the SEM), displays advertising, social media advertising, and smartphone ads are among the most common channels.

**How do drop shippers make money?**

Dropshipping businesses act like product curators, choosing the best dropshipping products for market to the customers; remember that marketing costs you incur, into both time & money, help the potential customers find, explain, & buy the right products. You will also have to include the cost of supporting customers whenever there is a product or a shipping problem. Last but not least is the original price for which the supplier sells a product. With all these prices to be accountable for, the dropshipping business mark up the individual products in exchange for the distribution. It's why the suppliers are okay with having drop shippers markets the products for those people — dropshipping stores also drive extra sales, which supplier would've missed out otherwise. it is good to find out how much this costs to "acquire" customer, & price the products with it in mind.

### Is dropshipping a legitimate business?

Dropshipping is essentially a fulfillment model, one used with many global distributors, and is completely legitimate. Satisfying consumer needs and creating brands that resonate with the right demographic is also vital for long-term growth, as with any company. Owing to a misconception of how dropshipping works, this question generally occurs. The bulk of discount shops at which you shop are most likely not to sell items they directly make. Dropshipping takes the curated approach & converts it into an online company-fit distribution model. of course, you must do more simple things to operate your business lawfully. To guarantee that you are doing business lawfully in your country, find a lawyer who has specialized in these matters.

Benefits of dropshipping

For emerging entrepreneurs, dropshipping is a perfect business model to start with because it's accessible. You can easily test multiple business concepts with a small drawback with dropshipping, which helps you learn a lot about picking and selling in-demand goods. In

2021, dropshipping is still a viable market opportunity. Since you don't need to spend in inventory or incur holding expenses, it's a sustainable business model. Combined with Oberlo, Shopify allows for a streamlined setup for dropshipping. On Oberlo, you can check for vendors and make items available on your branded Shopify site for sale. You make purchases, and your drop shipping provider will do the rest.

## Less capital is required

Stocking a warehouse takes a lot of money. By using dropshipping, you can eliminate the possibility of falling into debt to start your company. You can launch a dropshipping company with zero inventory instead of buying an extensive inventory and hoping it sells and start making money immediately. Perhaps the greatest bonus of dropshipping is that an e-commerce website can be opened without having to spend thousands of dollars in stock upfront. Traditionally, manufacturers have had to bind up large quantities of inventory with capital investments. For the dropshipping model, unless you have already made the sale and have been paid by the consumer, you do not have to buy a product. It is possible to start sourcing goods without substantial up-front inventory investments and begin a profitable dropshipping company with very little capital. And because you're not dedicated to selling, as in a typical retail company, there's less danger involved in launching a dropshipping shop without any inventory bought upfront.

## Easy to get started

Managing an e-commerce business is much easier as you don't have to deal with physical products. With drop shipping, you won't have to worry about:

Warehouse cost and management

Handling returns and inbound shipments

Packing and shipping of your orders

Keeping track of inventory for accounting purposes

Perpetually ordering products

Continuously managing stock level

**Low cost of inventory**

If you own and warehouse stock, inventory is one of the biggest costs you would have. You can end up with old inventory, causing you to find ways to reduce your inventory, or you may end up with very little inventory, resulting in stockouts and missed sales. Dropshipping lets you escape these challenges and concentrate on increasing your client base and developing your brand.

**Low Order Fulfillment Costs**

Usually, order fulfillment requires you to store, organize, label, select and carry and ship your inventory. Dropshipping lets all of it be taken care of by a third party. In this arrangement, the sole job is to ensure that they receive customer requests. They will do all the rest.

**Low overhead**

Your operating rates are minimal because you don't have to do with buying inventory or maintaining a warehouse. In reality, many popular dropshipping stores are managed as home-based enterprises, needing nothing more to run than a laptop and a few recurring costs. These costs are likely to escalate as you expand, but they will still be low relative to those of conventional brick-and-mortar companies.

## Flexible location

From just about anywhere with an internet connection, a drop shipping company can be managed. You can run and handle your company as long as you can effectively connect with vendors and clients.

## A wide selection of products to sell

Without the limitations of a physical inventory and the associated costs, dropshipping allows you to rapidly, comfortably, and cheaply upgrade your inventory. You will instantly deliver it to your customers without waiting for it to arrive in your factory if you know that a product is doing well for another store or reseller. Without the risk of bringing old products, dropshipping helps you to try new products. You're paying just for what you offer. Since you don't have to pre-purchase the items you sell, you can show your future buyers various trending products. If suppliers store an item, you can list it for sale at no added cost at your online store.

## Easier to test

Dropshipping is a valuable form of fulfillment for both the opening of a new store and for company owners looking to measure consumers' demand for additional types of items, such as shoes or whole new product ranges. Again, the primary advantage of dropshipping is the opportunity to list and likely sell goods before committing to purchasing a significant quantity of stock.

**Easier to scale**

For a typical retail organization, you would typically need to do three times as much work if you get three times the orders. By leveraging dropshipping vendors, suppliers will be responsible for most of the work to handle extra orders, helping you to improve with fewer growing pains and less gradual work. Sales growth can often bring extra labor, especially customer service, but companies that use dropshipping scale particularly well compared to conventional e-commerce companies

# Conclusion

Digital entrepreneurship may be clearly described as entrepreneurial businesses which are carried through a digital medium. Most studies proved that entrepreneurship a crucial driver for economic development & also for the reduction of unemployment. I's really important to grasp all the principles relevant to entrepreneurship. For meeting market competition & achieve the business target, every entrepreneur must be up to date with changes that arise in the customer's tastes & desires and even in the market. It is often important to use certain new digital technology & softwares to connect with the consumers and increase quality demand. As today's environment is largely dependent on national & global technology, it is important to have the sector's technologies. In this way, digital entrepreneurship plays a critical role in enabling the entrepreneur to conduct all the tasks accurately and efficiently. Using software apps allows any entrepreneur to increase the market demand for his or her product & grow the business both technologically and traditionally. As the Information & communication technologies (ICT) skills are crucial elements of digital enterprise success, it's significant to learn how it allows people to improve their business so that you can use the same for creating your own successful business. It will allow any person who engages in the business to learn about digital entrepreneurship in the Present world, changing dramatically in all fields, particularly in information & communication technology (ICT). In this case, the exponential growth of emerging technology with new creative functionalities is changing competitive environment, modifying the general market strategies, systems, and the procedure. For example, on networked economy motorized by new technologies, many businesses or company is becoming tinier with just one person where the partnerships are evolving. Digital Innovative technologies, including big data, social media, and mobile & cloud platforms, are giving rise to new ways of collaborating, exploiting capital, service/product design, creation, and deployments over the open standards & collaborative technologies. They're, in turn, impacting the market activities through generating job opportunities. Like, Alibaba.com is digital technology that allowed millions of Chinese people to be entrepreneurs. It is also responsible for the creation of employment.

Even digital technologies generate vast job opportunities. They're creating several challenges also. Emerging technologies are modernizing the labor market. Several countries are facing several obstacles, such as Australia, to face economic competition. To face the obstacles and eliminate the barriers, countries are recommended for taking over digital entrepreneurship & achieve an acceptable role. Digital entrepreneurship increases jobs across ICTs like Facebook, social computing, mobile technology, and digital channels. Many firms began digital businesses by selling the products online to meet competition in the industry. As this becomes necessary, focusing on how a business venture must be started is rising with utmost significance. People who need to start a digital company should know the differences between digital versus conventional opportunities, downfalls, entrepreneurship, and digital entrepreneurship challenges. The people need a format or digital entrepreneurship system that consists all information about the new digital enterprise, including its features and objectives.

# The 9+1 Best Home-Based Business Model of 2021

*Find Out how Millennials Have Built Millionaire Businesses from Home with Soap and Candle Making, Natural Cosmetics and much more*

**By**

**The Golden Inner Circle**

# Table of Contents

# Introduction

Karsanbhai Patel (Patel), the chemist at Mines and Geology Department of the Gujarat Government, produced synthetic powder of detergent phosphate-free in 1969 and began selling this locally. He priced the new yellow powder at 3.50rs per kg. It was at one time when Rs 15 was being charged for Hindustan Lever Limited (HLL) Surf. Soon, in Kishnapur (Gujarat), Patel's hometown, there was a big demand for Nirma. In 10x12 feet space in his home, he began preparing the formula. He had named powder after his daughter's name-Nirupama. On the way to the office by bicycle, about 15 kilometers away, Patel was able to sell around 15-20 packets a day. Thus, the new journey began. Hindustan Lever Limited (HLL) responded in a manner characteristic of many global corporations in the early 1970s, when washing powder Nirma was launched into the market of low-income. "That isn't our business," senior executives said of the new offering. "We don't have to be worried." However very soon, Hindustan Lever Limited (HLL) was persuaded by Nirma's performance in the detergent sector that this wanted to take a closer gaze at the less income market. Low-cost detergents & toilet soaps are almost synonymous with the brand name. Nirma, on the other hand, found that it would've to launch goods targeted at the higher end of the market to maintain the middle-class buyers as they moved up the market. For the luxury market, the firm introduced bathroom soaps. Analysts, on the other hand, claimed Nirma wouldn't be capable of duplicate its performance in the premium market. In the year 2000, the Nirma had a 15 percent share of the toilet soap market and a 30% share of the detergent market. Nirma's revenue for the year ended in March 2000 grew by 17 percent over the previous fiscal year, to 17.17rs. bn, backed by volume development and commissioning of backward integration projects. By 1985, in many areas of the world, washing powder Nirma became one of the most common detergent brands. Nirma was a global consumer company by 1999, with a wide variety of soaps, detergents, & personal care items. Nirma has brought in the latest technologies for the manufacturing facilities in six locations across India, in line with its ideology of delivering premium goods at the best possible costs. The success of Nirma in the intensely competitive market for soaps & detergents was due to its efforts to support the brand, which had been complemented by the sales scope & market penetration. The network of Nirma spread across the country, with over two million outlets of retail and 400 distributors. Nirma was able to reach out to even the smallest villages due to its vast network. Nirma spread to the markets overseas in 1999 after establishing itself in India. Via a joint venture called Commerces Overseas Limited, it made its first foray into Bangladesh. Within a year, the company had risen to the top of Bangladesh's detergent market. Other areas such as Middle East, Russia, China, Africa & additional Asian countries were also intended for the entry of the organization. Nirma became a 17 billion Rs company in 3 decades, beginning as a single-product single-man article of clothing in 1969. Under the umbrella name Nirma, the company had several production plants and a large product range. The mission of the organization to have "Better Product, Better Values and Better Living" added much to its growth. Nirma was able to outshine Hindustan Levers Limited (then HLL) and carve out a niche for oneself in the lower-ends of detergent & market toilet soap. HLL's Surf was the first to be used as a detergent powder in India in 1959. But by the 1970s, merely by making the product available at a reasonable price, Nirma led the demand for detergent powder. Nirma launched its Nirma Beauty soaps to the Indian toilet soap industry in 1990. Nirma had gained a 15% share of 530,000 tons per annum toilet soap industry by 1999, making it India's second-largest producer. Although it was way behind HLL's 65 percent share, the success of Nirma was impressive compared to Godrej, which had an 8 percent share. By 1999-2000, Nirma had already acquired a 38 percent share of India's detergent market of 2.4 million tonnes. For the same period, HLL's market share was 31%. In this book, we will study and analyze the case of Nirma and its rise to the top detergent companies of India. Besides, we will also give profitable ideas and options for starting a lucrative detergent soap, candle making, and natural cosmetics business.

# CHAPTER 1: The Nirma Washing Powder's Success Story

The success story of the famous Nirma washing powder began in a small Gujarati farmer's house. We'll tell you about a billionaire father who lost his daughter in a car crash and later discovered a way to get her back to life. When she was alive, only a few people knew of her daughter, but it was the sheer persistence and willpower of this man that made his daughter famous in the world, even though she was no more. This is the story of a man who was born into a poor farming family and turned his daughter's nickname into India's leading detergent, soda ash, and education brand. A man of valor and passion who showed that nothing will hinder you if you have the willpower. Here is the story of **"Sabki Pasand Nirma, Washing Powder Nirma."**

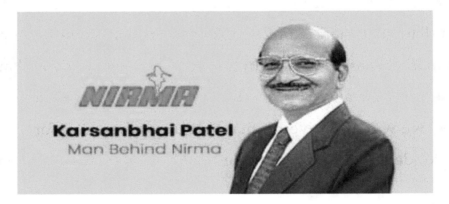

## 1.1 Invention of Nirma detergent?

Karsanbhai was born in Ruppur, Gujarat, to a farmer's family in 1945. He had earned a bachelor's degree in chemistry by the age of 21. He attempted to do a normal job like his colleagues at first. He served as a lab technician for the Lalbhai Group's New Cotton Mills, which is credited with launching the Indian jeans movement. He also took up a position at the Geology and Mining Department of the Gujarat government after this short stint. The year 1969 marked the start of a turning point in the career trajectory of Karsanbhai. It was at this time that Hindustan Lever Ltd (now Hindustan Unilever) formed a full monopoly on the Indian detergent market under the brand name "Surf." A Surf Pack was sold somewhere from Rs 10-15 back then. The USP was that, unlike normal washing soap bars, it eliminated stains from your clothes and didn't irritate your skin. However, for middle-class families, which had no other choice than to return to the old bar soap, this price point was not affordable. The tycoon in Karsanbhai noticed the issue and devised a plan. A young Karsanbhai will come home from work and dedicate all his time and energy to making a phosphate-free detergent in his yard. He wanted to bear in mind that he needed to produce a detergent with a low manufacturing cost so that everybody could afford it. Karsanbhai utilized a recipe for a yellow-colored detergent powder that could be marketed for a mere Rs 3 after several trials and failures. He chose to name the invention after Nirupama, his daughter. He finally got the formula right one day, and as an after-work business, he began making detergents in his 100-square-foot backyard. He will cycle around the neighborhoods, selling door-to-door homemade detergent packages. Patel set the price of his detergent at Rs. 3, almost a third less than Hindustan Unilever's well-known brand "Surf." The product's high quality and low price made it a success, and it was well-received by many who saw great benefit in purchasing it. Because of the business's high promise, Karsanbhai quit his government job three years later to pursue it full-time. Karsanbhai was so fond of the commodity that he called it Nirma, after his daughter Nirupama's nickname. To make sure that everybody remembers her, he used her picture (the girl in the white frock) on the pack and in TV advertisements. Such was a father's love for his daughter. While Karsanbhai Patel himself was not an MBA graduate, the techniques he adopted to expand his company left marketers bewildered and amazed. 'Nirma' was not only a game-changer but also a trendsetter for several small companies. Here are a couple of 'Washing Powder Nirma's' management lessons.

## 1.2 Karsanbhai Patel's sale policy for Nirma detergent

Karsanbhai Patel agreed to start marketing it once the product had a strong formula. On his cycle, he used to go door-to-door and neighborhood-to-neighborhood every day for three years, pitching the detergent. As it was a brand new product, if they found the product poor, he gave his consumers a money-back guarantee. Nirma has been the cheapest detergent in Ahmedabad at the time. As a result, Karsanbhai's product was an immediate hit. He left his government job three years later and set up a store in Ahmedabad to carry out this full-time enterprise. In some areas of Gujarat, his brand was doing very well, but there was a need to expand its scope. At the time, the standard was to offer the product to retailers on credit. This was a huge gamble because if the product didn't sell, Karsanbhai would have had to close down the company. At that time, he chose to try something different. He planned to spend a little money on advertising. These commercials, with their catchy jingles, were directed at housewives. And this bet paid off well. Nirma became a famous household brand and it had to be purchased by people. He did, however, remove 90% of the stock from the market at this time. Potential buyers had asked for the detergent at their local retailers for about a full month but would have to return empty-handed. During this time, retail store owners flocked to Karsanbhai, demanding that the detergent supply be increased. After another month, he eventually decided. Nirma was able to take over the sales and even beat Surf at their own game due to this approach. It went on to become the country's highest-selling detergent. It remained India's largest-selling detergent even after a decade,

## 1.3 Invest In Research and Development

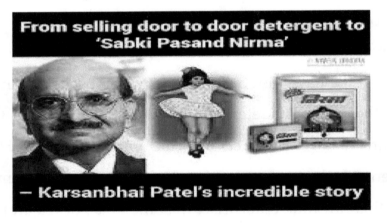

Karsanbhai Patel had little means and was not a man born with a silver spoon in his mouth. Karsanbhai loved experimenting with chemicals after completing a B.Sc. in Chemistry at the age of 21 and then working as a laboratory technician. He noticed that only MNCs in India were selling detergents and there was no economy brand detergent for the country. His excitement about bridging the distance grew, sensing a massive opening, and Karsanbhai began experimenting with chemicals. He quickly succeeded in manufacturing a detergent of high quality at a much cheaper price, which was an immediate success in the industry. Every good product needs a substantial expenditure in time, resources, and commitment in research and development.

## 1.4 No Higher Costs

Nirma had rewritten the rules of the game within a short time, by delivering high-quality goods at an unprecedentedly low price. Nirma's success was due to its cost-cutting policy. Patel had concentrated from the very beginning on delivering high-value goods at the lowest price possible. The corporation sought to keep improving efficiency while reducing prices. Nirma sought out captive processing plants for raw materials to keep production costs to a minimum. This led to the backward integration initiative, as part of which, at Baroda and Bhavnagar, which became operational in 2000, two state-of-the-art plants were established. This also led to a reduction in raw-material prices. Ahead of time and at a much smaller cost than anticipated, the two new plants were completed. The Baroda plant's second phase was finished 6 months ahead of schedule and at a cost of Rs.2.5 billion compared to the initial projected cost of Rs. 2.8 billion. Compared to the initial projected cost of Rs. 10.36 billion, the Bhavnagar plant was finished in a record period of 2 years at a cost of Rs.9.86 billion. This plant had a workforce of just 500 employees. Concerning Nirma's plant, Tata Chemical's plant, which had around twice the amount, employed ten times the number of workers. Almost

65000 tpa of N-Paraffin was produced by the Baroda plant for Linear Alkyl Benzene (LAB) and Synthetic detergents. Similarly, almost 4.20,000 tpa of soda ash could be produced by the Bhavnagar facility. Akzo Nobel Engineering in Holland produced the Akzo Dry Lime technology used in this factory. The plant had 108 kilometers of salt bunds, which would assist in the potential development of vacuum iodized salt. Patel said, "We have a processing potential of three lakh tons of pure salt. No one in the world had a related plant, but Tata Salt." Nirma had reduced its distribution costs by obviating the need for middlemen. The item went to the dealer straight from the manufacturer. Hiren K Patel (Hiren), CMD, explained to Nirma Customer Care Ltd., "An order is placed and the truck immediately leaves. It's similar to a bank account. We're sending stock, they're sending money." In states like Tamil Nadu, Andhra Pradesh, and southern Karnataka, the company-maintained depots, as it was often difficult to bring stocks to these regions. Stocks were shipped directly from the plants in states like Madhya Pradesh and Uttar Pradesh. In March 2000, Nirma opted for in-house packaging and printing by obtaining Kisan Factories at Moriya, near Ahmedabad, in a further cost-cutting exercise. Nirma hoped that this would increase the packaging's quality.

## 1.5 Be Proactive in your approach as it is beneficial for the business

Karsanbhai Patel was the only person who started this business and starting selling Nirma. He was educated and had a government career, but he was never afraid of selling door-to-door detergent. He was diligent in doing something and knew that the company was tiny and bootstrapping, so he had to consider everything and anything about his business that could be fruitful. There is no such thing as a small or large undertaking. And if you are the CEO, you should embrace the obligations that are valuable to the company without guilt.

## 1.6 Provide Customers with 'Value for Money'

Customers noticed the advantages of purchasing Nirma, and it became an immediate success. They considered the standard to be at par with the giant Surf brand, but to take advantage of the same perks, they just had to pay one-third of the amount. Customers would only appreciate the product if you show them the advantages and give them decent value for their money.

## 1.7 Define Your Segment

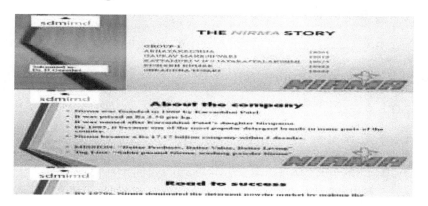

Karsanbhai Patel identified the target segment for his detergent almost as soon as he found the magical formula. He realized that a luxury brand sold in tier 1 cities was the alternative Surf brand, so he concentrated on marketing his brand in tier 2-3 cities. He priced his detergent low and made it a mass brand to get more consumer traction. People from the lower middle class and middle class quickly adopted the product, and it quickly rose in popularity. Where most firms adopted the conventional top-down strategy, i.e., spreading from metro towns to rural cities, Nirma did the reverse and changed the whole game. It is really important to evaluate the competitors for every company and define the most lucrative segment.

## 1.8 Focus on Building a Brand

It was failing to find vendors outside the city in the early 80s, although the commodity was approved on a small scale in Ahmedabad. Since clients were unaware of its presence, retailers were wary of keeping the detergent in their stores. It resulted in overdue payments, return on inventory, and large business losses. Karsanbhai Patel came up with a good publicity approach to handle the situation and launched a TV advertisement campaign. The popular "Washing powder Nirma, detergent tikiya Nirma" jingle became an anthem for the company and customers began to equate Nirma as a strong brand. The demand for Nirma soon peaked, and with his products, Patel flooded the retail stores. A good brand decreases a buyer's potential risk and increases the company's bargaining power.

## 1.9 Astutely Manage the Brand Wars

Nirma also had innovative marketing campaigns. Nirma successfully spread the name to other product segments in the mid-nineties, such as premium detergents (Nirma Mega Detergent Cake and Washing Powder), premium toilet soaps, and (Nirma Sandal, Nima Premium, Nirma Lime Fresh). In both the economy and luxury markets, it maintained its initial pricing and marketing plans. In 2000, with Nirma Beauty Shampoo, Nirma Shikakai, and Toothpaste, the firm entered the hair care market. Soaps, unlike detergents, were a private-care commodity. Many consumers had strong emotional attachments with their soap products. Furthermore, HLL segmented the market by price, fragrance appeal, and brand personality. So, against Lifebuoy, Nirma put Nirma Wash, Nirma Beauty Soap against Lux, Nima Rose against Breeze7, and Nima Lime against Jai Lime. Explaining how Nirma hoped to win this match, playing by the rules of HLL, Hiren said"Worldwide, there are only four or five channels that account for most of the soaps sold: floral, fashion, fitness, freshness." With the relevant scents, Nirma manufactured high-fatty-matter soaps and priced them much lower than other brands. As a result, the 'sub-premium' section was born. The game of controlling the geographical variety of market desires was also perfected by Nirma. The North, for instance, favored pink soaps, and green ones were favored by the South. In the South, sandal soaps were more common. Initially, the company's promotional budget, relative to other FMCG firms, was very poor. In contrast to the usual 6-10 percent, Nirma spent just 1.25-2 percent of its sales on ads. The firm used starlets such as Sangeeta Bijlani, Sonali Bendre, and Riya Sen, who were comparatively unknown at the time, to endorse soaps. The promotional messages were both transparent and centered on the product's benefits. Nirma still chose to first put the item on the shelf, get reviews, and then create a lasting ad campaign. Nirma used its tried-and-true tool, price, to introduce toilet soaps and detergents in the premium market. In these divisions, the company intended to rely on quantities as well. However, the margins granted to retailers had shifted. Unlike economic goods, where the cost advantages were passed on to customers, this advantage was passed on to retailers by Nirma. It provided them with massive profit margins. For instance, it offered 52 percent for Nirma premium soap and an incredible margin of 140 percent for Nirma shampoo. In the luxury segment of the soap industry, observers were pessimistic about Nirma's chances of success.

Unlike detergents, the demand for soaps and shampoos was incredibly fragmented. There were only 15-20 brands, and it was hard to get a considerable market share for any soap. This market was also less price sensitive. So, it was hard for any enterprise to support itself on price alone. Analysts thought that shifting the brand value of Nirma would take years. According to a survey conducted by Nirma's marketing agency, Samsika Marketing Consultancy, Nirma was viewed as a low-cost brand. Many people were almost afraid to say they used it. Nirma published corporate advertisements worth Rs 10 bn in India in the late nineties to shed this image. Analysts claim that the fast-growing shampoo market is a safer investment than luxury soaps. Just 30% of the population in India used shampoo, with more than 70% of this group living in urban areas. However, according to some researchers, while the rural market's presumed potential was very high, it was difficult to convince rural folk to use shampoos in actual practice. A further concern faced by Nirma was that of insufficient facilities. While it had a good presence in the smaller towns and villages, it lacked the requisite network for urban centers to penetrate. As a result, Nirma's foray into high-end soaps and shampoos proved to be a flop.

## 1.10 Diversify the Portfolio

For low-income groups, Nirma began with a low-cost detergent, but later introduced products for higher-income groups, such as Nirma Sandal soap, Nirma Beauty soap, etc.

Not just that, but in 2003, Karsanbhai Patel formed Nirma University to diversify the company's brand portfolio. The brand is currently exploring its options in the cement industry to grow its market. Diversifying the portfolio decreases the company's potential risk of loss while still allowing it to serve a broader variety of consumers.

## 1.11 Conclusion

While Nirma was best known as a manufacturer of goods for the low-cost economy, it was popular in the middle and upmarket segments. Yet rivalry was also growing at the same time. Although HLL continued to be a major threat, offensive initiatives were also introduced by P&G and Henkel SPIC. In the detergent and washing powder market, participants from the unorganized field were also introduced to the rivalry. Patel was confident of tackling the rivalry, though. "He added, "We keep the price line and the happy customer returns to us normally. Based on its growth strategy, the company has risen in demand and volume in the last three decades: "A buyer is not looking for one-time frills or feel-good variables. The landlord, on the other hand, is searching for a long-term solution to his or her issues." Karsanbhai Patel, who began with a vision of making his daughter famous through his brand and ended up being one of the greatest entrepreneurs of all time, exemplifies the relevance of this quotation. He began with an aim of creating his daughter famous through his brand and ended up becoming one of the greatest entrepreneurs of all time. His name not only gained tremendous respect but also became a trendsetter for many new firms. The brand has taught young entrepreneurs many useful lessons and has proven to be a valuable resource for the region. Karsanbhai Patel has shown that no goal is too lofty if you have the ambition and zeal to achieve it.

## 1.12 What Karsanbhai Patel and Nirma detergent did for the Indian Economy

Nirma's meteoric growth in prominence culminated in the introduction of a new economic market for detergent powder. It was of good quality and was inexpensive. Plus, contrary to the others, the fact that it was manufactured without phosphates made it the most environmentally-friendly detergent. In comparison, a labor-consuming process was the process of producing the detergent. And thus, Nirma went on to hire more than 14,000 workers and became the country's leading employer.

## 1.13 Karsanbhai Patel's ventures other than the Nirma detergent

Karsanbhai wanted to grow his FMCG business after Nirma dominated the detergent industry. Nirma launched its line of toilet soaps, beauty soaps, and even shampoos in the premium market.

While the latter venture failed, one of their products, edible salt Shudh, is still available and doing well. Overall, Nirma has a 20 percent market share in soap cakes and a 35 percent market share in detergents. That isn't it, however. In 1995, Karsanbhai Patel founded the Nirma Institute of Technology in Ahmedabad. Later, it became one of Gujarat's most prestigious engineering schools. After that, the whole structure was merged under the Nirma University of Science and Technology, which is supervised by the Nirma Education and Research Foundation, and in 2003, the entire structure was unified under the Nirma University of Science and Technology. This is overseen by the Nirma Education and Research Foundation. Since 2004, Karsanbhai's CSR initiative, Nirmalabs education, has aimed to train and incubate entrepreneurs. Karsanbhai Patel has now turned over the reins of his profitable company to his two sons. Pratibha Patil, the then-President of India, bestowed the Padma Shri on him in 2010. Nirma is now the world's biggest manufacturer of soda ash, and the company has been privately owned since 2012. Karsanbhai Patel invested his huge fortune on a six-seat chopper in 2013, which cost Rs 40 crore. After Gautam Adani (Adani Group) and Pankaj Patel (Zydus Group), he became the third Ahmedabad-based industrialist to purchase a helicopter. Nirma, on the other hand, is still one of India's most popular detergents. And the jingles will live on forever.

# CHAPTER 2: Start a Profitable Soap Making Business

As a soap manufacturer, you'll create your recipes for soaps and probably other personal cleaning and beauty products. Ecommerce, farmers markets, arts events, wholesale positioning in spas and boutiques, and even door-to-door sales are all options for selling the goods. You'll test several solutions and see if you can find a steady stream of clients. Learn how to launch a soap-making company of your own.

Steps for starting a soap making business

You've uncovered the ideal market opportunity and are now prepared to take the next step. There's more to launching a company than simply filing papers with the government. We've put together a list of steps to help you get started with your soap-making business. These measures will ensure that the new company is well-planned, legally compliant, and properly registered.

## Plan your business

As an entrepreneur, you must have a well-thought-out strategy. It will assist you in figuring out the additional data of your organization and uncovering any unknowns. Given below are some key points to consider:

What are the startup and recurring costs?

Who is the targeted audience?

What is the maximum price you will charge from the customers?

What would you name your company?

**What are the costs involved in opening a soap-making business?**

You've got a good start if you have a kitchen or workspace as well as a few simple kitchen utensils. Making soap isn't an expensive business to undertake, but you would need to invest in some basic equipment. Ingredients cost at least $200. Lye and fats or oils are used to make soap. That's a good start, but it'll be your special formula that sets you apart. For superior feel, fragrance, and lather, you can use coconut oil, olive oil, almond oil, and several fragrance oils, extracts, and natural additives. To keep materials costs down and simplify production, you could start with only one or two simple recipes. Equipment for producing soap will cost around $300. Your equipment specifications will be determined by the type of soap-making you do. Hot process, cold process, rebatching, and melt and pour are the four basic forms of processing, and each needs different equipment. But, regardless of the route you take, you'll almost definitely need soap molds, packing, and shipping items. You can get your basic ingredients, additives, equipment, and supplies from several online retailers. Marketing software will cost up to $750. A professional-looking website with enticing product images is key to the company's growth. Since your online consumers can't touch or smell your goods, they must be able to judge the good quality of what they see. That means recruiting a graphic designer and web developer to help you make the best out of your logo and online presence is a smart investment. To express your love and dedication to product quality, your visual imagery will be carried through in your labeling and branding. Skilled services will cost up to $200. Is it legal in your state and society for you to run this sort of business from home? Before you put up your shingle, meet with a lawyer for a quick consultation. The Handcrafted Soap & Cosmetics Guild charges a membership fee of $100 per year (HSCG). Small-batch soap makers will benefit from this organization's preparation, funding, and useful networking opportunities. Insurance for general liability and product liability would cost $265-$375 a year. This is also accessible via the HSCG.

## What are the ongoing expenses for a soap-making business?

The consumable commodity materials you'll need for ongoing development would be your greatest ongoing expense. Your increasing variable expenses would be more than offset by a rise in revenue if you've priced your offering correctly.

## Who is the target market?

While women make up the majority of the demand for homemade soaps, some firms have had success selling male-oriented soap scents. You may approach consumers who admire your product's consistency and luxury, or those who only purchase organic or vegan goods. Customers will note the difference in quality among your soaps and those sold on the shelves of a traditional supermarket.

## How does a soap-making business make money?

In the majority of the cases, all of your revenue shall be derived from the products you make or sell.

## How much can you charge customers?

Your goods could be sold for $5 or $6 a bar. This is more than your consumers are likely to spend for mass-produced retail soaps, but your product has a high perceived value. Other price points can be met by providing discounts on multiple orders, marketing multi-bar bundles, and extending the product range. Look at local rivals' websites to see what they're costing and how that would impact the pricing. Will you charge more to suggest a higher-end product range, or will you charge less to compensate for the lower per-unit sales margin with higher volume?

## How much profit can a soap-making business make?

There are a few well-known soap makers who began their careers in the same way you did. Take, for example, Burt's Bees. Others in your business run it as a side venture, something between a crafts hobby and a modestly profitable business. You will go as far as your dedication, imagination, promotional skills, and hard work can take you, as with many home-based companies.

## How can you make your business more profitable?

Many soap makers diversify their product range to include more exotic soaps (goat's milk soap is one example) or complementary goods. Making candles is a natural progression for soap makers who still use a hot process. Others are involved in home fragrances, lip balms, hair care, and even pet products. Focus on what else will cater to the consumer base when speaking about expanding your product mix. Many companies aim to maximize their net income by lowering the cost of goods produced. Growing the earnings by issuing bigger batches at a time is a cost-effective technique.

## 2.1 What will you name your business?

Choosing the correct name is vital and daunting. If you own a sole proprietorship, you should start using a separate company name from your own. We suggest reviewing the following references before filing a company name:

The state's business records

Federal and state trademark records

Social media sites

Web domain availability

It's important to have your domain name registered before anyone else does.

## 2.2 Form a legal entity

The sole proprietorship, partnership, limited liability company (LLC), and corporation are the most traditional corporate structures. If your soap manufacturing company is used, creating a legitimate business entity such as an LLC or corporation prevents you from being found legally accountable.

Register for taxes

Before you can start doing business, you'll need to apply for several state and federal taxes. You would need to apply for an EIN to pay for taxation. It's very basic and free.

## 2.3 Small Business Taxes

Depending on which business arrangement you select, you can have various taxation choices for your corporation. There could be state-specific taxes that apply to your business. In the state sales tax guides, you can read more about state sales taxes and franchise taxes.

## 2.4 Open a business bank account & credit card

Personal wealth security necessitates the use of dedicated company banking and credit accounts. If your personal and corporate accounts are combined, your personal properties (such as your house, vehicle, and other valuables) are put at risk if your company-issued. This is referred to as piercing the corporate veil in business law. Furthermore, learning how to create company credit will help you receive credit cards and other borrowings under your business's name (rather than your own), lower interest rates, and more credit lines, among other advantages.

## 2.5 Open a business bank account

This protects your assets from those of your business, which is essential for personal wealth security, as well as making accounting and tax reporting simpler.

## 2.6 Get a business credit card

It will help you achieve the following benefits:

It builds the company's credit background and will be beneficial for raising capital and profit later on.

It lets you differentiate personal and business expenditures by placing all of your business's costs under one account.

Set up business accounting

Understanding your business's financial results includes keeping track of your different costs and sources of revenue. Maintaining correct and comprehensive reports also makes annual tax filing even simpler.

## 2.7 Obtain necessary permits and licenses

Failure to obtain required permits and licenses will result in hefty fines or even the closure of your company. If you intend to market homemade soaps, you must first acquire a business license.

## 2.8 State & Local Business Licensing Requirements

Operating a handmade soap company can necessitate the procurement of some state permits and licenses. Furthermore, several states have varying laws governing the manufacturing of cosmetics and other body care goods. Visit the SBA's guide to state licenses and permits to read more about your state's licensing criteria.

## 2.9 Labor safety requirements

It is essential to comply with all Occupational Safety and Health Administration protocols. Pertinent requirements include:

Employee injury report

Safety signage

## 2.10 Certificate of Occupancy

A Certificate of Occupancy is normally required for businesses that operate out of a specific location (CO). All requirements concerning building codes, zoning rules, and local requirements have been followed, according to a CO. If you're thinking about renting a space, keep the following in mind:

Securing a CO is normally the landlord's duty.

Before signing a contract, make sure your landlord has or can get a legitimate CO for a soap-making operation.

A new CO is often needed after a significant renovation. If your company will be renovated before opening, add wording in your lease agreement that specifies that lease payments will not begin before a valid CO is issued.

If you intend to buy or build a place:

You would be responsible for securing a legal CO from a local government body.

Review all building codes and zoning standards for your soap-making business's place to ensure that you'll comply and eligible to get a CO.

## 2.11 Trademark & Copyright Protection

It is wise to protect your interests by applying for the required trademarks and copyrights if you are creating a new product, idea, brand, or design. The essence of legal standards in distance education is continually evolving, especially when it comes to copyright laws. This is a regularly revised database that can assist you with keeping on top of legal specifications.

## 2.12 Get business insurance

Insurance, including licenses and permits, are necessary for your company to run safely and legally. In the case of a covered loss, corporate insurance covers your company's financial well-being. There are several insurance schemes tailored for diverse types of companies with various risks. If you're not sure what kinds of risks your company might face, start with General Liability Insurance. This is the most popular form of coverage required by small companies, so it's a good place to start.

## 2.13 Learn more about General Liability Insurance

Workers' Compensation Insurance is another essential insurance scheme that many companies need. When your company hires staff, your state may mandate you to carry the Workers' Benefits Package.

## 2.14 Define your brand

Your company's brand is what it stands for, as well as how the general public perceives it. A good name would set the company apart from the market.

### How to promote & market a soap making business

Look for areas where you can stand out. Try having a larger-than-usual bar of soap or one that is formulated to last longer. Perhaps you should market a six-pack of sampler soaps in smaller sizes so that your customers can check out your whole product range and pick their preferences. Consider an uncommon fragrance or texture additive for applying to your soaps to make them stand out. When you've found a winning design, publicize it on your website and social media. Also, if you're showing your soaps at an exhibition, bring some unwrapped samples of your entire product line so consumers can touch them, see what they're made of, feel their textures, and experience the various scents.

### How to keep customers coming back

bear in mind that you're offering an aesthetic experience. Make sure your logo, labels and packages, and the name of your product line all cater to consumers looking for a low-cost luxury experience. One benefit is that the more your consumers like your stuff, the faster they can consume it and require more. Ensure that you retain contact with your clients and that they are aware of how to contact you. Request email addresses from all of your clients to obtain their approval to send out a monthly e-newsletter or catalog. It's important not to bother someone with so many promotional newsletters, but a monthly newsletter will keep consumers updated on all of the new items you have to sell. You might want to add a toll-free phone number for orders as your company expands.

## Establish your web presence

Customers can learn more about your business and the goods or services you deliver by visiting your website. One of the most successful ways to build your web presence is through press releases and social media.

## 2.15 Soap Making Plan

If you live in the jungle and love your body odor, you would not need soap. It is a regular need and one of the common goods. As a result, soap has a huge demand. There are various varieties of soaps available due to the wide range of skin types. Soaps are manufactured in a multitude of ways to suit the needs of all. One of the most promising FMCGs is soap production. Perhaps this is why so many people are drawn to this sector year after year. Every day, in a country like India, there is a massive demand for soap. However, there are only a few competitors in the business. We have a few ideas for you if you want to launch your own soap company. Let's get this started.

## Tips for soap making using the cold process method

Soap making is easy at the most fundamental level. The cold process approach is the most common way to produce soap. It's "cold" because the ingredients aren't heated before being combined. Using the "hot process" technique, you can make soap with heat. We will use the cold process. Soap is made by mixing fats and oils with a lye and water solution in the most basic form. Soap is made from a combination of water, lye, fats, and oils. The fun starts as you change the components and quantities of the various materials. But, to keep things simple, note that soap is essentially a solution of fats and oils, lye, and water. It's as plain as that.

## Is making soap without lye possible?

Is it possible to produce soap without lye? Not at all. Soap bases that can be heated and poured into molds can be purchased. You didn't have to use lye to make the base as everyone else did. However, you have no idea what's in those bases. Sodium hydroxide is the lye used to produce bar soap. Soft soaps are made of potassium hydroxide. Leaching lye from wood ashes is an easy way to create it. This form of lye results in a smoother soap. Unless you have access to a chemical supply house, lye is typically difficult to come by locally. It is, however, simple to put an order. Lye is highly caustic, and it can sear the skin and strip color from whatever surface it comes into contact with. If it gets into your eyes, it will blind you. This is a toxic drug and can never be used in a place where children may reach it. Adults, on the other hand, would have no trouble with the lye if they take simple precautions. When dealing with lye, please wear safety goggles. Long sleeves and protective gloves are also recommended. Leave lye or lye mixtures unattended at all times. Uncured soap should be used similarly to lye.

**Fats and oils required for making the cold process soap**

Another fundamental to producing soap can be found here. To turn oils and fats into soap, different quantities of lye are needed. Every fat that is likely to be used in soap making has a known amount of time it takes to turn oil or fat into soap. Simply look up the amount of lye needed to produce soap from a certain oil in a table. The volume of lye used in each recipe is then determined based on the oils used. Using a little less lye than is needed to transform all of the oils into soap. This is achieved as a precautionary step to ensure that all of the lye is absorbed during the process. The lye discount is the volume of lye used that is reduced. It's normal to use around 5% less lye than is needed to completely transform the oils into soap. Coconut, palm, and olive oils are the most common oils used in soap making. If you just use those three oils to make soap, you will make amazing results. Each of these oils has its collection of characteristics that make it useful as a soaping oil. You can produce a soap with only one of the oils, but the results won't be as strong as if you used all three. This is why. If you want a lot of bubbles in your soap, coconut oil is the way to go. It's the root of a slew of big, light bubbles. However, soap made entirely of coconut oil cleans so well that it extracts much of the oil from the skin, leaving it dry. This is why it can only account for about 30% of the soap oils. Palm oil is important for hard, long-lasting bars, but it isn't as clean or bubbly as coconut oil. This fat is often referred to as "vegetable tallow," but it is similar to beef tallow in any way. If you don't want to eat meat fats, use them instead of beef fat. Then you should ask about olive oil. Just olive oil is used to produce castile soap conventionally. If you've ever used this form of soap, you know how good it is as a skin conditioner. It's amazing. However, if olive oil is the only oil used in the soap, the effect is tiny little bubbles and bars that fade away quicker than you'd like. As a result, this type of oil is only used to make up about 40% of the oils in a recipe. Granted, soap can be made from almost any form of fat or oil, and there are several alternatives.

**Adding ingredients for premium luxury results**

If you choose to use other oils, just apply a small amount during the final stages of the soap-making process. you'll find that you can use almond oil in your example recipe. Simply raise the amount of olive oil in the formula and leave out the almond oil. It was chosen because it brings a little more to the bar's feel and quality. Soap can be used for a lot more than just producing pure soap. All of the additives are what make soap production so exciting. Clays, natural oils, medicinal products, colors, patterns, and a slew of other alternatives are available as additives. The first step to perfect soap is to get the fundamentals correctly, which can be achieved fast and effectively. After learning the fundamentals of soap manufacturing, the soap manufacturer progresses to using a range of exotic ingredients.

How to make soap?

We'll go into the fundamentals of how the soap is made. Bear in mind that this is just the first step. Following that, you may need additional materials and a special recipe to distinguish the product from competitors.

Ingredients

Given below are the following ingredients that would be required for preparing soap:

Take 2/3 cup of coconut oil (that will create lather) and the same amount of olive oil. Moreover, 2/3 cup almond, safflower oil, or grape seed will also be needed.

Then you'll need a quarter cup of lye, which is sodium hydroxide in its purest form. Finally, you'll require 3/4 cup of cool water that is distilled or pure.

You'll also need oatmeal, aloe vera gel, cornmeal, clay, salt, and any other items you choose to use.

**Instructions**

Listed below are the step-by-step directions that you must follow in the preparation of soap:

Put on your gloves and pour lye and water into a canning jar. Allow them to sit for a few minutes after they've been stirred gently and the water has begun to clear.

Now pour in the oil from the pint jar. Then Stir well, then put the jar in a warm pan of the water that is bubbling (and/or you may microwave it, when you do, place temperature to one hundred and twenty degrees F).

Remove the lye after that is finished. Allow the lye to cool. Remove pint jar & allow your oil to cool as well. Both can achieve a temperature of 95 to 105 degrees Fahrenheit. If the temperature drops below 95 degrees F, the soap will begin to crumble.

Pour them into a mixing bowl until they've hit the ideal temperature and whisk until fully combined. After stirring for five minutes, mix it with an immersion blender.

Then, to make the soap special, apply herbs, essential oils, & any other things that go with it. They can be thoroughly combined so they appear coarse. Place them in molds & cover with a towel.

After a day check the soap and let it stay for an additional 12 to 24 hours if it's either warm or soft.

When the soaps are fully cured, wrap them in the paper wax & lock them in an airtight jar for a week. Since this soap contains oil on its own, we'll need an airtight jar. As a consequence, interaction with air will cause it to pick up debris and dust.

**Soap making machine and price**

 fiber covered mixing machine will cost you at least about US$ 1000. This price includes a fiber-covered mixing machine capable of producing 200 kilograms of detergent powder.

**Where to get soap making machine?**

Online, you can buy a soap-manufacturing machine. Soap manufacturing machines are available from several online retailers.

These websites sell the requisite appliances, including the microwave, blender, wrapper, mold, and labeler, also the main device. A soap-making unit, for example, can be bought for the US $ 5000. This item can be used to produce toilet soaps and detergent cakes. If you're searching for something less costly, say under the US $ 1500 apiece, you can easily find it on the market. It can be used to produce soap for bathing purposes. There are also other products of varying price points. However, the budget may start at one dollar an item. You'll get a good detergent maker for this amount.

## Soap making raw material and price

The Soap-making ingredients may be bought for a very cheap price. It is much less costly if you buy them in bulk. If you may get the price correct upfront, the rest of the company will be a breeze later on. As a consequence, we prefer bulk raw materials. Alkali and fat are the two main raw materials used to produce soap. the raw material which is most commonly used in soap manufacture is sodium hydroxide. Potassium hydroxide, on the other hand, maybe used. The latter makes a soap that is more soluble in water. As a result, potassium hydroxide creates "warm soap." Locally, raw products are available at a reduced quality. You can discover raw materials for manufacturing soaps online or in your neighborhood with a fast Google search. People typically buy this locally so it cuts the price even further. Rest assured that rates can differ depending on your needs. It depends solely on how much you're making & how much of the raw material you'll need. Caustic soda costs about US $ 150-250 per metric ton on the market. The price of 1000 grams of laundry soap ranges between US$1 and $1.25.

## Soap making formulae

legitimate chemical formulae for the soap's $C_{17}H_{35}COONa$. Its chemical name is thus sodium stearate. However, it is important to note that it's for the common soap that is used for personal purposes only. For the detergents, there are normally long chains of carboxylic acid as well as sulfonate salts or ammonium salt.

## 2.16 Soap selling process

Let us now go through the packaging, distribution, marketing, and promotion processes.

## Colorful wrappings

Choose a bright & eye-catching label that will guarantee that the product is noticed. To set it apart from the competition, style it & use the proper design.

## Branding

Make the most of this opportunity to build your brand through packaging. Choose a design that you think best reflects your business.

## Go simple

Today's entrepreneurs aim for simplicity. Examine the performance of POP displays as well. If they don't live up to your standards, it's time to make a change.

## Soap marketing strategy

You can use the following strategies for marketing soap:

## Email marketing

And the ones who also sign up for your offer are truly interested in the soaps, email marketing is the perfect way to market. It's also becoming highly customizable and cost-efficient these days.

## Blogging

The next logical move is to start blogging. You'll need to hunt down some prominent bloggers who may help you spread the word about the business. You may even invite them to write a review on their blog about a sample of the product.

## Social media

Due to availability of the social media, it is now easier to create a brand. Furthermore, guess what? It's the shortest and least expensive alternative. The secret is to make something go viral. this could be the merchandise, online presence, or your ads.

## 2.17 Soap making supplies

To make it function properly, you'll need some modernized tools equipment, as well as a lot of the space. You will need to find rental space to make the soap. Some of the typical things you'll need to get started include cyclone, mixing vessels, perfumers, blowers, reactors, furnaces, weighing scales, and blenders.

## 2.18 Marketing area for soap

The marketing region you select will be decided by the audience you're targeting. You would be able to segment your customers depending on age and demographic in social media marketing. Your marketing field can be decided by the type of soap you sell. If you're selling detergent cakes, for example, they're mainly aimed at homemakers of different ages. As a consequence, you will show the commercial depending on age & gender. Marketing is successful on a variety of measures. It simply depends upon whether you've online or a physical company. In any case, it's better to entrust this to a practitioner.

## 2.19 Total investment

The Investment isn't based on raw materials. Just As mentioned above, different raw materials are used for personal and detergent soaps. Therefore investment will be different for each category.

You must take into consideration the size and place of the business for starting the business. So You need minimum money of US $ 20,000to purchase the machinery along with primary raw materials –if you decide to start with little.

Raw materials shall cost the US $ 2500 per month. Moreover, making unit rentals would charge not less than the US $ 1000 per month. In addition to the above-mentioned costs, the salary of the plant manager is expected to be around the US $ 500. Equipment shall cost around the US $ 10,000 or more.

In addition to the above prices, you need the US $ 500 for license & registration. Moreover, you will need another US $ 800 to cover the accidental coverage. the Marketing might cost you approximately US $ 500 per month.

## 2.20 Selling price

Supply, materials, brand, packaging, and other factors impact soap pricing. When you're only starting, keep the rates comparable to those of your rivals.

Prices are determined by several factors. A lower-cost soap is generally assumed to be of lower quality. As a result, we won't keep prices very low about market prices.

Additionally, too high prices could decrease overall demand. As a consequence, we will arrive at the golden middle & retain it just marginally, so at all, below current levels.

## 2.21 Profit margin

Measure profit margins through factoring in your annual manufacturing expenses. You must also remember manpower, raw materials, utilities, and maintenance costs.

This business has a high-profit margin, but it also has a lot of competition from well-known brands. As a result, profit margins would be dictated by the price of the goods.

Know more about your rivals' prices and, as a result, determine which would give the greatest return – find the "golden value point" for the sales.

## 2.22 Precaution

It is important to obtain insurance. it is why, in addition to other necessities, insurance must still be part of the investment.

Another crucial step's to understand the company's legal framework. Obtain both the "consent to establish" and "consent to operate."

## 2.23 Risk

In the soap industry, the risk is not creating a large enough brand to compete with the rivals. There are a lot of competitors in the business, so making a name for your company can be challenging.

Another danger is that the company will collapse due to a lack of consumer awareness. To run a good soap company, you must first select the right market.

## 2.24 Conclusion

Soap production, as satisfying as this is, necessitates thorough study and measured risk-taking. Seeking your niche and launching a company are just simple activities. However, careful preparation and intervention are necessary to make this a success. Make sure you don't undersell yourself & that you also stand out.

## 2.25 Advantage of starting a soap making business at home

Soap making requires little investment to start with

The supplies needed to make soap can be easily acquired

Equipment required can also be easily acquired

It is comparatively much easier to learn the making of soap

There is already good demand for handmade soap and people are willing to purchase handmade soap,

You can easily specialize in your particular field

It's rather easier to make soap that is both distinctive and different from the existing ones

You can create other products that can gel in with your existing products

You can generate handsome profits by selling soap

It is very easy to locate a market for the soaps

## 2.26 How Much Money Can You Make Making Soap?

That's a tough question to answer because so much depends on you. And, just to be clear, producing soap is not lucrative. Of course, the

money is in the soap sales. To make money selling a product, much as with any other business endeavor takes a lot of time and commitment.

# CHAPTER 3: Start a Profitable Candle Making Business

Candlemakers are extremely professional artisans who pay particular attention to the sensory aesthetics of their products and experienced business people who know how to entice consumers with innovative marketing tactics. Learn how to launch a candle-making company of your own.

## 3.1 Steps for starting a candle making business

You've uncovered the ideal market opportunity and are now prepared to take the next step. There's more to launching a company than simply filing papers with the government. We've put together a list of steps to help you get started with your candle-making business. These measures will ensure that the new company is well-planned, legally compliant, and properly registered.

**Plan your business**

As an entrepreneur, you must have a well-thought-out strategy. It will assist you in figuring out the additional data of your organization and uncovering any unknowns. Given below are some key points to consider:

What are the startup and recurring costs?

Who is the targeted audience?

What is the maximum price you will charge from the customers?

What would you name your company?

**What are the costs involved in opening a candle-making business?**

You will be able to start your business at home, based on local zoning rules, making use of your kitchen heat source as well as utensils. Many online retailers, including Candle Science and CandleChem, offer a starter kit of items. To start, your candle materials shouldn't cost more than a few hundred dollars. This includes:

Paraffin, gel, soy, beeswax, or other wax

Wicks

Jars, tins, or other containers (though bear in mind that if you're just selling pillar candles, you won't need containers)

Fragrance oils

Coloring agents

Packaging materials

Transportation costs of raw goods in and finished products out

Web growth, which can cost anywhere from nothing to a few hundred dollars based on the expertise in the industry and at least properly contributes to some other start-up costs. A booth will cost $100 per day if you intend to showcase your goods at different exhibits and festivals, plus you'll have to pay for fuel and other travel expenses. You can also contact an insurance provider first. Since there is a chance of a fire accident, you can ensure that your company is fire-proofed and that you have a fire extinguisher onboard. You can also have an initial consultation with a lawyer to decide what licenses or permits are required in your region.

**What are the ongoing expenses for a candle-making business?**

The majority of the business revolves around different varieties of wax, your containers, and paint and scent additives. You can purchase these goods in bulk at lower per-unit prices once you've established your business model is viable. Wax, for example, can be ordered in 25-pound sizes for as little as a dollar per pound. Wicks are sold in 100-foot spools. Bulk amounts of containers, such as glass pots, mason jars, and tins, are also available.

**Who is the target market?**

Anyone who needs candles is your end customer. Some may have specific concerns, such as lights in the case of a power outage, and others are searching for a more sensory experience. Churches that use candles to decorate prayer offerings or stores that wish to bring a dramatic effect to their showrooms are often fantastic consumers. You may also approach resellers that can order the goods in vast quantities. Shop owners from the neighborhood and beyond will be among them. Customers like these are usually seen at arts and crafts shows. Try renting stalls at arts and crafts shows, flea markets, festivals and fairs, and other similar venues if you love seeing your customers face to face in an atmosphere where they can truly appreciate the aesthetics of your goods.

**How does a candle-making business make money?**

Candlemakers market candles to customers directly or indirectly through resellers such as boutiques, gift stores, and other arts and crafts shopping outlets. Since candle making is such a wide field, differentiate yourself by the types of candles you sell (pillar, floating, votive, tea, etc.) or the quality of your offering. Experiment with scents, textures, and molds to come up with something unique that is worth premium pricing. Furthermore, for optimum profit margins on your sales, you can still be on the lookout for low-cost raw material suppliers. To widen your target audience, think of related products or candle styles.

## 3.2 How much can you charge customers?

Your goods could sell for as little as a few bucks or as much as $20 or more per unit. Pricing will be dictated by the nature and reach of your product line, as well as your target market, marketing plan, and competitiveness. If you want to be the lowest vendor, make sure you're buying your raw materials at a discount and that you're still aware of what your rivals are charging. To save the most cost per unit, you'll want to buy wax, wicks, coloring agents, scents, and other products in bulk. If your goal is to market a higher-end product line, price is less important as long as your goods are visually pleasing. If you find a retail reseller that can move a lot of your product, you might want to consider giving deep discounts on prices.

### How much profit can a candle-making business make?

Profit margins of 50% or more are not out of the question. While the cost of materials is not especially high, make sure you have the resources to devote to making your company profitable.

### How can you make your business more profitable?

Consider expanding the product offerings once you've perfected the principles of candle-making. For example, learning how to mold or carve candles into any shape will improve the cost and revenue potential. Alternatively, you might start selling fancy oil lamps made from liquid candles. Find scented soaps and incense as well as other sensory items. You might be able to learn how to make these additions to your expanding product line, or you might be able to figure out where to purchase them for resale. Consider offering candle-making lessons if you have the requisite space in your workshop. You might contact the local community center or community college in this effort and see if they'd be involved in adding your class to their program. Finally, is the company prosperous enough that you might consider franchising it? You have to give this important factor a thorough consideration if you want to enhance your profits.

**What will you name your business?**

Choosing the correct name is vital and daunting. If you own a sole proprietorship, you should start using a separate company name from your own. We suggest reviewing the following references before filing a company name:

The state's business records

Federal and state trademark records

Social media sites

Web domain availability

It's important to get your domain name registered before anyone else. After registering a domain name, you should consider setting up a professional email account (@yourcompany.com).

**Form a legal entity**

The sole proprietorship, partnership, limited liability company (LLC), and corporation are the most traditional corporate structures. If your candle manufacturing company is used, creating a legitimate business entity such as an LLC or corporation prevents you from being found legally accountable.

**Register for taxes**

Before you can start doing business, you'll need to apply for several state and federal taxes. You would need to apply for an EIN to pay for taxation. It's very basic and free.

**Small Business Taxes**

Depending on which business arrangement you select, you can have various taxation choices for your corporation. There could be state-specific taxes that apply to your business. In the state sales tax guides, you can read more about state sales taxes and franchise taxes.

## Open a business bank account & credit card

Personal wealth security necessitates the use of dedicated company banking and credit accounts. If your personal and corporate accounts are combined, your personal properties (such as your house, vehicle, and other valuables) are put at risk if your company-issued. This is referred to as piercing the corporate veil in business law. Furthermore, learning how to create company credit will help you receive credit cards and another borrowing under your business's name (rather than your own), lower interest rates, and more credit lines, among other advantages.

## Open a business bank account

This protects your assets from those of your business, which is essential for personal wealth security, as well as making accounting and tax reporting simpler.

## Get a business credit card

It will help you achieve the following benefits:

It builds the company's credit background and will be beneficial for raising capital and profit later on.

It lets you differentiate personal and business expenditures by placing all of your business's costs under one account.

## Set up business accounting

Understanding your business's financial results includes keeping track of your different costs and sources of revenue. Maintaining correct and comprehensive reports also makes annual tax filing even simpler.

## Labor safety requirements

It is essential to comply with all Occupational Safety and Health Administration protocols. Pertinent requirements include:

Employee injury report

Safety signage

## Certificate of Occupancy

A Certificate of Occupancy is normally required for businesses that operate out of a specific location (CO). All requirements concerning building codes, zoning rules, and local requirements have been followed, according to a CO. If you're thinking about renting a space, keep the following in mind:

Securing a CO is normally the landlord's duty.

Before signing a contract, make sure your landlord has or can get a legitimate CO for a soap-making operation.

A new CO is often needed after a significant renovation. If your company will be renovated before opening, add wording in your lease agreement that specifies that lease payments will not begin before a valid CO is issued.

If you intend to buy or build a place:

You would be responsible for securing a legal CO from a local government body.

Review all building codes and zoning standards for your candle-making business's place to ensure that you'll comply and eligible to get a CO.

## Trademark & Copyright Protection

It is wise to protect your interests by applying for the required trademarks and copyrights if you are creating a new product, idea, brand, or design. The essence of legal standards in distance education is continually evolving, especially when it comes to copyright laws. This is a regularly revised database that can assist you with keeping on top of legal specifications.

## Get business insurance

Insurance, including licenses and permits, are necessary for your company to run safely and legally. In the case of a covered loss, corporate insurance covers your company's financial well-being. There are several insurance schemes tailored for diverse types of companies with various risks. If you're not sure what kinds of risks your company might face, start with General Liability Insurance. This is the most popular form of coverage required by small companies, so it's a good place to start.

Define your brand

Your company's brand is what it stands for, as well as how the general public perceives it. A good name would set the company apart from the market.

## How to promote & market a candle making business

The first and most crucial step is to decide who you intend to reach. Is your average customer a cost-conscious shopper, or is she more concerned with the sensory experience? If your target market is the former, you should be able to deliver fair prices. If it's the latter, make sure your product range is well-presented and that your color and scent options are pleasing. Try building an online presence on sites including eBay, Amazon, and Etsy. Since these platforms have a lot of competition, keep the costs as low as possible. There is a slew of other arts and crafts marketplaces, but they aren't as well-known as Etsy (and therefore potentially less populated with competitors). Among them are ArtFire, Big Cartel, and Craft Is Art, to name a few.

## How to keep customers coming back

You aim to not only retain buyers but to keep them coming back. Since candles are consumable goods that must be replaced daily, the current consumer partnerships may become profitable over time. As a result, make sure you fulfill their needs so that they appreciate the quality of your goods and know-how to reach you if stocks run out. As a consequence, any order must provide easy-to-find contact information, such as your website, email address, or phone number (or all three). As part of the packaging, you could add a business card or sticker with this detail. Make sure shoppers and passers-by alike get your business card when approaching clients in people, such as at art shows or flea markets. Often, get their names and permission to connect them to an email list you give out, maybe before peak candle-buying seasons like the holidays or Mother's Day.

## Establish your web presence

Customers can learn more about your business and the goods or services you deliver by visiting your website. One of the most successful ways to build your online presence is through press releases and social media.

## Top of Form

## Bottom of Form

## Is this Business Right For You?

The perfect candle maker is passionate about the craft and has experience in sales and promotion. Candlemakers may start small, with a minimal budget and inventory, in the kitchen and storage room of their home or apartment. Since candles are always thought of as commodity products, you must continually search for ways to brand your line to set yourself apart from the competition. Excellent image photography, a solid web presence, and savvy sales expertise can help you highlight your product line attractively.

## What are some skills and experiences that will help you build a successful candle-making business?

The bulk of people get into this business as hobby candle builders. You should appreciate the aesthetics of making candles and related products and have a clear understanding of how to mark your business. You should be familiar with the principles of eCommerce and how to build an online presence. If you sell from a booth at a fair, your display presentation skills are relevant both online (in the quality of your images and written product descriptions) and in physical displays. If you plan to market your product line in person, either to consumers personally or to resellers, personal sales skill is important. You must trust in the goods and be able to convince people to do so as well.

## What is the growth potential for a candle-making business?

A good full-time candle maker could earn between $25,000 and $50,000 per year. However, if you sell to a big reseller, you might make more money. Consider franchising your organization once it has become popular enough for others to choose to follow in your footsteps. Candle making is an easy business to launch on your own. However, your ambition likely is to become so well-known that you'll need assistance with crafting, selling, and/or shipping your merchandise. Begin by enlisting the support of friends or family members if required, such as to match seasonal revenue spikes. Don't recruit permanent full-time support once you've been through ample revenue periods to realize that you'll be able to easily reach payroll over the year. Also, contact the accountant to hear about all the hidden expenses.

## Candles Pricing

From a business standpoint, you'll need to find out how much you need/want to receive every hour and how many candles you can make in that time. Divide the hourly wage by the number of units (candles) generated to get a figure to add to the basic cost of the supplies used to manufacture each candle until you have these two numbers. Consider the following scenario: You pay $50 on ingredients (not equipment) and can make 20 candles from them. For the supplies, you paid $2.50 per candle. Making candles is a way for you to earn $20 per hour. Since the 20 candles you made took two hours to make, the overall cost is two times $20, or $40. Then you divide $40 by 20 to get a $2 per candle labor rate. When you apply the $2 labor cost to the $2.50 content cost, you get $4.50 per candle. This isn't a great example because you'll need to pay for other expenses like the additional utilities needed to produce the candles and the expense of importing supplies like boilers, pots, and jugs.

## How much should you charge for candles?

This is based on the sort of brand you choose to be affiliated with. If you intend to sell bulk candles at a low price, you should expect your company to turn out a huge amount of low-cost candles with a slight but steady profit per candle. Votive candles are cheap and can be ordered for as little as $0.50 each. This approach can be very successful, particularly when several cheap candles are purchased in bulk, resulting in several sales for each customer. The drawback is that you would have to bring in a lot of money to make a big profit. You'll almost definitely need to expand, recruiting someone to help you achieve your broad production goals. Another choice is to create your brand. This means catering to a more discerning public able to pay a premium price for a candle. Some high-end artisanal candles will cost upwards of $200 each. For a brand, you'd have to worry about the packaging theme and what you're encouraging your clients to do with their candles.

## 3.3 Benefits of candle making business

If you've ever visited a big shopping center, you've probably seen a variety of candle shops. There are whole areas devoted to candles in several major department stores. To give you an example of how strong the candle business is, over 1 million pounds of wax are used to produce candles for the US market alone every year. The candle industry is worth around $2.3 billion a year without additional products such as candlesticks, ceramic pots, and so on. Who makes the most candle purchases? Seasonal holidays account for just 35% of overall sales, making them an outstanding all-year-round investment. Outside of these days, candles are purchased for 65 percent of the year. The most popular motives for buying a candle as a present include a seasonal gift, a housewarming gift, a dinner party gift, a thank you gift, and adult birthday presents. People nowadays believe fragrance to be the most important consideration when buying a candle. Make sure the candles you're thinking of selling have high-quality scents since this can be the difference between success and failure in the candle industry.

# Conclusion

In 1969, in a period when India's domestic detergent industry had very few competitors, predominantly multi-national firms, which targeted the affluent of India, Karsanbhai launched Nirma. The detergents were not affordable for most middle-class and poor citizens. Karsanbhai began producing detergent powder in the backyard of his home in Khokra, near Ahmedabad and selling it door to door for Rs 3 per kg, while other brands were charging Rs 13 per kg. Business Standard reported how Karsanbhai came up with a genius idea during the early 1980s, when the Nirma was still struggling with the sales, for drying out market of the goods collecting all the due credits. This was accompanied by a huge ad campaign featuring his daughter singing the iconic Nirma jingle in a white frock. Customers were flocking to markets, only to return empty-handed. Karsanbhai flooded the industry with his goods as the demand for Nirma peaked, leading to huge sales. Nirma's sales peaked that year, making it the most successful detergent, well outselling its closest competitor, Hindustan Unilever's Surf. As Karsanbhai purchased the cement firm LafargeHolcim for 1.4 billion dollars that year, he showed once again that the business appetite is away from over. Mint reported how the deal in Rajasthan and the surrounding area would help Nirma achieve a stronger grip. While a media-shy guy, Karsanbhai, an entrepreneur in the truest sense, has a sharp eye for nation-building. In 1995, he founded the Nirma Institute of Technology, which was followed by the Nirma University of

Science and Technology, which was founded in 2003 and is supervised by the Nirma Education and Research Foundation. He initiated the education project Nirmalabs in 2004, aimed at educating and incubating entrepreneurs in India. Karsanbhai Patel received the Padma Shri award in 2010. Just like Nirma, you can also transform your soap and candle-making business into large corporate businesses with the help of your ingenious marketing and creative skills, dedication, perseverance, and unfearfulness of new and challenging situations.

CPSIA information can be obtained
at www.ICGtesting.com
Printed in the USA
BVHW011153160321
602550BV00020B/418

9 781801 846493